W9-ACR-639

GED® TEST
SOCIAL STUDIES
REVIEW

LEARNINGEXPRESS®

NEW YORK

Cataloging-in-Publication Data is on file with the Library of Congress.

ISBN-13: 978-1-61103-088-4

Printed in the United States of America

9 8 7 6 5 4 3 2 1

For more information on LearningExpress, other LearningExpress products, or bulk sales, please write to us at:
224 W. 29th Street
3rd Floor
New York, NY 10001

CONTENTS

CONTENTS

GED® TEST
SOCIAL STUDIES
REVIEW

1 ▶ INTRODUCTION TO THE GED® SOCIAL STUDIES TEST

The test of General Education Development, or GED® test, measures how well you understand high-school-level math, reading, writing, science, and social studies. Passing a GED® test in a specific area proves you have a high-school-level education in that subject. If you pass all four of the GED® tests, you will be awarded a GED® diploma, the equivalent of a high school diploma.

The four separate modules of the GED® test include
1. Reasoning through Language Arts
2. Social Studies
3. Science
4. Mathematical Reasoning

To pass each test, not only will you need to know the basics of each subject, but you'll also need to use critical thinking, writing, and problem solving skills.

If you would like to receive a high school diploma, but you are unable or do not wish to graduate via the traditional path of attending high school, the GED® test might be a great fit for you.

About the GED® Social Studies Test

The GED® Social Studies test consists of 35 multiple-choice questions. The questions on the exam are based on relevant social studies materials, including brief texts, maps, graphics, and tables. Many of the brief texts featured will be drawn from materials reflecting the Great American Conversation, which includes U.S. founding documents, such as the Declaration of Independence, and other documents and speeches from U.S. history that have shaped the country.

The topics tested on the exam are broken down as follows:

- civics and government (50% of the exam)
- U.S. history (20% of the exam)
- economics (15% of the exam)
- geography and the world (15% of the exam)

Each question on the GED® test is assigned a different point value depending on its difficulty, and a minimum score of 145 is required for passing the test. You'll have 70 minutes to complete the test. Use this time effectively and wisely to ensure you earn your best possible test score.

The GED® Social Studies test measures how well you can apply problem solving, analytical reasoning, and critical thinking skills alongside your understanding of high-school-level social studies. Although a good grasp of the core facts, events, and terms commonly taught in social studies classrooms is essential for success on the GED® test and beyond, the test takes it a step further. It measures your ability to analyze key information and apply your knowledge of fundamental social studies concepts in a variety of realistic scenarios. The test also attempts to gauge your level of readiness for success beyond the high school classroom, including college and a career.

This book is designed to get you started on a path to do your best on the GED® Social Studies test, which assesses important ideas in the following two ways:

1. Every question tests a social studies practice skill. These skills measure the critical thinking and reasoning skills that are essential to social studies success.
2. Each question is drawn from one of the four main content areas in social studies—civics and government, U.S. history, economics, and geography and the world.

How Is the Test Delivered?
You will take your GED® test on a computer at an official testing center. Although you do not need to be a computer expert to pass the GED® test, you should be comfortable using a mouse and typing on a keyboard.

The GED® Testing Service has put together a useful GED® Test Tutorial to familiarize test takers with important aspects of the exam. It's important to watch this tutorial in order to

- learn how to use the computer to navigate the questions on the test,
- learn how to operate the online calculator that will be provided during the GED® test,
- become familiar with the five different styles of questions that will be on the exam, and
- understand how to access and use several different math reference tools that will be available during your GED® Science Test.

You can find this useful tutorial at http://www.gedtestingservice.com/2014cbttutorial view/

When and Where Can I Take the Test?

Now that the GED® tests are given online, the testing dates are no longer restricted to just three times a year. The first step is to create an account at www.ged.com. Use this account to select an official Testing Center, a date, and the time that you would like to take any of the four different tests. If you do not pass a particular module on your first attempt, you may take that test up to two more times with no waiting period between test dates. If you still do not pass on your third attempt, you will need to wait 60 days before you can retake that particular test.

GED® Social Studies Test Structure

You will see a variety of question types on test day.

Multiple-Choice Questions

Multiple choice, the main question type on the GED® Social Studies test, is designed to evaluate your ability to apply general social studies concepts to various problem-solving and critical-thinking questions. Each multiple-choice question is followed by four answer choices labeled A through D. You will be instructed to select the best answer to the question. There is no penalty for guessing.

Fill-in-the-Blank Questions

For fill-in-the-blank questions, you will be given a sentence or a paragraph that includes a blank. You must manually type your answer into this blank. There will be no choices from which to select your answer.

Drag-and-Drop Questions

For drag-and-drop items, you will need to click on the correct object, hold down the mouse, and drag the object to the appropriate place in the problem, diagram, chart, or graph.

Here's what a computerized drag-and-drop question might look like on the GED® test.

Drag-and-Drop

Drag-and-drop questions have two areas—one area shows all of the answer choices, and the other area is where you will move the correct answers. You will need to drag one or more answer(s) from the first area to the second area.

To answer a drag-and-drop question, click and hold the mouse on an answer and move it (drag it) to the correct area of the screen. Then let go of the mouse (drop it). You can remove an answer and switch it with another answer at any time.

Try the practice question below.

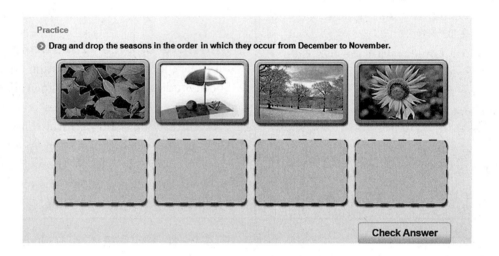

Hot Spot Questions

Hot-spot questions require you to click on an area of the screen to indicate where the correct answer is located. For instance, you may be asked to plot a point by clicking on a corresponding online graph. You can change your answer by simply clicking on another area.

Hot Spot

Hot spot questions ask you to choose a certain place on an image.

To answer the question, click on the correct spot of the image provided. You can change your answer by simply clicking on another area.

Now, you try.

Practice

❯ Plot the number 2.5 on the number line below.

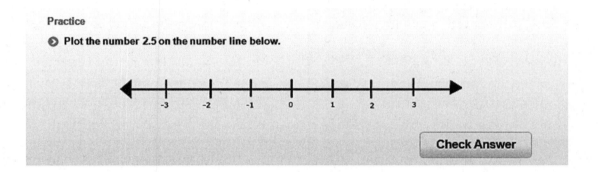

Check Answer

Drop-Down Questions

Drop-down questions will have one or more drop-down menus with options that you can select to complete a sentence or problem. To answer the question, click your mouse on the arrow to show all of the answer choices. Then click on your chosen answer to complete the sentence or paragraph.

Practice

❯ Select the appropriate word from each drop-down menu to complete the sentence correctly.

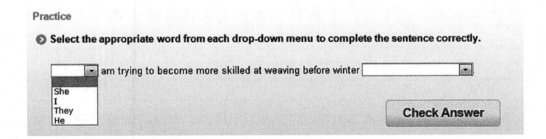

Check Answer

NOTE

Most of the information you will need to answer the questions on the GED® Social Studies test is actually within the passages, graphs, or maps themselves. The GED® test questions test your ability to read and comprehend information; they do not test your memory or knowledge of social studies. The focus of the exam isn't to assess your social studies content knowledge; it's to test your critical reasoning and thinking skills in a social studies context. On the test, you will never encounter a question that asks you to provide your own definition of a specific social studies term or concept. However, according to the GED® Testing Service, you should be "broadly and generally familiar" with each of the basic social studies concepts covered on the test.

The review chapters in this book will give you a solid background of the social studies topics you must know to succeed on the exam, so you can read the passages with ease and clarity. The review chapters in this book will also give you practice reading test-like passages and reviewing test-like graphs, maps, and charts, and the practice questions throughout will test your ability to comprehend what you have read, just as the GED® test asks you to do.

How to Use This Book

In addition to this introduction, *GED® Test Social Studies Review* also contains the following:

- **A Diagnostic Exam.** It's always helpful to see where your social studies skills stand. Therefore, we recommend taking the diagnostic test before starting on the content chapters. By taking the diagnostic test, you should be able to determine the content areas in which you are strongest and the areas in which you might need more help. For example, if you miss most of the economics questions, then you know that you should pay extra attention to the review and questions in Chapter 6.

  The diagnostic test does not count for any score, so don't get caught up on how many you got right or wrong. Instead, use the results of the diagnostic test to help guide your study of the content chapters.

- **Social Studies Practices.** In chapter 3, we will review social studies practice skills in detail. These are the critical thinking and reasoning skills that are essential to social studies success. Reviewing these skills is key to doing well on the GED® Social Studies test.

- **Content Chapters.** Chapters 4, 5, 6, and 7 include a basic review of the four social studies areas covered on the GED® Social Studies test: civics and government, U.S. history, economics, geography and the world. These chapters form the heart of the book. To help you understand all these ideas, every chapter has sample questions, helpful tips, and summaries, as well as explanations of the concepts being discussed. We recommend reading these chapters in order and not skipping around, as many of the concepts in the earlier chapters are built on in the later chapters.

- **Practice Test.** After you've completed your review, take another full-length practice test to assess how much you've learned and what you still need to go over before test day. Every answer has a full-length explanation that tells you why every choice is right or wrong. Don't skip these explanations—they'll give you insight into the types of tricky wrong answers the testmaker often uses to steer you in the wrong direction. Then, when you're done, spend the days/weeks/months before your test reviewing the areas that are giving you the most trouble.

Let's get started with reviewing what you need to do well on the GED® Social Studies test!

C H A P T E R

2 ▶ GED® SOCIAL STUDIES DIAGNOSTIC TEST

This practice test is modeled on the format, content, and timing of the official GED® Social Studies test and, like the official exam, presents a series of questions that focus on the fundamentals of social studies reasoning.

You'll be asked to answer questions based on brief texts, maps, graphics, and tables. Refer to the information provided as often as necessary when answering the questions.

- Work carefully, but do not spend too much time on any one question. Be sure to answer every question.
- Set a timer for 70 minutes, and try to take this test uninterrupted, under quiet conditions.

35 total questions
70 minutes to complete

Please use the following passage to answer questions 1–3.

This excerpt is from a speech by George W. Bush given on March 19, 2008.

Operation Iraqi Freedom was a remarkable display of military effectiveness. Forces from the U.K., Australia, Poland, and other allies joined our troops in the initial operations. As they advanced, our troops fought their way through sandstorms so intense that they blackened the daytime sky. Our troops engaged in pitched battles with Fedayeen Saddam, death squads acting on the orders of Saddam Hussein that obeyed neither the conventions of war nor the dictates of conscience. These death squads hid in schools, and they hid in hospitals, hoping to draw fire against Iraqi civilians. They used women and children as human shields. They stopped at nothing in their efforts to prevent us from prevailing, but they couldn't stop the coalition advance.

Aided by the most effective and precise air campaign in history, coalition forces raced across 350 miles of enemy territory, destroying Republican Guard divisions, pushing through the Karbala Gap, capturing Saddam International Airport, and liberating Baghdad in less than one month.

Because we acted, Saddam Hussein no longer fills fields with the remains of innocent men, women, and children. . . . Because we acted, Saddam's regime is no longer invading its neighbors or attacking them with chemical weapons and ballistic missiles.

1. Based on the primary-source excerpt concerning a central idea of American foreign policy since 9/11, what was Bush's purpose for launching Operation Iraqi Freedom?
   a. to liberate Baghdad in less than one month by destroying Republican Guard divisions
   b. to liberate Iraqi people from a brutal regime and remove Saddam Hussein from power
   c. to stop Saddam Hussein from invading other nations
   d. to join countries in aiding Saddam Hussein's control of the Iraqi people's natural rights

2. Which of the following statements is an opinion, NOT a fact?
   a. "[C]oalition forces raced across 350 miles of enemy territory, . . . liberating Baghdad in less than one month."
   b. "Forces from the U.K., Australia, Poland, and other allies joined our troops in the initial operations."
   c. "Our troops engaged in pitched battles with Fedayeen Saddam, death squads acting on the orders of Saddam Hussein."
   d. "Operation Iraqi Freedom was a remarkable display of military effectiveness."

3. Based on the primary-source excerpt, what can be concluded about the credibility of Bush's choice to launch Operation Iraqi Freedom?
  a. The operation was not justified and Bush makes this clear in his speech.
  b. Bush feels that the operation was justified, but the realities of Saddam's regime discredit any justification.
  c. The operation was justified in trying to bring down a detrimental and brutal regime.
  d. The actions of Saddam's regime justify the operation, but Bush expresses his concern that the operation may not have been justified in his speech.

Please use the following passage to answer questions 4–6.

This excerpt is from the U.S. Constitution.

> The President shall be Commander in Chief of the Army and Navy of the United States, and of the Militia of the several States, when called into the actual Service of the United States . . . He shall have Power, by and with the Advice and Consent of the Senate, to make Treaties, provided two thirds of the Senators present concur.

4. In this portion of the U.S. Constitution, which branch of the government checks the power of which other branch of government by a two-thirds agreement?
  a. the executive checks the power of the legislative
  b. the judicial checks the power of the executive
  c. the legislative checks the power of the executive
  d. the legislative checks the power of the judicial

5. Why is it important for the U.S. Constitution to include rules, such as the one in the excerpt, that allow for power checking between the different branches of government?
  a. to ensure that the legislative branch has power over the executive and judicial branches
  b. to ensure a separation of power that balances the powers of the three branches in order to prevent any one person or group from holding too much or all power
  c. to ensure that the president has the ability to check the power of all other branches
  d. to ensure that the president does not have the power to make treaties without some say from the Senate

6. Based on the excerpt from the U.S. Constitution, what can you infer would be the effect of a failure to receive a two-thirds agreement from the Senate in this instance?
  a. the Senate could not make a treaty but the president could make a treaty
  b. the Senate could make a treaty
  c. the president could not make a treaty because the Senate does not agree
  d. the president could make a treaty

7. What is the difference between a government ruled by popular sovereignty and a government ruled by a dictatorship?

   a. A government ruled by popular sovereignty means that the authority has the consent of the governed to rule, and a government ruled by a dictatorship means that the authority is held by one individual.

   b. A government ruled by a dictatorship means that the authority has the consent of the governed to rule, and a government ruled by popular sovereignty does not have consent.

   c. Popular sovereignty means that the government is ruled by the most popular individual, and a dictatorship means that the government is ruled by the least popular individual.

   d. A dictatorship means that the government is ruled by the most popular individual, and popular sovereignty means that the government is ruled by the least popular individual.

8. Determine whether each aspect of the federal government listed below is associated with the executive, legislative, or judicial branch of government. Write your answers in the boxes below.

   The Supreme Court
   The House of Representatives
   The Senate
   The president's Cabinet
   The president

Executive Branch	Legislative Branch	Judicial Branch

Please use the following passage to answer questions 9 and 10.

This excerpt is from a speech by Bill Clinton given on July 19, 1995.

The purpose of affirmative action is to give our Nation a way to finally address the systemic exclusion of individuals of talent on the basis of their gender or race from opportunities to develop, perform, achieve, and contribute. Affirmative action is an effort to develop a systematic approach to open the doors of education, employment, and business development opportunities to qualified individuals who happen to be members of groups that have experienced longstanding and persistent discrimination.

It is a policy that grew out of many years of trying to navigate between two unacceptable pasts. One was to say simply that we declared discrimination illegal and that's enough. We saw that that way still relegated blacks with college degrees to jobs as railroad porters and kept women with degrees under a glass ceiling with a lower paycheck.

The other path was simply to try to impose change by leveling draconian penalties on employers who didn't meet certain imposed, ultimately arbitrary, and sometimes unachievable quotas. That, too, was rejected out of a sense of fairness.

So a middle ground was developed that would change an inequitable status quo gradually but firmly, by building the pool of qualified applicants for college, for contracts, for jobs, and giving more people the chance to learn, work, and earn. When affirmative action is done right, it is flexible, it is fair, and it works.

9. According to the excerpt from Clinton's speech, in which he speaks out against this, affirmative action is a partial solution to which long-standing societal problem that has affected history?
   a. slavery
   b. discrimination
   c. unemployment
   d. poverty

10. According to the excerpt, what changes would affirmative action cause to come about for minority groups that suffer from discrimination?
   a. It will give more people in these minority groups the chance to work, learn, and earn a living by increasing the number of qualified applicants from these groups who are accepted for job positions and places in college.

   b. It will give fewer people in these minority groups the chance to work, learn, and earn a living by decreasing the number of qualified applicants from these groups who are accepted for job positions and places in college.

   c. It will change nothing for minority groups and will instead only reduce penalties on employers who do not meet a certain quota of minority workers in their workplaces.

   d. It will reduce the pay of women in the workplace and decrease the number of minority groups in universities.

Please use the following two documents to answer questions 11 and 12.

This excerpt is from the Declaration of Independence.

> We hold these truths to be self-evident, that all men are created equal, that they are endowed by their Creator with certain unalienable Rights that among these are Life, Liberty and the pursuit of Happiness. That to secure these rights, Governments are instituted among Men, deriving their just powers from the consent of the governed. That whenever any Form of Government becomes destructive of these ends, it is the Right of the People to alter or to abolish it, and to institute new Government, laying its foundation on such principles and organizing its powers in such form, as to them shall seem most likely to effect their Safety and Happiness.

This excerpt is from the U.S. Constitution.

> We the People of the United States, in Order to form a more perfect Union, establish Justice, insure domestic Tranquility, provide for the common defence, promote the general Welfare, and secure the Blessings of Liberty to ourselves and our Posterity, do ordain and establish this Constitution for the United States of America.

11. Analyze the two excerpts taken from key historical documents that have shaped American constitutional government. Based on these excerpts, which of the following ideas is incorporated into both documents?
a. the equality of men
b. the right to abolish destructive government
c. the abolition of slavery
d. the right to liberty

12. In the excerpt from the Declaration of Independence, what concept is being described in the following sentences?

"That to secure these rights, Governments are instituted among Men, deriving their just powers from the consent of the governed. That whenever any Form of Government becomes destructive of these ends, it is the Right of the People to alter or to abolish it, and to institute new Government, laying its foundation on such principles and organizing its powers in such form, as to them shall seem most likely to effect their Safety and Happiness."
a. federalism
b. popular sovereignty
c. popular socialism
d. capitalism

13. The table below displays the number of men killed, wounded, and captured during two battles of the Revolutionary War on both the American and British sides.

Date	Engagement	Commander	Troops	Killed	Wounded	Captured
April 19, 1775	Lexington/Concord	American: Capt. John Parker, et al.	3,763	49	41	0
		British: Lt. Col. Francis Smith	1,800	73	174	7
June 17, 1775	Bunker (Breed's) Hill	American: Gens. Putnam & Ward	2,000	140	271	30
		British: General William Howe	2,400	226	826	0

Based on this information, what was the mean value of men killed in both engagements? Write your answer in the box below. (You may use a calculator to answer this question.)

14. The graph shows the changes in unemployment rates for nonfarm workers between 1926 and 1947.

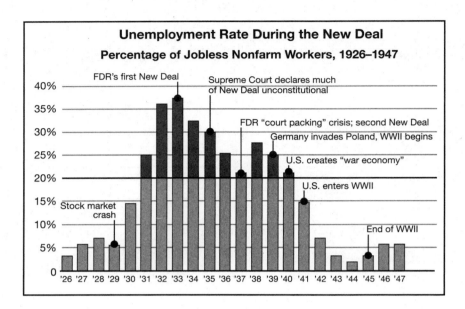

Based on the information shown, select the event that led to the greatest drop in the unemployment rate the following year for nonfarm workers.
a. FDR's first New Deal
b. the United States enters World War II
c. the stock market crash
d. Germany invades Poland, World War II begins

15. Read the following definition of capitalism.

Capitalism is an economic and political system that allows a country's trade and industry to be controlled by private owners for profit.

Based on this definition, write the appropriate word in the box that makes the following statement true.

Capitalism gives _____ owners the freedom to make a profit from control of the country's trade and industry.

16. The graph shows the percentage of citizens affiliated with each U.S. political party.

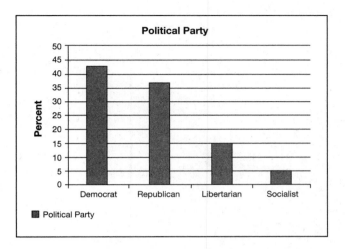

Which political party has the most members, and how does the graph show that?

a. The Democratic Party has the most members. Political parties are labeled on the x-axis, and the percentage of members in those parties is labeled on the y-axis. The bar for percentage of Democrats is highest.

b. The Democratic Party has the most members. Political parties are labeled on the y-axis, and the percentage of members in those parties is labeled on the x-axis. The bar for percentage of Democrats is highest.

c. The Libertarian Party has the most members. Political parties are labeled on the x-axis, and the percentage of members in those parties is labeled on the y-axis. The bar for percentage of Libertarians is highest.

d. The Libertarian Party has the most members. Political parties are labeled on the y-axis, and the percentage of members in those parties is labeled on the x-axis. The bar for percentage of Libertarians is highest.

17. Based on this map of China, select the answer that correlates to a gray triangle surrounded by a circle.

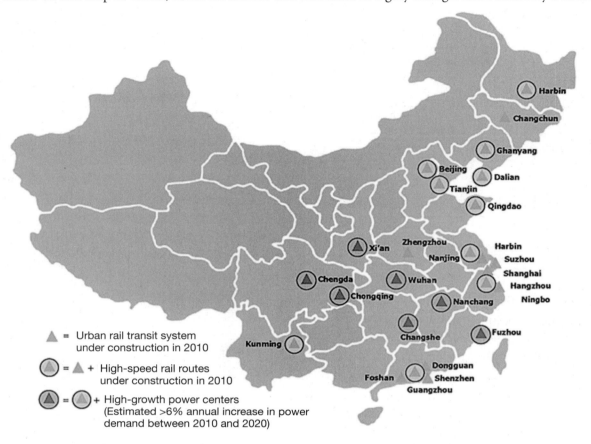

a. urban rail transit system under construction in 2010
b. urban rail transit system and high-speed rail routes under construction in 2010
c. high-speed rail routes under construction in 2010
d. high-growth power centers

18. The graph shows the total campaign expenditures by candidates for the California State Legislature between 1975 and 1998.

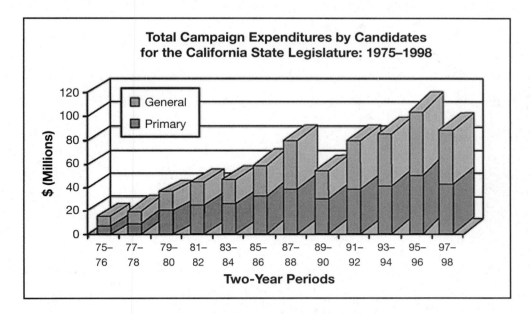

What was the trend in expenditures by candidates for the California State Legislature from 1983 to 1988?

a. decreasing

b. increasing then decreasing

c. decreasing then increasing

d. increasing

Please use the following passage to answer questions 19 and 20.

This excerpt is from a speech by Barack Obama announcing his candidacy for president in Springfield, Illinois, in 2007.

All of us know what those challenges are today—a war with no end, a dependence on oil that threatens our future, schools where too many children aren't learning, and families struggling paycheck to paycheck despite working as hard as they can. We know the challenges. We've heard them. We've talked about them for years.

What's stopped us from meeting these challenges is not the absence of sound policies and sensible plans. What's stopped us is the failure of leadership, the smallness of our politics—the ease with which we're distracted by the petty and trivial, our chronic avoidance of tough decisions, our preference for scoring cheap political points instead of rolling up our sleeves and building a working consensus to tackle big problems.

For the last six years we've been told that our mounting debts don't matter, we've been told that the anxiety Americans feel about rising health care costs and stagnant wages are an illusion, we've been told that climate change is a hoax, and that tough talk and an ill-conceived war can replace diplomacy, and strategy, and foresight. And when all else fails, when Katrina happens, or the death toll in Iraq mounts, we've been told that our crises are somebody else's fault. We're distracted from our real failures, and told to blame the other party, or gay people, or immigrants.

And as people have looked away in disillusionment and frustration, we know what's filled the void. The cynics, and the lobbyists, and the special interests who've turned our government into a game only they can afford to play. They write the checks and you get stuck with the bills, they get the access while you get to write a letter, they think they own this government, but we're here today to take it back. The time for that politics is over. It's time to turn the page.

19. Based on the excerpt from Obama's speech announcing his candidacy for president, which of the following sets of words represents instances of loaded language?
a. hoax, frustration
b. today, decisions
c. void, lobbyists
d. page, diplomacy

20. The paragraph starting with "For the last six years . . ." could be viewed as an example of which of the following?
a. economic chart
b. campaign speech
c. statistical data
d. campaign promise

Please use the following passage to answer questions 21 and 22.

This is an excerpt from a speech about healthcare delivered to Congress by President Barack Obama on September 9, 2009.

Then there's the problem of rising cost. We spend one and a half times more per person on health care than any other country, but we aren't any healthier for it. This is one of the reasons that insurance premiums have gone up three times faster than wages. It's why so many employers, especially small businesses, are forcing their employees to pay more for insurance or are dropping their coverage entirely. It's why so many aspiring entrepreneurs cannot afford to open a business in the first place and why American businesses that compete internationally, like our automakers, are at a huge disadvantage. And it's why those of us with health insurance are also paying a hidden and growing tax for those without it, about $1,000 per year that pays for somebody else's emergency room and charitable care.

Finally, our health care system is placing an unsustainable burden on taxpayers. When health care costs grow at the rate they have, it puts greater pressure on programs like Medicare and Medicaid. If we do nothing to slow these skyrocketing costs, we will eventually be spending more on Medicare and Medicaid than every other government program combined. Put simply, our health care problem is our deficit problem. Nothing else even comes close. Nothing else.

21. In the excerpt from Obama's speech on health-care, what type of statement is "we aren't any healthier for it"?
   a. supported fact
   b. statistic
   c. warning
   d. opinion

22. According to the excerpt from Obama's speech on healthcare, what does he think will be the eventual effect of unchecked added pressure being put on Medicare and Medicaid from rapidly increasing healthcare costs?
   a. the government spending less on Medicare and Medicaid than every other program combined
   b. the government spending more on Medicare and Medicaid than every other program combined
   c. the shutdown of Medicare and Medicaid instead of other programs
   d. the government no longer spending any money on Medicare and Medicaid

23. Why did Christopher Columbus set sail in 1492 on an expedition that would eventually bring him into contact with the Americas for the first time?

    a. He was attempting to claim new territory in the Americas for Spain.

    b. He was going to the Americas to trade with the native peoples.

    c. He was attempting to find a new route to Asia for trade purposes.

    d. He was going to the Americas in order to start a settlement.

24. Based on the pie chart showing the number of women working in the U.S. military during World War II, fill in the box in the following statement to make it correct.

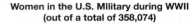

**Women in the U.S. Military during WWII
(out of a total of 358,074)**

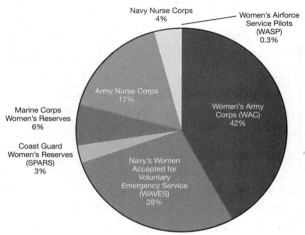

During World War II, the number of women who joined _____ was almost equal to the combined number of women who joined WASP, the Army and Navy Nurse Corps, SPARS, and the Marine Corps Women's Reserve.

25. The map shows the division of European countries according to political alignment during most of the Cold War.

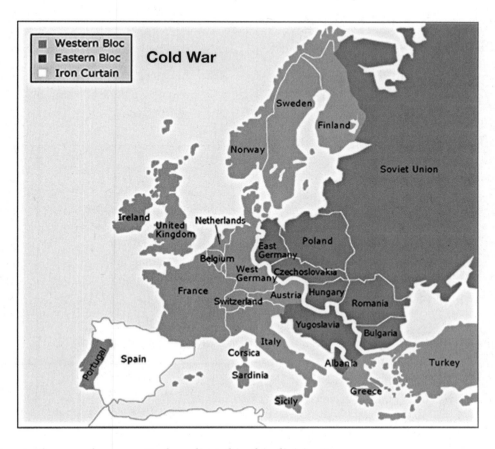

According to the map, how was Turkey aligned in this division?
a. with the Western Bloc
b. with the Eastern Bloc
c. with the Iron Curtain
d. with the United States

26. This excerpt is from a speech by George W. Bush given on March 19, 2008.

> To ensure that military progress in Iraq is quickly followed up with real improvements in daily life, we have doubled the number of Provincial Reconstruction Teams in Iraq. These teams of civilian experts are serving all Iraqi—18 Iraqi Provinces, and they're helping to strengthen responsible leaders and build up local economies and bring Iraqis together, so that reconciliation can happen from the ground up. They're very effective. They're helping give ordinary Iraqis confidence that by rejecting the extremists and reconciling with one another, they can claim their place in a free Iraq and build better lives for their families.

Based on the excerpt from Bush's speech, you can infer which of the following is NOT a reason that it was important to have civilian expert teams in Iraq after the military action in the area?
a. to strengthen the local leadership and economy
b. to take control of the local leadership and economy
c. to help give confidence to the people of Iraq
d. to help the Iraqi people build a free Iraq

27. If a company purchases a product for $1 and sells it to consumers for $2.35, the $1.35 that the company receives is an example of what economic concept?
a. monopoly
b. expense
c. profit
d. loss

28. Write the word in the box that completes the following definition.

A _____ is a tax or duty a government places upon imported or exported goods.

29. This excerpt describes the eligibility requirements for a Stateside Union Bank College Credit Card.

> To qualify for a Stateside Union Bank College Credit Card, a student must be at the age of majority in the state of residence, and show proof of enrollment in an accredited college or university.
>
> Applicants must have a minimum income greater than $4,000. Applicants who do not meet this criterion will need a co-applicant with an ability to repay the debt.

Based on the excerpt, in which of the following situations would someone NOT qualify for the card?
a. age 20, student at the University of Texas, income of $5,000
b. age 14, high-school student, no income
c. age 24, graduate student at Rice University, income of $11,000
d. age 18, student at Baylor University, income of $4,250

30.

Government spending during war that is associated with wartime expenses has short-term positive economic benefits because high levels of spending associated with conflict increase economic growth. However, after the war is over, unintended residual effects of that heightened wartime spending, which is no longer taking place, tend to cause long-term impediments to economic prosperity.

Based on the information above, choose the best description of the economic effects of war.
a. short-term negative effects followed by positive long-term effects
b. wars produce neither positive nor negative economic effects
c. short-term positive effects followed by negative long-term effects
d. wars produce short-term and long-term negative effects

31. The graph shows the correlation between metal exploration budgets in the United States and the prices of metals between 1989 and 2008.

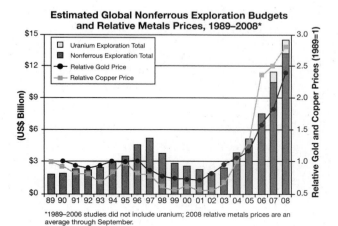

Estimated Global Nonferrous Exploration Budgets and Relative Metals Prices, 1989–2008*

*1989–2006 studies did not include uranium; 2008 relative metals prices are an average through September.

Based on the graph, how did the price of gold and copper correlate to U.S. exploration spending from 2006 to 2008?
a. as the price of gold and copper increased, the amount that the United States spent on exploration increased
b. as the price of gold and copper increased, the amount that the United States spent on exploration decreased
c. as the price of gold and copper decreased, the amount that the United States spent on exploration increased
d. as the price of gold and copper decreased, the amount that the United States spent on exploration decreased

32. These two excerpts are taken from separate sources about the Industrial Revolution.

> The era known as the Industrial Revolution was a period in which fundamental changes occurred in agriculture, textile and metal manufacture, transportation, economic policies and the social structure in England . . . The year 1760 is generally accepted as the "eve" of the Industrial Revolution. In reality, this eve began more than two centuries before this date. The late eighteenth century and the early nineteenth century brought to fruition the ideas and discoveries of those who had long passed on, such as Galileo, Bacon, Descartes and others.

> Industrial Revolution, in modern history, is the process of change from an agrarian, handicraft economy to one dominated by industry and machine manufacture. This process began in England in the eighteenth century and from there spread to other parts of the world.

What is the discrepancy between what is stated in these two passages?
a. the date of the eighteenth century as the time period
b. defining the time period as a time of fundamental change
c. the real start beginning two centuries before the eighteenth century
d. the revolution starting and growing in England

33. The map shows the major ethnic regions of Pacific Asia.

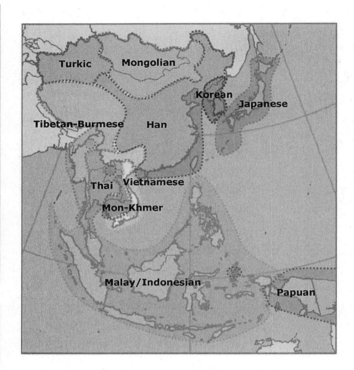

What is the label for the region on the map that covers one island that borders the Korean ethnic region and is located north of the Malay/Indonesian and Papuan ethnic regions?
a. Turkic
b. Thai
c. Han
d. Japanese

Please use the following maps to answer questions 34 and 35.

These maps are based on information from the U.S. Census Bureau.

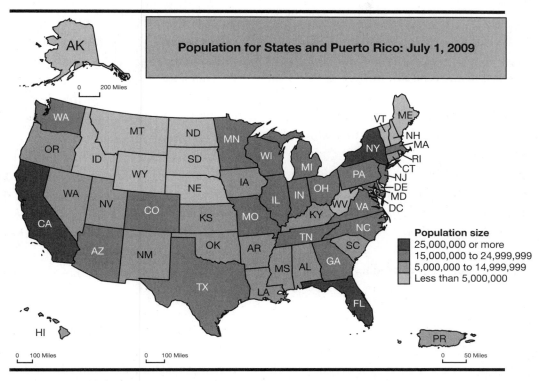

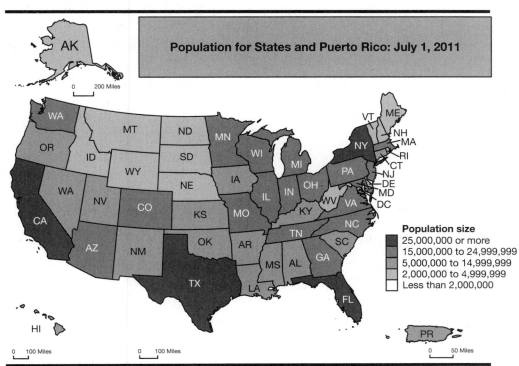

34. Based on the maps showing the population of American states in 2009 and 2011, what has been the population trend between those years for the state of Texas?

    a. increased

    b. stayed the same

    c. decreased

    d. increased then decreased

35. Based on the 2011 Census map, how does the population of California relate to the population of Texas?

    a. population two categories larger than Texas

    b. in the same population category as Tennessee

    c. population two categories smaller than Texas

    d. in the same population category as Texas

Answers and Explanations

1. Choice b is correct. The liberation of the Iraqi people from a brutal ruling regime and the removal of Hussein from power are both goals that would have the ability to bring about all of the changes for Iraq that Bush mentions came about after the success of the operation. Therefore, it is safe to say that this choice represents the main purpose of the launching of the operation by Bush.

Choice **a** is incorrect. While the liberation of Baghdad led to Operation Iraqi Freedom's success, it alone was not the purpose of the operation. The capture of this one city would not have been enough to bring about the other changes and freedoms for the Iraqi people that Bush mentions, such as those in the excerpt's final paragraph.

Choice **c** is incorrect. Stopping Hussein from invading nations was an outcome of the operation's success in removing Hussein from power, not the actual purpose of the operation. That purpose would be to remove Hussein, which would result in this beneficial outcome.

Choice **d** is incorrect. These nations joined forces for the common cause of the operation to stop Saddam Hussein's control of the Iraqi people's natural rights.

2. Choice d is correct. This statement is an opinion held and expressed by Bush. He uses the term "remarkable," which is inherently a term of opinion. Bush may feel that the operation "was a remarkable display of military effectiveness," but this is an opinion, not a fact.

Choice **a** is incorrect. All of these events are facts that are confirmed by the actions and technicalities of the operation. All of these actions were actually carried out during the operation.

Choice **b** is incorrect. This is once again a fact. These forces did all join with the U.S. in the beginning of the operation.

Choice **c** is incorrect. This is another fact of the actions carried out during the operation when troops actually did battle Saddam's death squads.

3. Choice c is correct. All of the atrocities carried out by Saddam that Bush mentions in his speech serve to show the justification for the operation and show just how brutal Saddam's regime was and how detrimental it was to the citizens of that regime who were exposed to atrocities. Bush mentions in the end all the negative things that have been stopped due to the operation, once again bolstering its justification.

Choice **a** is incorrect. Everything that Bush says about the operation in this part of his speech implies that the operation was justified and successful. He mentions on many occasions the brutality of Saddam's regime and gives examples. He then goes on to list atrocities that have been stopped due to the operation.

Choice **b** is incorrect. Everything that Bush says would imply that he feels the operation was justified. However, the realities of Saddam's regime that Bush mentions only lend credit to this justification. Instead of discrediting the operation, the atrocities that Saddam imposed on his people only bolster the idea that it was justified.

Choice **d** is incorrect. While the atrocities of Saddam's regime that Bush mentions justify the operation, Bush does not disagree with that justification. The fact that he mentions all of said atrocities implies that he agrees that the operation was justified, and in the last paragraph he goes on to mention all of the atrocities that have been stopped due to the operation. He never expresses any doubts about the operation's justification.

4. Choice c is correct. The legislative branch involves the Senate and the House of Representatives, and the executive branch consists of the president and his administration. The fact that the Senate must have a two-thirds agreement in order to allow the president to make a treaty means that the legislative branch is checking the power of the executive branch so that the president does not have full and unopposed power to make treaties.

Choice **a** is incorrect. The president is part of the executive branch, and that branch is not checking the powers of any other branches but actually having its own powers checked.

Choice **b** is incorrect. The judicial branch involves the courts, and this branch is not even mentioned in this section of the Constitution.

Choice **d** is incorrect. The judicial branch does not even factor into this section of the Constitution.

5. Choice b is correct. The system of checks and balances in the U.S. government is meant to separate the powers of the branches of government and provide a balance to those powers so that one person or group does not hold all power, which could then be abused and exploited.

Choice **a** is incorrect. The idea behind checks and balances between the branches of government is to keep a balance of power, not to allow the legislative branch to have power over the executive or judicial branches. In the excerpt, this check on the power of the president does not imply that the Senate has power over the president or courts, but rather it is a balance of power.

Choice **c** is incorrect. If the president had the ability to check the power of all the other branches, his power would be more like a dictatorship than a presidency. The system of checks and balances is meant to prevent this. Also, the excerpt shows that the president does not have this power due to the fact that the Senate is actually checking the president's power in this example.

Choice **d** is incorrect. While the example in the excerpt does refer to this check on the power of the president, this is only an example of one instance of checks and balances in the U.S. government and not the actual point of this system. There are many other examples of checks and balances written into the U.S. Constitution.

6. Choice c is correct. Without a two-thirds agreement in the Senate, the president cannot make a treaty. This is part of the system of checks and balances in the U.S. government. It is a check on the power of the executive branch. Choice **a** is incorrect. The president is the one who makes treaties with the consent of the Senate. Therefore, failure to receive a two-thirds agreement would make a treaty impossible, not just in the Senate but for the president as well. Choice **b** is incorrect. The Senate does not make the treaties; the president does. The Senate consults with the president and must agree with the treaty in order for it to be made. Choice **d** is incorrect. Without a two-thirds agreement in the Senate, the president cannot make a treaty. This is part of the system of checks and balances in the U.S. government. It is a check on the power of the executive branch.

7. Choice a is correct. The concept of popular sovereignty implies that the government holds authority through the consent of the governed, and if the governed fail to approve of said authority, the people can change it. A dictatorship does not take the consent of the governed into account, and one individual rules without consent.

Choice **b** is incorrect. The concept of popular sovereignty implies that the government holds authority through the consent of the governed and if the governed fail to approve of said authority, the people can change it. A dictatorship does not take the consent of the governed into account and one individual rules without consent.

Choice **c** is incorrect. The concept of popular sovereignty does not necessarily mean that the government is run by the most popular person, but rather that the leader of the government has consent of the governed. A dictatorship does not necessarily mean that the government is run by the least popular person, but rather that said person does not take the consent of the governed into account.

Choice **d** is incorrect. A dictatorship does not mean that the government is run by the most popular person, but rather that the leader of the government does not take the consent of the government into account. The concept of popular sovereignty does not mean that the government is run by the least popular person, but rather that said person has the consent of the governed.

8. The executive branch is made up of the **president** and the **president's Cabinet**.

The legislative branch is made up of the **Senate** and the **House of Representatives**, collectively known as Congress.

The judicial branch is made up of the **Supreme Court**.

9. Choice b is correct. Right at the beginning of the excerpt, Clinton references the problems of discrimination from the past and says that it continues to plague the country. He makes it apparent that affirmative action is a way to lessen this discrimination and hopefully solve many problems that it creates for minority groups.

Choice **a** is incorrect. Slavery was a problem that has been abolished by law since the Civil War and Reconstruction. Affirmative action is not addressing slavery or a solution.

Choice **c** is incorrect. While unemployment can be caused by discrimination, affirmative action addresses discrimination, which could then inadvertently help with unemployment as a side effect. Affirmative action is not directly addressing unemployment or providing a direct solution to it.

Choice **d** is incorrect. While poverty can be caused by discrimination, affirmative action addresses discrimination, which could then inadvertently help with unemployment and poverty as a side effect. Affirmative action is not directly addressing poverty or providing a direct solution to it.

10. Choice a is correct. According to Clinton, affirmative action will benefit minority groups "by building the pool of qualified applicants for college, for contracts, for jobs, and giving more people the chance to learn, work, and earn. When affirmative action is done right, it is flexible, it is fair, and it works."

Choice **b** is incorrect. This change is the opposite of the purpose of affirmative action and is the opposite of the correct answer. According to Clinton, affirmative action will benefit minority groups "by building the pool of qualified applicants for college, for contracts, for jobs, and giving more people the chance to learn, work, and earn. When affirmative action is done right, it is flexible, it is fair, and it works."

Choice **c** is incorrect. Clinton mentions that the idea to have penalties for employers who fail to meet high quotas was actually rejected and affirmative action helps to keep this from happening. However, affirmative action has as its main goal the improvement of conditions for minority groups. Therefore, the idea that it would not change anything for minority groups is wrong.

Choice **d** is incorrect. Both of these statements represent things that affirmative action is trying to fix. Affirmative action would increase the number of minority groups in college, not decrease their numbers. According to Clinton, affirmative action will benefit minority groups "by building the pool of qualified applicants for college, for contracts, for jobs, and giving more people the chance to learn, work, and earn. When affirmative action is done right, it is flexible, it is fair, and it works."

11. Choice d is correct. Both excerpts mention the importance of liberty for all citizens. The Declaration of Independence says all men have the right to liberty, and the Constitution says that the government must "secure the Blessings of Liberty to ourselves and our Posterity."
Choice **a** is incorrect. The concept of all men being equal is mentioned only in the excerpt from the Declaration of Independence.
Choice **b** is incorrect. The right to abolish destructive government is mentioned only in the excerpt from the Declaration of Independence.
Choice **c** is incorrect. Neither excerpt mentions anything about slavery or the need to abolish it. Furthermore, the Declaration of Independence was made during a time when slavery was still very prominent.

12. Choice b is correct. Popular sovereignty refers to a government run by the people, where the people have the ability to affect, change, and replace their government as they see fit. This is what the excerpt is essentially describing.
Choice **a** is incorrect. Federalism refers to the concept of a federal government. This excerpt references the ability to replace the government; it doesn't describe a federal system of government.
Choice **c** is incorrect. Socialism deals with a centralized control of wealth in order to make the spread of wealth more equal. This has nothing to do with the ability to replace the government. The term *socialism* is not preceded by the word *popular*.
Choice **d** is incorrect. Capitalism deals with the idea of free markets and private ownership in the economy. This is an economic system, not a system of replacing a destructive form of government.

13. The correct answer is 122.
The mean is the average. Therefore, you add up all of the numbers in the column listing the number of men killed: 49 + 73 + 140 + 226 = 488.
Then divide the answer by the number of values given: $\frac{488}{4} = 122$.

14. Choice b is correct. The United States entering World War II took the rate from 14.5% in 1941 to 7% in 1942, or a 7.5% decrease.
Choice **a** is incorrect. FDR's first New Deal took the rate from 37% in 1933 to 33% in 1934, or a 4% drop. This was not the largest decrease.
Choice **c** is incorrect. The stock market crash *increased* the unemployment rate by 9%, from 5.5% in 1929 to 14.5% in 1930.
Choice **d** is incorrect. In the year following the German invasion of Poland, the unemployment rate dropped from 25% to 21%, or a 4% drop. This was not the largest decrease.

15. The answer is **private**, based on an understanding and a comprehension of the definition and logical reasoning to understand how it can fit into the statement.

16. Choice a is correct. The Democrat bar is the highest and is shown on the graph with political parties being labeled on the *x*-axis (horizontally) and the percentage of members labeled along the *y*-axis (vertically). This allows a viewer to see that the Democratic Party has the highest percentage of members.

Choice **b** is incorrect. While the Democratic Party does have the most members based on the percentages, the political parties are labeled on the *x*-axis, not the *y*-axis. Also, percentages are labeled on the *y*-axis, not the *x*-axis.

Choice **c** is incorrect. While the political parties are labeled on the *x*-axis and percentages are labeled on the *y*-axis, which shows, through the use of bars, which party has the most members, the Libertarian Party does not have the highest bar. Therefore, it does not have the most members.

Choice **d** is incorrect. The Libertarian Party does not have the highest bar representing percentage of members and consequently does not have the most members. Also, political parties are labeled on the *x*-axis, not the *y*-axis, and percentages are labeled on the *y*-axis, not the *x*.

17. Choice b is correct. The key indicates that a circle surrounding a gray triangle includes **both** "urban rail transit system under construction in 2010" and "high-speed rail routes under construction in 2010."

Choice **a** is incorrect. The symbol for "urban rail transit system under construction in 2010" is a simple gray triangle.

Choice **c** is incorrect. The key indicates that a circle surrounding a gray triangle includes both "urban rail transit system under construction in 2010" and "high-speed rail routes under construction in 2010."

Choice **d** is incorrect. High-growth power centers are designated by a circle surrounding a black triangle.

18. Choice d is correct. The bars indicating expenditures for that time period are increasing. They increase from around $40 million to $80 million based on the dollar amount labeled on the *y*-axis (vertical) and years labeled on the *x*-axis (horizontal).

Choice **a** is incorrect. The bars indicating expenditures for that time period are not decreasing. They increase from around $40 million to $80 million based on the dollar amount labeled on the *y*-axis (vertical) and years labeled on the *x*-axis (horizontal).

Choice **b** is incorrect. The bars indicating expenditures for that time period are increasing, but they never decrease during that time. They increase from around $40 million to $80 million based on the dollar amount labeled on the *y*-axis (vertical) and years labeled on the *x*-axis (horizontal).

Choice **c** is incorrect. The bars indicating expenditures for that time period are increasing, and they never decrease during that time. They increase from around $40 million to $80 million based on the dollar amount labeled on the *y*-axis (vertical) and years labeled on the *x*-axis (horizontal).

19. Choice a is correct. Loaded language means language that is highly emotive and used to gain support, sway emotions, degrade others, or push an agenda. *Hoax* and *frustration* are words that are being used by Obama to sway voters against the previous political administration in order to win the presidency in the coming election.

Choice **b** is incorrect. Loaded language means language that is highly emotive and used to gain support, sway emotions, degrade others, or push an agenda. *Today* and *decisions* are not words that serve this purpose in this excerpt.

Choice **c** is incorrect. Loaded language means language that is highly emotive and used to gain support, sway emotions, degrade others, or push an agenda. *Void* and *lobbyists* are not words that serve this purpose in this excerpt.

Choice **d** is incorrect. Loaded language means language that is highly emotive and used to gain support, sway emotions, degrade others, or push an agenda. *Page* and *diplomacy* are not words that serve this purpose in this excerpt.

20. Choice b is correct. Obama is publicizing a point of view or political cause. He does not acknowledge who has been telling Americans this but implies that it is coming from members of the government. Obama wants to replace these members by hopefully winning the presidency. This speech announces his political campaign for president.

Choice **a** is incorrect. Obama is stating his opinions. Obama wants the people hearing him to feel he is right about these issues. He does not present an economic chart.

Choice **c** is incorrect. Obama is stating his opinions. Obama wants the people hearing him to feel he is right about these issues. He does not present statistical facts.

Choice **d** is incorrect. The third paragraph of Obama's speech does not mention anything that he promises to do when he becomes president.

21. Choice d is correct. In the excerpt, Obama does not give any factual evidence to support this statement. Therefore it falls into the category of an opinion or unsupported claim.

Choice **a** is incorrect. In the excerpt, Obama does not give any factual evidence to support this statement.

Choice **b** is incorrect. A statistic is a piece of data that typically comes from a study involving a large amount of numerical data. Obama does not mention any numbers in this statement.

Choice **c** is incorrect. Obama's statement is not a warning that something will happen.

22. Choice b is correct. If Medicare and Medicaid are struggling, then the government would have to spend more on them in order to help the programs. Obama explicitly says, "We will eventually be spending more on Medicare and Medicaid than every other government program combined."

Choice **a** is incorrect. If Medicare and Medicaid are struggling, then the government would have to spend more on them in order to help the programs, not less. Obama explicitly says, "We will eventually be spending more on Medicare and Medicaid than every other government program combined."

Choice **c** is incorrect. While Obama mentions that Medicare and Medicaid are struggling due to rapidly increasing healthcare costs, he never mentions that this would lead to the shutdown of these programs. As government programs, it is much more likely that the government would spend more money on them instead of shutting them down. Also, due to the fact that so many people rely on these programs, it would take a lot more to actually shut them down.

Choice **d** is incorrect. This is the exact opposite of what Obama implies will happen. As government programs, the government would spend more money on them to help them when they are struggling. If the government stopped spending money on them, their struggles would increase to the point where they could no longer function. Also, Obama explicitly says, "We will eventually be spending more on Medicare and Medicaid than every other government program combined."

23. Choice c is correct. This was the goal of Columbus' expedition in 1492. The spice trade was very lucrative at the time, and Columbus had the idea that he could sail in the direction of the Americas and eventually reach Asia, thereby avoiding overland trade routes in the other direction. He did not realize that there was a large landmass in the way, and this is how he discovered the Americas.

Choice **a** is incorrect. His first expedition in 1492 had nothing to do with finding new territory. He did not know that the Americas existed since this expedition brought him into contact with the land for the first time. While he did eventually make future expeditions to the Americas on behalf of Spain, this was after he knew it existed.

Choice **b** is incorrect. He did not know that the Americas existed since this expedition brought him into contact with the land for the first time. While he did eventually make future expeditions to the Americas for goods on behalf of Spain, he could not be planning an expedition to trade with native peoples he did not know existed.

Choice **d** is incorrect. His first expedition in 1492 had nothing to do with creating a new settlement for Spain in the Americas. He did not know that the Americas existed since this expedition brought him into contact with the land for the first time, and he could not be looking to make a settlement in a place he didn't know existed. While he did eventually make future expeditions to the Americas on behalf of Spain, this was after he knew it existed.

24. The correct answer is **Navy's Women Accepted for Voluntary Emergency Service**, or **WAVES**. Based on the pie chart, 0.3% of the women joining the military during World War II were Women's Airforce Service Pilots or WASP, 4% were Navy Nurse Corps, 17% were American Nurse Corps, 6% were Marine Corps Women's Reserves and 3% were Coast Guard Women's Reserves, or SPARS. The combination of all of those percentages comes out to 30.3% of women joining the military. This is closer to the 28% of the Navy's Women Accepted for Voluntary Emergency Service rather than to the 42% that was the Women's Army Corps.

25. **Choice a is correct.** The map shows countries in the Eastern Bloc in darker gray and the Western Bloc in lighter gray. Turkey is colored lighter gray and is, therefore, part of the Western Bloc.

Choice **b** is incorrect. The map shows countries in the Eastern Bloc in darker gray and the Western Bloc in lighter gray. Turkey is colored lighter gray and is, therefore, part of the Western Bloc.

Choice **c** is incorrect. The Iron Curtain is a dividing line. Therefore, it is not one of the divisions that countries could be put into during the Cold War. It is shown as a white line, which Turkey only barely touches.

Choice **d** is incorrect. This map does not give any information about Turkey's relationship with the United States. The United States is not depicted on the map.

26. **Choice b is correct.** Bush never mentions that the goal is to control the local leadership and economy in Iraq, but rather the goal is to help the Iraqi people eventually be able to completely control their own government. Therefore, this is not a reason that it was important to have civilian experts in Iraq.

Choice **a** is incorrect. Bush explicitly states, "They're helping to strengthen responsible leaders and build up local economies." Therefore, this choice is a reason that it was important to have civilian experts in Iraq.

Choice **c** is incorrect. Bush explicitly states, "They're helping give ordinary Iraqis confidence." Therefore, this choice is a reason that it was important to have civilian experts in Iraq.

Choice **d** is incorrect. Bush explicitly states, "They can claim their place in a free Iraq." Therefore, this choice is a reason that it was important to have civilian experts in Iraq.

27. **Choice c is correct.** A profit is a financial gain. Since the company only spent $1 on the product and then sold it for $2.35 to consumers, the company makes a financial gain of $1.35 every time that a consumer purchases the product. The company makes a profit of $1.35.

Choice **a** is incorrect. A monopoly is an entity that has exclusive control over a product or service. A dollar amount cannot be an example of something that has complete control over a product or service. Also, the example gives no indication that the company has exclusive control of the product.

Choice **b** is incorrect. The $1.35 would only be a part of the expense for the consumer, not an expense for the company. The company's only expense was the $1 that it spent on the product before selling it.

Choice **d** is incorrect. Since the company only spent $1 on the product and then sold it for $2.35 to consumers, the company makes a financial gain of $1.35 every time that a consumer purchases the product. The company makes a profit of $1.35, not a loss.

28. **The correct answer is tariff.**

A tariff is a tax or duty placed on imports or exports.

29. **Choice b is correct.** The person in this situation would not qualify for the card. He or she is not old enough, is a high-school student, not a college student, and does not have an income greater than $4,000.

Choices **a**, **b**, and **c** are incorrect. The people in these situations would qualify for the card. They are old enough, are students of an accredited university, and have an income greater than $4,000.

30. **Choice c is correct.** The excerpt mentions that the economy benefits in the short term from substantial spending increases during the conflict; however, this leads to negative residual effects that hurt the economy in the long term after the war is over and there is no longer a spending boom related to the conflict.

Choice **a** is incorrect. The excerpt mentions that the economy benefits in the short term from substantial spending increases during the conflict; however, this leads to negative residual effects that hurt the economy in the long term after the war is over and there is no longer a spending boom related to the conflict.

Choice **b** is incorrect. The excerpt mentions that the economy benefits in the short term from substantial spending increases during the conflict; however, this leads to negative residual effects that hurt the economy in the long term after the war is over and there is no longer a spending boom related to the conflict. Therefore, wars definitely have economic effects.

Choice **d** is incorrect. The excerpt mentions that the economy benefits in the short term from substantial spending increases during the conflict; however, this leads to negative residual effects that hurt the economy in the long term after the war is over and there is no longer a spending boom related to the conflict. The effects are not all negative due to the positive short-term effects.

31. **Choice a is correct.** Dark gray bars represent the amount that the United States spent on metal exploration. The two lines represent the price of gold and copper. Based on this information, between the years 2006 and 2008 the prices of gold and copper along with U.S. spending on metal exploration all increased. Choices **b**, **c**, and **d** are incorrect. Dark gray bars represent the amount that the United States spent on metal exploration. The two lines represent the price of gold and copper. Based on this information, between the years 2006 and 2008 the prices of gold and copper along with U.S. spending on metal exploration all increased.

32. **Choice c is correct.** The quote from the first source says, "In reality, this eve began more than two centuries before this date," while the quote from the second source does not mention this idea.

Choice **a** is incorrect. Both quotes mention that the time period of the Industrial Revolution was the eighteenth century.

Choice **b** is incorrect. Both quotes define the Industrial Revolution as a time of great change. "The era known as the Industrial Revolution was a period in which fundamental changes occurred" and "Industrial Revolution, in modern history, is the process of change from an agrarian, handicraft economy to one dominated by industry and machine manufacture."

Choice **d** is incorrect. Both sources mention that England is where the Industrial Revolution began and grew. "The era known as the Industrial Revolution was a period in which fundamental changes occurred in agriculture, textile and metal manufacture, transportation,

economic policies and the social structure in England" and "This process began in England in the eighteenth century and from there spread to other parts of the world."

33. **Choice d is correct.** The Japanese region covers an island, borders the Korean region, and is north of the Malay/Indonesian and Papuan regions.

Choice **a** is incorrect. The Turkic region is above the Malay/Indonesian and Papuan regions, but it is not covering an island and does not border the Korean region.

Choice **b** is incorrect. The Thai region is above the Malay/Indonesian and Papuan regions, but it is not covering an island and does not border the Korean region.

Choice **c** is incorrect. The Han region is above the Malay/Indonesian and Papuan regions and borders the Korean region, but it is not covering an island.

34. **Choice b is correct.** The map key shows that states labeled with the darkest gray have a population size of 25,000,000 or more, and the states labeled with one shade lighter have a population size of 15,000,000 to 24,999,999. In the 2009 map, Texas is colored the second to darkest shade and in the 2011 map it is colored the darkest shade. Therefore, its population increased from the 15,000,000–24,999,999 range to the 25,000,000 or more range.

35. Choice d is correct. Texas and California are both colored the darkest shade of gray, representing a population of 25,000,000 or more. Therefore, the population of California is in the same category as the population of Texas according to the information given in the map. Choice **a** is incorrect. California does not have a larger population than Texas. Both are colored the darkest shade of gray, representing a population of 25,000,000 or more. Therefore the population of California is in the same category as the population of Texas according to the information given in the map. The map does not show exact population numbers, so there is no way to determine which one actually has a slightly larger or smaller population. Choice **b** is incorrect. Texas and California are both colored the darkest shade of gray, representing a population of 25,000,000 or more. Tennessee has a smaller population than either Texas or California.

Choice **c** is incorrect. Texas and California are both colored the darkest shade of gray, representing a population of 25,000,000 or more. Therefore, the population of California is in the same category as the population of Texas according to the information given in the map. The map does not show exact population numbers, so there is no way to determine which one actually has a slightly larger or smaller population.

CHAPTER 3 ▶ SOCIAL STUDIES PRACTICES

This chapter focuses on reviewing and building the skills you need to master for test day. It covers what the GED® Testing Service refers to as social studies practices—the critical thinking and reasoning skills that are essential to social studies success.

These social studies practices are:

- **Reading and Writing in a Social Studies Context:** 30% of the GED® Social Studies test
- **Applying Important Social Studies Concepts:** 40% of the GED® Social Studies test
- **Applying Mathematical Reasoning to Social Studies:** 30% of the GED® Social Studies test

Becoming familiar with these skills and how the GED® test measures them is important for doing your best on test day. In addition to the social studies practices, this chapter provides you with an overview and practice for the extended response question found on the GED® Social Studies test. The answers and explanations for all practice questions are found at the end of the chapter.

Reading and Writing in a Social Studies Context

The GED® Social Studies test addresses reading and writing skills as they relate to the social studies content areas (civics and government, U.S. history, economics, and geography and the world). About 30% of the questions on the test assess these skills. This means that doing well on the GED® Social Studies test requires you to be able to apply reading skills to a broad range of social studies topics.

Your reading skills will be mostly tested through questions related to reading passages. These passages can be as short as a sentence or two, but they are more often one or two paragraphs. Rarely are passages longer than three paragraphs.

The passages used on the GED® Social Studies test include primary source materials, such as speeches, letters, laws, excerpts from the U.S. Constitution, and other documents. Passages may also include secondary source materials in which an author provides an overview of an event, a person, or a geographic region, for example. In addition to reading passages, social studies reading skills may be assessed in written information provided in tables, charts, or other stimuli.

Passages may be paired with just one question, or they may have several questions. The questions are intended to assess your understanding of the passage and related social studies concepts.

Questions related to reading in a social studies context focus on the central ideas, the meaning of words and phrases, the author's point of view, the arguments that are made in the passage, and the evidence that supports those arguments. Sometimes a pair of passages is provided on the same topic, and you will be asked to compare and contrast them.

The best approach for questions related to passages is to look carefully at the clues provided in the passage.

- Read the passage carefully. Think about what the author is saying, the conclusions that are being drawn, the arguments that are being made, and the details used to support these arguments.
- Read the question and consider your answer options.
- Go back and find specific details in the passage that are related to the question.

Determining Details to Make Logical Inferences or Valid Claims

Making logical inferences sounds complicated, but it's not. In fact, you make inferences every day without thinking about it. When you hear "Happy Birthday" being sung, you infer that it is someone's birthday—even if you know nothing else about this person. If you see a school bus with yellow flashing lights, you would logically infer several things: there is a bus stop nearby. The school bus is about to stop. The traffic going both ways is about to stop. These are all logical inferences—they follow from the evidence provided. Inferences can be illogical, too. If you used what you know about school buses and yellow flashing lights to infer that bus drivers love yellow, this would be an *illogical* inference. It would not be a valid claim.

When taking the GED® test, the inferences and claims you make must be based on the information that is provided. When dealing with reading passages, this is a two-step process.

Step 1: Determine Clearly Stated Details

The first thing you need to do is to focus on the details that the author includes. These may be facts, definitions, examples, or other evidence. This is the information that you will use to make logical inferences or claims. Other than a basic understanding of social studies, you will not need a lot of other technical or factual information outside of what you'll find in the passage.

Step 2: Make Logical Inferences or Valid Claims

This step focuses on how you use the information that has been provided in the passage. Some questions will ask you whether you can make a logical inference from the facts, definitions, examples, and other details that have been provided. An **inference** is a conclusion that is drawn from the evidence provided. It is the conclusion that you reach logically from following the author's reasoning. A **claim** is a statement based on this inference. A **valid claim** is a statement that is reasonable or that can be supported by evidence, in this case by the evidence provided in the passage.

INFERENCES VERSUS CLAIMS

- An **inference** is a conclusion that is drawn from the evidence provided. It is the conclusion that you reach logically from following the author's reasoning.
- A **claim** is a statement based on this inference.
- A *valid* claim is a statement that is reasonable or that can be supported by evidence.

The GED® Social Studies test assesses your ability to make inferences in a variety of ways. Questions might ask about the context in which a speech or primary source document was written. Other questions might ask about the opinions or priorities of the author. You might even be asked what likely happened as a result of the speech or document.

Practice

Carefully read the following excerpt from a speech by George Washington and answer the question that follows.

EXCERPT

Friends and Citizens:

The period for a new election of a citizen to administer the executive government of the United States being not far distant, and the time actually arrived when your thoughts must be employed in designating the person who is to be clothed with that important trust, it appears to me proper . . . that I should now apprise you of the resolution I have formed, to decline being considered among the number of those out of whom a choice is to be made.

1. Based on the excerpt, when did George Washington make this speech?
   a. during his tenure as general of the Continental Army
   b. at the Constitutional Convention
   c. prior to his first presidential nomination
   d. during his second term as president

Once you have made your inference, check your answer. Ask yourself: Do the facts and evidence point to this conclusion? In this case, the facts do support the conclusion that Washington made this speech during his second term in office.

As you can see from the example, making inferences may require your knowledge of social studies concepts. You could not determine the context of a speech by George Washington without knowing who Washington was, for instance.

That said, it is important to focus on the evidence provided in the passage without involving your own assumptions or prejudices. Inference questions often ask about how an author—or in the last example, a speaker and a president of the United States—feels about a topic or historical event. When reading an excerpt from a speech by George Washington, how you feel about Washington or the presidency is not important; how Washington feels about his presidency *is*.

Determining Central Ideas

The GED® Social Studies test will also require you to determine the main ideas of excerpts from primary or secondary source documents. A **primary source** is an original piece of writing or art. Some good examples are diary entries, letters, speeches, the texts of laws, and literary passages. A **secondary source** is a document that discusses a primary source. An example is an academic article about a novel. Questions may ask about the main idea of a passage as a whole or a section, paragraph, or other part of the passage.

The **main idea** is a general statement that sums up what the author is saying. To determine the main idea, ask yourself the following questions:

- What is the passage (section/paragraph) mostly about?
- What is the author trying to tell me?

The main idea is often included in the first sentence, but this is not always the case. An author may include an introductory paragraph to set the scene and then introduce the main idea. Or the author may build up to his or her point, causing the main idea to be found near or at the end of the passage or paragraph.

Have you ever heard the expression that someone "can't see the forest for the trees"? This means that when you are focused on the small stuff (trees), you miss the bigger picture (the forest). This can happen with the main idea as well. To find the main idea, you need to look at the forest—the passage as a whole. This can be somewhat counterintuitive: rather than reading each word carefully, you may be better

able to assess the main idea by reading the entire passage as a whole.

Practice

2. Read the following paragraph and underline the sentence that shows the main idea.

When Christopher Columbus landed in the New World, he brought with him horses, cattle, and seeds for planting. Over the next decades, European explorers and settlers brought to the New World other domesticated animals and plants. Wheat and other grains soon became a staple crop in North America. Meanwhile, from the New World to the Old went corn, squash, turkeys, tomatoes, and the ever-important potato. This transfer of plants, animals, and diseases, known as the Columbian Exchange, transformed the diets and lifestyles of people on both sides of the Atlantic.

Figuring Out the Meaning of Words and Phrases

As with any type of study, the social studies disciplines—economics, geography, history, and government—all have words and phrases that are somewhat unique to them. While you should study and learn common social studies terms, you are not expected to know more specific vocabulary terms. What you are expected to be able to do, however, is to figure out the meaning of these words in context.

What does this mean? Basically, you become a detective on the hunt for clues in the rest of the passage. When you come upon an unfamiliar word or phrase, look at the words around that word or phrase. Often, they can unlock the meaning. Then move outward from there, looking for clues in the other parts of the sentence, other sentences, and finally other parts of the passage. In some cases, the word may be defined in a passage. In other cases, its meaning may become clear from the examples that are used. In still others, meaning may be discerned by looking at the greater context—that is, the overall meaning of the sentence, paragraph, and/or passage.

Some words have more than one meaning. You may be expected to figure out how a word with different meanings is used in a sentence or phrase. Take the word *convention*, for example. A convention can mean a formal assembly or gathering, a political meeting at which candidates are selected, an agreed-upon contract, the customary way of doing things, or a familiar or preferred writing style.

Practice

Read each of the following sentences, and then match it to the correct definition of *convention* from the choices listed.

3. The organization will hold its 45th annual *convention* in June.

4. The military government clashed with the *conventions* of the native peoples.

5. One of the reasons it can be difficult to read historical documents is that they follow different *conventions* from those used today.

Definitions:
a. customary way of doing things
b. formal assembly or gathering
c. familiar or preferred writing style

As you can see, you need to think about how a word is used in context to figure out what it means.

Points of View and Purposes

Understanding a text often goes beyond the words in front of you. You must also consider how and why it was written. This involves two things: point of view and the author's purpose (or the purpose of the document).

Point of view is simply the perspective from which someone writes something. A person's point of view is based on his or her background, experiences, and understanding of events and is tied to his or her opinions. For example, the American colonists and the British Parliament clearly had very different points of view regarding the American Revolution and the events leading up to it, and therefore had very different opinions about the Revolution itself. You will often know quite a bit about an author's point of view by knowing who the author is.

Author's purpose is simply the reason that an author is writing something. In some cases, it will help to consider who the intended audience is. Is the document meant for the whole population, or is it written for a certain group, such as the members of Congress? What does the document want to accomplish? Is it trying to cite facts to support a proposal? Is it trying to call people to take action?

Ask yourself the following questions:

- Why did the author write this?
- Who is the audience?
- What is this document intended to accomplish?

Practice

Read the following excerpt from an 1884 Congressional hearing and then answer the following question.

EXCERPT

They who say that women do not desire the right of suffrage, that they prefer masculine domination to self-government, falsify every page of history, every fact in human experience. It has taken the whole power of the civil and canon law to hold woman in the subordinate position which it is said she willingly accepts.

6. Think about who would have written the passage and why. The purpose of this passage is to _____.

Fact and Opinion

Just because something is stated in a passage does not mean that it is true. Most written material has some bias. **Bias** is just a preference for one thing or another or one point of view over another. Since almost everyone has personal opinions about everything from food to television shows, bias will probably be a part of anything you read, even if the writer tries very hard to be neutral. A good reader must notice bias and tell the difference between facts and opinions.

A **fact** is a statement that can be verified. Examples typically include the dates on which events took place and the names of the people involved.

An **opinion** is a belief held by one person or a group of people. It cannot be verified or proven. Even if the majority has the same opinion, it does not make it a fact.

To differentiate between facts and opinions, consider the following questions:

- Would everyone agree with this statement?
- Can it be verified by a trustworthy source?

The answer to both of these questions must be "yes" for it to be a fact.

RECOGNIZING OPINIONS	
Be alert to common words that may introduce a statement of opinion:	
likely	believe
possibly	say
probably	charge
should/could	attest
think	feel

Facts and opinions may occur in a wide range of primary and secondary source materials. Editorials by definition include an author's opinion, but they also often include facts that support this opinion. Encyclopedias and social studies textbooks, on the other hand, focus on presenting facts with as little bias as possible.

Differentiating between facts and opinions is not always as easy as it appears. Sometimes this is because we bring our own perspectives and biases to the equation. Consider the following statement.

The American Revolution was a necessary fight for freedom.

You may agree with this statement. Most of the people you know may agree with this statement. There may be many facts and reasons that support this statement. But it is still an opinion. It cannot be verified by any sources.

Sometimes words will be used to emphasize that it is the author's opinion, such as when an author writes "I think . . ." or "we believe." A recommendation for a change is also typically an opinion, although it may be based on very real facts. Look also for comparative or superlative terms (he was the *best* president; there is *too much/not enough* attention paid to this issue).

Practice

Look at the following statements and decide whether each is a fact or an opinion.

7. The United States has a population that exceeds 316 billion. _____

8. The U.S. population is growing too quickly. _____

9. The fastest-growing segment of the U.S. population is adults over the age of 65. _____

Determine the Validity of Hypotheses

A **hypothesis** is a statement that has not been proven to be true or false. Some hypotheses are assumed to be true, but they cannot be proven. In social studies, hypotheses may include what might have happened if an event had not occurred or if someone else had been the leader when an event occurred. People may have many hypotheses about what might have happened had the United States not developed the atomic bomb, for instance. In this case, the hypothesis cannot be proven since this has already happened. People can also have hypotheses about what will happen in the future. For instance, "The threat of terrorism will continue to grow" or "The Republican Party will splinter into two factions" are hypotheses that will prove true or untrue over time.

The GED® Social Studies test assesses your ability to tell whether a hypothesis is based on evidence. What is evidence? **Evidence** is simply the facts and reasons that point to a conclusion. To support the hypothesis that World War II would have dragged on had the United States not developed the atomic bomb, an author might provide evidence about the numbers of casualties prior to the atomic bomb, the readiness plans of Japan and other combatants, letters revealing the impact of the atomic bomb, and so forth.

To decide whether a hypothesis is based on evidence, ask the following questions:

- What is the author saying? What is his or her hypothesis? (This will often be provided as the question.)
- What reasons, facts, and evidence does the author provide?
- Do these reasons, facts, and evidence logically support the author's hypothesis?

Practice

Read the passage and answer the question that follows.

MACHU PICCHU

Machu Picchu is an ancient stone city situated on a mountain ridge high in the Peruvian Andes, above the Sacred Valley. The Incas built the city around 1450, at the height of their empire. The city follows a strict plan in which agricultural and residential areas are separated by a large square. Most archeologists believe that Machu Picchu served as a religious and ceremonial center of the Incan empire.

The Incas chose Machu Picchu for its unique location and features. Getting to Machu Picchu requires a journey up a narrow path. This makes it easily defended, as no one could approach without being spotted.

Machu Picchu was abandoned shortly after Spanish conquistadors vanquished the Incan empire. Over the next several centuries, the jungle reclaimed the site on which Machu Picchu lay. The site was once again discovered by an American historian and explorer in 1911. Since then, archeologists have flocked to the site to see what they can learn about the Incas. Today, Machu Picchu—the Lost City of the Incas—is the most visited site in Peru.

10. Which hypothesis is supported by the evidence in this passage?

    a. The Incas would have expanded their empire had Columbus not discovered the Americas.

    b. If Machu Picchu had not been discovered in 1911, we would not know anything about the Incas.

    c. Machu Picchu would have survived many more years had Columbus not discovered the Americas.

    d. If the Incas had built fortified centers on lower ground, they would have been able to beat the conquistadors.

Compare Two Sources on the Same Social Studies Topic

Comparing social studies texts is no different from comparing two movies or two television programs. In some cases, the sources to be compared will express opposite opinions, with one author expressing an opinion *in favor of* a cause and another *against* it, for instance. In other instances, one passage may be a primary source written by an eyewitness or participant in an event, while another might be a secondary source that analyzes that event. In these cases, the differences between the authors' positions might not be as easy to identify.

Regardless of what types of sources are being compared, the approach is the same: comparing and contrasting will require you to look for similarities and differences between them. This will often require you to examine both sources more than once.

For example, you might see pieces of two famous documents from U.S. history, such as a passage from the Declaration of Independence of 1776 and a portion of the Alien and Sedition Acts of 1798.

EXCERPT FROM THE DECLARATION OF INDEPENDENCE, 1776

We hold these truths to be self-evident, that all men are created equal, that they are endowed by their Creator with certain unalienable Rights, that among these are Life, Liberty and the pursuit of Happiness. That to secure these rights, Governments are instituted among Men, deriving their just powers from the consent of the governed, That whenever any Form of Government becomes destructive of these ends, it is the Right of the People to alter or to abolish it, and to institute new Government, laying its foundation on such principles and organizing its powers in such form, as to them shall seem most likely to effect their Safety and Happiness. . . . [W]hen a long train of abuses and usurpations, pursuing invariably the same Object evinces a design to reduce them under absolute Despotism, it is their right, it is their duty, to throw off such Government, and to provide new Guards for their future security.

EXCERPT FROM THE ALIEN AND SEDITION ACTS, 1798

SECTION 1. Be it enacted by the Senate and House of Representatives of the United States of America, in Congress assembled, That if any persons shall unlawfully combine or conspire together, with intent to oppose any measure or measures of the government of the United States, which are or shall be directed by proper authority, or to impede the operation of any law of the United States, or to intimidate or prevent any person holding a place or office in or under the government of the United States, from undertaking, performing or executing his trust or duty, and if any person or persons, with intent as aforesaid, shall counsel, advise or attempt to procure any insurrection, riot, unlawful assembly, or combination, whether such conspiracy, threatening, counsel, advice, or attempt shall have the proposed effect or not, he or they shall be deemed guilty of a high misdemeanor. . . .

SECTION 2. And be it farther enacted, That if any person shall write, print, utter or publish, or shall cause or procure to be written, printed, uttered or published, or shall knowingly and willingly assist or aid in writing, printing, uttering or publishing any false, scandalous and malicious writing or writings against the government of the United States, or either house of the Congress of the United States, or the President of the United States, with intent to defame the said government, or either house of the said Congress, or the said President, or to bring them, or either of them, into contempt or disrepute; or to excite against them, or either or any of them, the hatred of the good people of the United States, or to stir up sedition within the United States, or to excite any unlawful combinations therein, for opposing or resisting any law of the United States, or any act of the President of the United States, done in pursuance of any such law, or of the powers in him vested by the constitution of the United States, or to resist, oppose, or defeat any such law or act, or to aid, encourage or abet any hostile designs of any foreign nation against United States, their people or government, then such person . . . shall be punished by a fine not exceeding two thousand dollars, and by imprisonment not exceeding two years.

In this case, it is helpful to remember some United States history. Thomas Jefferson, who later became the third president of the United States, wrote the Declaration of Independence, which was approved by the Continental Congress in 1776. John Adams, the second president of the United States, signed the Declaration of Independence. Adams was president when the Alien and Sedition Acts were written, and he approved them.

But even if you do not know this context, you would recognize that these two documents emerged during the earliest part of the history of the United States—a period of revolution. Read both carefully and ask yourself: "What do these two passages have in common?" It is clear they are talking about governments and how citizens should behave toward their governments. You don't have to read too far into the Declaration of Independence to know what it is about. In fact, it's clear from the title. Jefferson is arguing that it is the *right* and *duty* of the people to overthrow an unjust government. However, the portion of the Sedition Act above makes it illegal to *com-*

bine or conspire together, with intent to oppose any measure or measures of the government of the United States.

Summary of Reading and Writing in a Social Studies Context

As you can see, the reading skills assessed in the GED® Social Studies test are interrelated. These are the same skills that are needed by a reader in any other discipline. Most social studies passages will be fairly straightforward, but you will need to make inferences based on the passage and an overall understanding of social studies. You may be asked—explicitly or implicitly—to identify the main idea(s) and/or determine the author's point of view and purpose. Other questions may focus on the opinions and claims of the author and whether these are supported by the details.

- **Be a detective.** Look for clues that will help you better understand the text. In addition to the passage itself, look for the title, the date it was written, and the background of the person who wrote it—all of these can provide you with valuable information.
- **Be an active reader.** Ask questions as you read. Stop and reread things that you don't understand.
- **Check your instincts.** In most cases when taking any type of test, your first instinct is correct. But before you submit it, check your answer by looking back at the text to find details that support it.

Applying Important Social Studies Concepts

The GED® Social Studies test asks you to apply reasoning skills to the social studies content areas (civics and government, U.S. history, economics, and geography and the world). About 40% of the questions you'll encounter on the test require these skills.

Success on this part of the test will require you to think logically about arguments, events, and ideas. You may need to look at the evidence and find details that support a claim that is made. You may need to consider the bias or point of view evident in a written excerpt, political cartoon, propaganda poster, or other visual element. Some questions may require you to look at two events and decide whether the first event caused the second or to identify the cause or effect from a list of items.

Let's look in more detail at how more specific reasoning skills may apply to the test.

Use Evidence to Support Inferences or Analyses

The GED® Social Studies test will assess your ability to find evidence in written material to support an inference or a claim. As discussed in the previous section, an **inference** is a conclusion that is drawn from the evidence provided. In addition to making inferences, the GED® Social Studies test will ask you to find the details, facts, or other information to support these inferences.

There are some words and phrases that authors often use to introduce evidence in support of an opinion or main idea. Look for phrases (e.g., *for example, for instance, in particular, a reason is, in one case*) that suggest the author is providing you with a reason or supporting detail.

Charts, graphs, or political cartoons are also sometimes used to assess this skill. For instance, you may be asked to find specific information on a graph that suggests something has happened.

Take a look at the following graph.

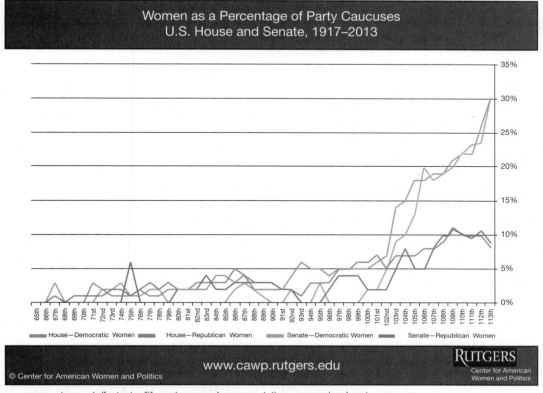

Women as a Percentage of Party Caucuses
U.S. House and Senate, 1917–2013

House—Democratic Women   House—Republican Women   Senate—Democratic Women   Senate—Republican Women

www.cawp.rutgers.edu

RUTGERS
Center for American
Women and Politics

© Center for American Women and Politics

www.cawp.rutgers.edu/footnotes/life-party-women's-representation-congressional-party-caucuses

First, let's break this chart down. The *x*-axis—the bottom line—contains a tick mark for each Congress from 1917 to 2013, which are the 65th through the 113th congressional sessions. The *y*-axis—the vertical line—denotes the percentages. The various lines represent women Democrats and women Republicans in the House of Representatives and women Democrats and women Republicans in the Senate.

On the GED® Social Studies test, a graph like this one will often be accompanied by a question like the following. Select the choice that you think is correct, and then we'll analyze each choice to see if there is evidence in the graph to support it.

Which statement about the data presented on this chart is correct?

a. More women run for Congressional seats as Democrats than as Republicans.

b. The number of women Republicans in the Senate has increased steadily since 1917.

c. The percentage of Congressional Democrats who are women has increased sharply since the 102nd Congress.

d. Republicans have tended not to vote for female Congressional candidates since the 102nd Congress.

Choice **c** is the correct answer. To answer this question correctly, you have to consider whether there is evidence in the chart that clearly supports the statement.

Let's start with choice **a**:

a. *More women run for Congressional seats as Democrats than as Republicans.*

This may be an attractive choice because it is clear that female Democrats (the lighter lines in the chart) represent a larger proportion of their party in Congress than Republican women. But we cannot conclude based only on this chart that this is because more Democratic women run for office.

Next, let's look at choice **b**:

b. *The number of women Republicans in the Senate has increased steadily since 1917.*

This might look possible at first glance, but it is important to remember that this is a chart that shows the percentage of Republicans in Congress that are women. It does not show the exact number of women Republicans that were serving in Congress at any given time. Even so, the chart shows that women Republicans as a percentage of all Congressional Republicans has varied widely over time.

Moving on to choice **c**:

c. *The percentage of Congressional Democrats who are women has increased sharply since the 102nd Congress.*

This choice is clearly supported by the chart and is thus correct. Look at the lighter lines in the chart and you can see a sharp upturn in both starting around the 102nd Congress. The percentage of Congressional Democrats who are women increased from around 5% to around 30% in that time span.

Finally, let's examine choice **d**:

d. *Republicans have tended not to vote for female Congressional candidates since the 102nd Congress.*

There is no evidence to support this statement. The chart does not give us any information about the number of women who have run for a Congressional seat on the Republican ticket, and there is no evidence in the chart that would allow us to make speculations about Republican voting preferences. Thus, this choice is incorrect.

Describe Social Studies Concepts and Connections between Them

Some of the questions on the GED® Social Studies test will ask you to describe relationships between or among people, places, environments, processes, or events. Sometimes these questions will stand on their own, but other times there will be a short reading passage or graphic—or both—for you to consider. Being able to sum up or describe quickly what you read is an important skill.

Practice

Read the paragraph and answer the question that follows.

REDUCING CARBON FOOTPRINT

Jim Blanchard is looking for ways to reduce his carbon footprint. He takes his own bags to the grocery store and avoids anything that is packaged in plastic. He also collects recyclables and takes them to the recycling center. Jim does not own a car. He uses mass transit to reach most places he needs to go to. He also owns an electric scooter, so he does not use gasoline.

11. How would you describe Jim Blanchard? Complete the following sentences.

Jim Blanchard is a(n) _____.

He is concerned about _____.

Now try examining the following two charts and describing them as we did previously with the passages.

**Causes of Deforestation in the Amazon
Rain Forest, 2006–2012**

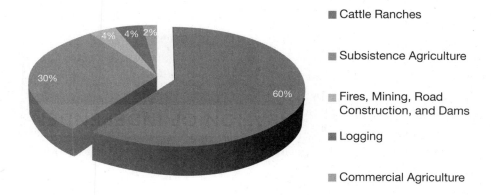

- Cattle Ranches
- Subsistence Agriculture
- Fires, Mining, Road Construction, and Dams
- Logging
- Commercial Agriculture

Beef Exports
OECD-FAO Projections, 2006 and 2015

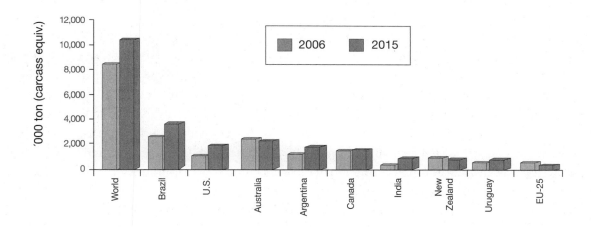

12. Describe, in one sentence, what is depicted in the pie chart.

_____

_____

13. Describe, in one sentence, what is depicted in the bar graph.

_____

_____

Now put it all together and answer the following question.

14. About 60% of the Amazon rain forest is in Brazil. What prediction about the deforestation of the Amazon rain forest can you make based on these charts?
   a. Subsistence agriculture will become an increasing cause of deforestation by 2015.
   b. Commercial agriculture will become an increasing cause of deforestation by 2015.
   c. Brazil's success as a beef exporter will lead to continued deforestation by 2015.
   d. Argentina's lack of success as a beef exporter will lead it to preserve the rain forest in 2015.

Put Events or Steps in Order

Some questions on the GED® Social Studies test will ask you to put historical events in the order in which they occurred. You may also be asked to understand the order of steps in a social studies process, such as how a bill becomes a law.

Some of these questions may use a time line or flowchart to provide a visual depiction of the order of events or steps in a process. A time line is a chart that organizes events or activities in the order in which they occur.

When writers use time as their main organization principle, it is called **chronological order**. They describe events in the order in which they did happen, will happen, or should happen. Much of what you will read on the GED® Social Studies test will be organized in this way, including historical texts, instructions and procedures, and essays about personal experiences.

Passages organized by chronology typically use a lot of transitional words and phrases. The **transitions** help us see when things happened and in what order. They help us follow along when the passage shifts from one period of time to another.

The following is a list of some of the most common chronological transitions:

- *first, second, third, (etc.), before*
- *after, next, now*
- *then, when, as soon as*
- *immediately, suddenly, soon*
- *during, while, meanwhile*
- *later, in the meantime, at last*
- *eventually, finally, afterward*

Practice

15. Put the events listed in the correct order.
   How a Bill Becomes a Law

   1. _____

   2. _____

   3. _____

   4. _____

   5. _____

   6. _____

- The differences are ironed out in a Conference Committee.
- The bill is then presented to the president.
- The House and Senate pass different versions of the bill.
- The bill is introduced to Congress.
- The president signs the bill.
- The bill returns to Congress, where it must be passed through both houses.

Analyze Cause-and-Effect Relationships

The GED® Social Studies test will ask you to identify the relationships between events. Often, historical events are connected to situations that came before them. There are several things to keep in mind when you are considering cause-and-effect relationships:

- There may be multiple causes for an event.
- There may be multiple effects of an event.

■ Just because events occur near the same time or in the same place does not mean they are related or that one caused the other.

■ Sometimes the question of what is considered a cause can be controversial.

Cause-and-effect questions are often associated with a written excerpt, but they may also ask about data presented in a time line or other chart or graph, or a combination of both.

Practice

Look at the time line, read the excerpt from the declaration made by South Carolina when it seceded from the Union, and then answer the question that follows.

Civil War Time Line, 1860–1865

December 20, 1860   South Carolina is the first to secede from the Union.

April 12, 1861   The first shots of the Civil War are fired at Fort Sumter.

January 1, 1863   Lincoln issues the Emancipation Proclamation.

April 9, 1865   General Robert E. Lee surrenders at Appomattox Courthouse in Virginia.

EXCERPT

The people of the State of South Carolina . . . declared that the frequent violations of the Constitution of the United States, by the Federal Government, and its encroachments upon the reserved rights of the States, fully justified this State in then withdrawing from the Federal Union. . . .

We affirm that these ends for which this Government was instituted have been defeated, and the Government itself has been made destructive of them by the action of the non-slaveholding States. Those States have assumed the right of deciding upon the propriety of our domestic institutions. . . . They have encouraged and assisted thousands of our slaves to leave their homes; and those who remain, have been incited by emissaries, books and pictures to servile insurrection.

16. Based on the time line and excerpt, which is a factor that contributed to South Carolina's decision to secede from the Union?
    a. President Lincoln freed the slaves.
    b. The Union fired upon the Confederacy at Fort Sumter.
    c. Abolitionists were encouraging slaves to rebel.
    d. The Confederacy offered greater protection from foreign aggression.

Compare Sets of Ideas

The GED® test will also assess your ability to compare differing sets of ideas. These ideas might have to do with civics or economics. For instance, you might be asked to compare ideas about how to organize an economy or govern a country.

Practice

The U.S. political landscape is dominated by the Republican and Democratic parties. Review the table and answer the following question.

REPUBLICAN PARTY	DEMOCRATIC PARTY
Free market economy	Minimum wages and labor unions
Limited government	Higher tax rates for wealthy citizens
Strong national defense	Government support for social programs

17. Based on the table, which party would be most likely to cut the food stamp program in order to reduce the deficit?
   a. Republican
   b. Democratic

Identify Bias and Propaganda

The next skill we will look at involves identifying bias and propaganda. Let's first learn about bias.

Bias

Bias is a prejudice in favor of or against one thing, person, or group compared with another, usually in a way considered to be unfair. You can think of bias as a personal preference.

Everyone has personal preferences. Even if writers try not to show these preferences, there is likely to be some bias in what they write. Bias is closely related to an author's point of view. For instance, someone who grew up in a family in which multiple adults served in the military might have a tendency to respect service members and believe them to be honorable and courageous. Someone who grew up in a war-torn area where soldiers behaved violently toward civilians might have a strong bias against members of the armed forces.

To detect bias, watch for words that try to tell the reader how to think or behave. These are called **prescriptive words** and include terms such as *should*

and *must*. Also, watch for strongly worded statements that include terms like *always* or *never*; these often represent strong viewpoints that are prone to bias. Bias can also be shown by using words with positive associations when referring to things the writer agrees with or supports and using words with negative associations when referring to things the writer disagrees with.

Practice

Read the following passage. Then answer the question that follows.

TOUGH TIMES

With the economy lagging, many Americans are out of work. Unemployment benefits should be extended to help citizens weather these tough times. At the same time, the United States cannot afford to turn its back on the elderly, children, and poor families who have always relied on government assistance. Despite the downturn in the economy, the rich continue to get richer. The best way—perhaps the only way—to help the country succeed is to increase revenue by raising taxes for those who can afford to pay higher taxes.

18. What bias is evident in this passage? Write your answer on the following lines.

_____

_____

_____

Propaganda

Propaganda refers to techniques that try to influence opinions, emotions, and attitudes in order to benefit an organization or individual. Propaganda uses language that targets the emotions—fears, beliefs, values, prejudices—instead of appealing to reason or critical thinking. Advertising, media, and political campaigns use propaganda techniques to influence others. To detect propaganda, ask yourself the following questions about the information:

- Whom does it benefit?
- What are its sources?
- What is the purpose of the text?

You should be aware of a number of propaganda techniques:

Bandwagon: The basic message of bandwagon propaganda is: "Everyone else is doing something, so you should do it, too." It appeals to the desire to join the crowd or be on the winning team. Phrases like "Americans buy more of our brand than any other brand" or "the brand that picky parents choose" are examples of the bandwagon technique. To evaluate a message, ask these questions:

- Does this program or policy serve my particular interests?
- What is the evidence for or against it?

Common man: This approach tries to convince you that its message is just plain old common sense. Politicians and advertisers often speak in everyday language and present themselves as one of the people to appeal to their audience. For example, a presidential candidate campaigning in New Hampshire may wear a plaid shirt and chop wood or visit a mill in order to look like an ordinary citizen. To determine if the common-man technique is being used, ask yourself these questions:

- What ideas is the person presenting? Are the ideas presented differently than the person's usual image or language?
- What are the facts?

Euphemisms: Instead of emotionally loaded language that rouses its audience, these terms soften an unpleasant reality. Terms that soften the nature of war are often used. In the 1940s, for example, the U.S. government renamed the War Department the Department of Defense. Stay alert to euphemisms. What facts are being softened or hidden?

Generalities: This approach uses words and phrases that evoke deep emotions. Examples of generalities are *honor*, *peace*, *freedom*, and *home*. These words carry strong associations for most people. By using these terms, a writer can appeal to the emotions so that the reader will accept his or her message without evaluating it. Generalities are vague so that you will supply your own interpretations and not ask further questions. An example might be: "The United States must further restrict immigration in order to preserve freedom and liberty."

Try to challenge what you read and hear. Ask yourself:

- What does the generality really mean?
- Has the author used the generality to sway my emotions?
- If I take the generality out of the sentence, what are the merits of the idea?

Labeling or name-calling: This method links a negative label, name, or phrase to a person, group, belief, or nation. It appeals to hate and fears. Name-calling can be a direct attack, or it can be indirect, using ridicule. Labels can evoke deep emotions, such as *Commie*, *Nazi*, or *terrorist*. They can be negatively charged, depending on the situation: *yuppie*, *hipster*, *slacker*, *liberal*, or *reactionary*. When a written text or speech uses labeling, ask yourself these questions:

- Does the label have any real connection to the idea being presented?

- If I take away the label, what are the merits of the idea?

Testimonials: In advertising, athletes promote a range of products, from cereal to wristwatches. In politics, celebrities endorse presidential candidates. Both are examples of testimonials. A testimonial uses a public figure, expert, or other respected person to endorse a policy, organization, or product. Because you respect or admire a person, you may be less critical and accept what he or she says more readily. Ask yourself these questions:

- Does the public figure have any expert knowledge about this subject?
- Without the testimonial, what are the merits of the message?

Practice

19. Who was the intended audience for this poster?

_____

20. What was the goal of this poster?

_____

Analyze How Historical Circumstances Shape Point of View

Questions on the GED® Social Studies test may ask you to consider how historical circumstances shape an author's point of view. You may also need to assess how believable an author is based on an understanding of his or her bias.

When you come across information, consider point of view and bias by asking the following questions:

- Who wrote the text?
- Who is the intended audience?
- Under what circumstances was the text written?
- What is the purpose of the text?

In short, the more you know about the text, the more you will understand its point of view and/or bias.

Point of view is how someone looks at an event. A person's point of view is based on his or her background, experiences, and understanding of events. For example, a person who grew up in a family that had little money might think buying an expensive car or jewelry is wasteful. From that person's point of view, spending a lot of money on something that isn't a necessity is bad.

Practice

Read the following excerpt from the speech "Ain't I a Woman?" delivered in 1851 by African-American abolitionist and women's rights activist Sojourner Truth, and then answer the question that follows.

EXCERPT

Well, children, where there is so much racket there must be something out of kilter. I think that 'twixt the Negroes of the South and the women at the North, all talking about rights, the white men will be in a fix pretty soon. But what's all this here talking about?

That man over there says that women need to be helped into carriages, and lifted over ditches, and to have the best place everywhere. Nobody ever helps me into carriages, or over mud-puddles, or gives me any best place! And ain't I a woman? Look at me! Look at my arm! I have ploughed and planted, and gathered into barns, and no man could head me! And ain't I a woman? I could work as much and eat as much as a man, when I could get it, and bear the lash as well! And ain't I a woman? I have borne thirteen children, and seen most all sold off to slavery, and when I cried out with my mother's grief, none but Jesus heard me! And ain't I a woman?

Then they talk about this thing in the head; what's this they call it? [A member of the audience whispers, "Intellect."] That's it, honey. What's that got to do with women's rights or negroes' rights? If my cup won't hold but a pint, and yours holds a quart, wouldn't you be mean not to let me have my little half measure full?

21. In this excerpt, the point of view that Sojourner Truth is expressing when she repeatedly asks "And ain't I a woman?" is
    a. that former female slaves deserve the same courtesies as white women.
    b. that women deserve equal rights because they are as capable as men.
    c. that all men will suffer if they do not offer women equal rights.
    d. that intellect should influence whether a woman deserves equal rights.

Summary of Applying Important Social Studies Concepts

The most important thing when taking the GED® Social Studies test is to think carefully about what the question is asking. You will find that you can answer a lot of the questions by applying simple common sense to a basic understanding of social studies concepts.

Many of the questions will be based on a written excerpt, a graph, a political cartoon, a picture, or a combination of these things. Regardless of the types of passages or graphics you encounter, take the following steps:

- Look at the title or titles (if there are any): What do they tell you about the main idea?
- Look for the date or source of the information: What does this tell you about the context?
- Look at the author: What do you know about his or her background that may influence the point of view?
- Read the passage or visual element carefully: Look for the main idea and supporting details.
- Step back and consider the big picture: What is the author or illustrator trying to tell you?
- Finally, when you are ready to answer the question, look again at the passage or visual stimulus to make sure your initial impulse is correct.

Applying Mathematical Reasoning to Social Studies

The GED® Social Studies test asks you to apply basic mathematical skills to the social studies content areas (civics and government, U.S. history, economics, and geography and the world). About 30% of the questions on the GED® test require these skills.

Success on this part of the test does not require you to be a mathematician. However, you will need to know basic mathematical principles and terms, such as what an *average* means. You will also need to be able to apply basic principles, perhaps by figuring out the average of two or more numbers. Keep in mind that these questions are designed to assess your ability to use math to address *social studies* problems, not such computation skills as adding or multiplying.

Many of these skills are assessed by having you look at information presented in tables, charts, graphs, and maps. You may also be asked to apply mathematical reasoning to a political cartoon, photograph, or short passage. As a basic example, a map or chart may provide statistical data on population growth within individual states, but you may need to use your own knowledge about where the states are located to assess regional trends or how population growth is likely to affect a particular issue.

Let's look in more detail at how mathematical skills are applied to the social studies discipline.

Analyze Information Presented Visually

The GED® Social Studies test will assess your ability to analyze information that is presented visually. This information may be presented in maps, tables, charts, or other stimuli used to organize and present information in a logical manner. You may also be asked to analyze information in a political cartoon, a photograph, an advertisement, or a propaganda poster, for example.

Reading and understanding a map, chart, graph, or other stimulus is very similar to reading a passage. You want to look for clues about the meaning. Ask yourself the same questions as when trying to understand the main idea of a reading passage:

- What is this mostly about?
- What is the author (or illustrator) trying to tell me?

With many types of visual stimuli, the title can provide valuable clues. Often, the year (or years) represented in the map, chart, or graph will be included in the title. If not, look for this information elsewhere.

Tables

Tables organize information in columns and rows. Labels in the first column describe the information contained in the rows to the right of the first column. The labels at the top (column heads) describe the information in the columns below.

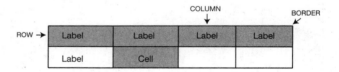

Here is an example of the type of table you will see on the GED® Social Studies test.

World Energy Consumption, 1970–2020	
Year	Quadrillion Btu Consumed
1970	207
1975	243
1980	285
1985	311
1990	346
1995	366
1999	382
2005	439
2010	493
2015	552
2020	612

Bar Graphs

A **bar graph** is one way to present facts visually. A bar graph features a vertical axis (running up and down on the left-hand side of the graph) and a horizontal axis (running along the bottom of the graph).

The horizontal axis is known as the *x*-axis. The vertical axis is known as the *y*-axis. The graph represents quantities in strips or bars. Graphs are especially useful for showing changes over time or comparing two or more quantities or trends.

To construct a bar graph from the table "World Energy Consumption, 1970–2020," mark the five-year increments on the bottom horizontal axis (*x*-axis) and the units of energy consumed (by increments of 100 quadrillion Btu) on the vertical axis (*y*-axis). By representing the table's data in a bar graph, you can visualize the world's energy consumption trend more easily.

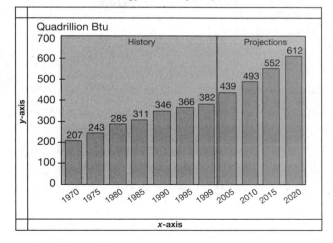

World Energy Consumption, 1970–2020

Line Graphs

Next, let's look at a **line graph**. It is similar to a bar graph because there is information presented along the *x*-axis and *y*-axis, and you'll need to look at both to understand the graph.

Immigrants Admitted to the United States, Fiscal Years 1900–2000

As you can see, line graphs are good for showing changes over time. In this case, we have a chart that depicts the number of immigrants admitted into the United States between 1900 and 2000. The line is useful because it shows not only an increase in the number of immigrants admitted, but the years in which the numbers increased dramatically or stayed relatively stable. Noticing these kinds of changes will help you interpret line graphs on the GED® Social Studies test because sharp increases and decreases shown on a line graph are usually significant to the question you are facing.

Circle Graphs/Pie Charts

Circle graphs, also called **pie charts**, look nothing like bar and line graphs; they even lack an *x*-axis and a *y*-axis. Circle graphs display information so that you can see relationships between parts and a whole. The information on a circle graph can be presented as percentages or as actual numbers. The circle is divided into parts, or pie slices, that together add up to the whole. To understand a circle graph, first read the title. What does the graph represent? Read all other headings and labels. What does each portion of the circle represent? Now you are ready to see how the parts relate to each other.

The following circle graph illustrates the items making up the entire amount of bakery goods sold by the Grainville Baking Company. Notice that this graph includes a title, labels, and a legend.

Breakdown of Breakfast Sales

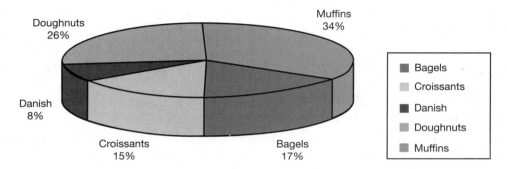

Maps

Maps are printed or drawn representations of a geographic area. Social scientists use different types of maps to understand the natural or cultural facts about an area. Maps can visually display many kinds of information, such as the physical features of the land, political boundaries between nations, or population densities.

- **Topographic maps** show the physical features of land, including land elevations and depressions, water depth, rivers, forests, mountains, and human-made cities and roads.
- **Political maps** display political divisions and borders.

- **Special-purpose maps** can depict a wide range of information about an area, from average rainfall, crop distribution, or population density to migration patterns of people.

To read a map, carefully review each of the following:

- **Title** describes what the map represents.
- **Legend or key** is a table or list that explains the symbols used in a map.
- **Latitude and longitude:** Latitude refers to the lines on a map that are parallel to the *equator*; longitude refers to lines parallel to the *prime meridian* that run north and south through

Greenwich, England. These lines help to locate specific areas on a map.

- **Scale** shows the map's proportion in relation to the actual area it represents. For example, on a topographic map, the scale might show the distance on the map that equals a mile or a kilometer on land.

Analyze Numerical, Technical, and Written Materials on a Common Topic

Some of the questions on the GED® Social Studies test will include more than one type of stimulus. They might include both a passage and a chart, for example. You may have to figure out whether different types of information go together—in other words, whether the information that is presented in a chart, graph, or other format goes with information in the written material, and vice versa.

These types of questions should be fairly easy; don't overcomplicate them. Look for the main idea of the passage that is provided. What is it mostly about? Then look at the main idea of the chart, graph, or other stimulus that is provided. Is it about the same topic?

Other questions may ask you to point out differences between two types of information on the same topic. For instance, a question might present two sets of information about immigration—from different centuries or focused on different countries. You might then be asked to point out similarities and differences in the information.

Create Tables, Graphs, and Charts

Some questions on the GED® Social Studies test will ask you to take written information and put it into a table or graph. Again, the key here is not to overcomplicate things. Take the following steps:

- Read the excerpt. Look for the numbers and statistics that are included.

- Look at the labels on the table or chart. Note how the information is organized.
- Transfer the numbers and statistics to the table or chart.

Questions may ask you to provide the labels for a chart or graph. The types of labels needed will vary depending on the chart or graph.

- **Line graphs** typically include labels for the x-axis and the y-axis. If the line graph shows a trend over time, the years are typically represented on the x-axis, with the item being measured shown on the y-axis.
- **Bar graphs** typically include a series of bars across the graph. They will need labels for the x-axis and y-axis.
- **Circle graphs** (or **pie charts**) show elements in relation to one another and to the whole. They often use a legend to show what the elements are, but labels may or may not be used to spell out the actual numbers or percentages.

Charts and graphs, like other visual stimuli, will also include titles. Some questions may ask you to add a title to a chart or graph. Again, all you need to do to answer these kinds of questions is to look for the main idea. You may also need to look at the legend to see what years or other categories are included in the graph.

Interpret Graphs and Use Data to Predict Trends

On the GED® Social Studies test, you'll have to do more than understand a chart. You'll need to interpret the data. This just means that you will take the numbers or other information provided and put them into words. It may also require you to relate one number to another, noting that it has decreased, increased, or doubled, for example. Finally, the information may require you to predict trends based on the chart. For example, if a population chart shows that the population of a country has doubled every 50 years, you might be asked what you would expect the population to be 100 years from now.

If you understand what the graph is showing, you should have no trouble with these types of questions. Again, familiarizing yourself with various types of graphs will help.

Practice

The following chart shows the price of SuperSport Sneakers since they were introduced to the U.S. market in 1990. Review the chart and answer the question that follows.

SuperSport Sneakers

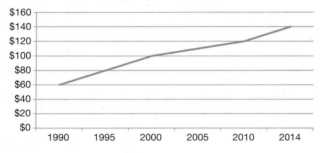

22. Based on the information in the chart, you would expect the price of SuperSport Sneakers to
   a. increase steadily.
   b. increase dramatically.
   c. decrease somewhat.
   d. remain the same.

Analyze How Variables, Events, or Actions Are Related

The GED® test will also assess your ability to determine whether different elements, events, or actions are related. Some of these questions will provide a chart or graph and ask you to make a valid conclusion or assess a claim regarding the impact of one variable on another. This will require you to

determine whether they are dependent or independent variables.

- A **variable** is just an object, event, idea, or other category that is being measured. For example, the time at which the sun rises could be a variable.
- A **dependent variable** is a variable that changes if another variable changes—it is dependent upon that variable. If some factor can change a variable, it is a dependent variable. The average life expectancy of a country may be a dependent variable if it is connected to factors such as famine or war.
- An **independent variable** is an element that is not affected by how the values of other variables may change. For example, your age is an independent variable. At a given time, nothing changes the exact number of days you have been on the planet.

Questions on the GED® Social Studies test may present information in a chart along with a written passage. You would then be asked to determine whether one factor has influenced the other. For instance, a question may include a graph that shows a sudden increase in average life expectancy along with a passage that talks about some trends in that country. You could be asked what factor or factors might have contributed to the change in life expectancy. Another question might present a set of data and ask you to assess the validity of one or more claims, requiring you to determine whether one thing relates to another. For instance, there may be a graph showing changes in the federal budget over time coupled with a passage discussing trends in the country. You may be asked to determine whether any connections are supported by the information given.

Closely related to this skill is determining cause and effect. This may involve determining whether one historical event led to another. A tricky part about analyzing cause and effect is that it is tempting to decide something is a cause just because it comes right before some change or effect. Often, so many factors might contribute to a change of some sort that it is impossible to point out a single cause. The key is to think logically about the issue.

Practice

Read the passage and examine the chart that accompanies it, and then answer the question that follows.

A DEADLY WAR

World War I (1914–1918) was one of the deadliest conflicts of the twentieth century. It involved the use of modern weaponry never before used in battle. This allowed combatants to kill each other on a scale that had been impossible in earlier wars. Most of the countries involved in the war were European nations, although the United States and the Ottoman Empire were also involved. Approximately 60 million Europeans fought over the course of the war. About 9 million combatants were killed. At the same time, a global epidemic of a deadly strain of influenza known as the Spanish flu killed some 50 million people around the world.

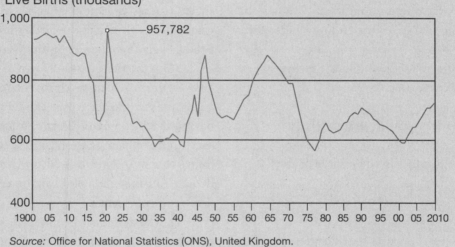

Live Births: England and Wales, 1900–2010

Live Births (thousands)

957,782

Source: Office for National Statistics (ONS), United Kingdom.

23. Which factor was most responsible for the first sharp drop in the birth rate in England and Wales in the early part of the twentieth century?
   a. The Spanish flu epidemic killed most English and Welsh women.
   b. World War I introduced advanced technology.
   c. Millions of English and Welsh men were fighting in World War I.
   d. Women in England and Wales were unable to afford to feed children.

Calculate Mean, Median, Mode, and Range

The final mathematical skill we'll discuss involves mean, median, mode, and range.

Mean

The **mean** is the same as the average. To find the mean, take the values, add them up, and divide by how many values you have.

Here's an example. Find the mean of the following numbers: 9, 14, 22, 11, and 10.

- Add the values. The sum is 66 (9 + 14 + 22 + 11 + 10 = 66).
- Count up how many items or values you have added: 5.
- Divide the sum of the values (66) by the number of values (5), and you get 13.2 (66 ÷ 5 = 13.2).

The mean, or average, is 13.2.

Median

The **median** is the value in the middle of your list of values. To find the median, reorder the values from lowest to highest. The median will be the number in the middle. If you have an even number of values, the median will be the average of the two numbers in the middle.

Let's find the median of the following list of numbers: 9, 14, 22, 11, and 10.

- First, put in order from smallest to largest: 9, 10, 11, 14, 22.
- Then, find the number in the middle of the list: 11.

Mode

The **mode** refers to the value that occurs most frequently in the list. If you have a list of three numbers and one occurs twice, that will be the mode. In longer lists, it will again help to put the values in order. Then, it's simple! Just look for the number that occurs most often.

Find the mode of the following list of numbers: 18, 12, 10, 2, 9, 6, 18, 42, 18, 2.

- Put in order from smallest to largest: 2, 2, 6, 9, 10, 12, 18, 18, 18, 42.
- Look for the number that occurs most often: there are three 18s, more than any other number.
- The mode is 18.

Range

The **range** is the difference between the largest and the smallest values.

Let's find the range of the previous set of numbers: 18, 12, 10, 2, 9, 6, 18, 42, 18, 2

- The largest number is 42.
- The smallest number is 2.
- The difference between them is 40.

Summary of Applying Mathematical Reasoning to Social Studies

Keep in mind that the GED® Social Studies test is not designed to assess your computational skills, just the mathematical skills directly related to the social studies discipline. You'll have access to a calculator, and social studies questions that require mathematical calculation will usually provide choices, so you will be less likely to make a computational error.

Many of the question formats provide a set of answers from which to choose. Look at each of the answer choices to see if you can figure it out without having to do the math. For instance, a question that asks for the mean or average of a series of numbers may not require you to add up the values and then divide. You may be able to figure out the answer by using common sense.

That said, one of the things that you will need to pay attention to is how numbers work. You should be able to move fairly readily between percentages and fractions, for instance. You should recognize that 1% is equal to $\frac{1}{100}$, meaning that something occurs 1 out of every 100 times. You should know that 50% is the same as one-half of something. Reviewing these basic mathematical principles, as well as the types of graphs you will likely come across, can help you focus on the content of the question that is asked.

Social Studies Practices Review

Use the following to answer questions 1–5.

Read the excerpt from a 1940 speech by Winston Churchill and answer the questions that follow.

EXCERPT

I speak to you for the first time as Prime Minister in a solemn hour for the life of our country, of our Empire, of our Allies, and, above all, of the cause of Freedom. A tremendous battle is raging in France and Flanders. The Germans, by a remarkable combination of air bombing and heavily armored tanks, have broken through the French defenses. . . . They have penetrated deeply and spread alarm and confusion in their tracks. . . .

In the air . . . the relative balance of the British and German Air Forces is now considerably more favorable to us than at the beginning of the battle. In cutting down the German bombers, we are fighting our own battle as well as that of France. My confidence in our ability to fight it out to the finish with the German Air Force has been strengthened by the fierce encounters which have taken place and are taking place. At the same time, our heavy bombers are striking nightly at the taproot of German mechanized power. . . .

We must expect that as soon as stability is reached on the Western Front, the bulk of that hideous apparatus of aggression which gashed Holland into ruin and slavery in a few days, will be turned upon us. I am sure I speak for all when I say we are ready to face it; to endure it; and to retaliate against it. . . .

Having received His Majesty's commission, I have found an administration of men and women of every party and of almost every point of view. We have differed and quarreled in the past; but now one bond unites us all—to wage war until victory is won, and never to surrender ourselves to servitude and shame, whatever the cost and the agony may be.

1. Which best explains Winston Churchill's purpose in this speech?
   a. to give an update on the latest battles
   b. to ask for support from other countries
   c. to galvanize popular support for the war
   d. to commemorate the soldiers fighting for freedom

2. Which statement can you infer from this passage?
   a. Germany will win the war at any cost.
   b. Holland has allied itself with Germany.
   c. The German army is advancing toward Britain.
   d. The British counterattack requires support from France.

3. Which of the following expresses the main idea of the second paragraph?

  a. *At the same time, our heavy bombers are striking nightly at the taproot of German mechanized power.*

  b. *My confidence in our ability to fight it out to the finish with the German Air Force has been strengthened by the fierce encounters which have taken place and are taking place.*

  c. *[T]he relative balance of the British and German Air Forces is now considerably more favorable to us than at the beginning of the battle.*

  d. *In cutting down the German bombers, we are fighting our own battle as well as that of France.*

4. During what war was this speech made?

_____

5. The third paragraph refers to *that hideous apparatus of aggression*. To what does this term refer? _____

Use the following passage to answer questions 6–8.

AIR POLLUTION IN MEXICO CITY

In 1992, Mexico City topped the United Nations' list of most polluted cities in the world. The air was so toxic that birds dropped in midflight. Air pollution was taking a toll on human health as well. Experts attributed roughly 1,000 deaths and 35,000 hospitalizations a year to the high ozone level.

The city's location has contributed to its air pollution problems. The city is located on a lake basin that was originally drained in the 1600s and is 7,000 feet above sea level. There are lower levels of oxygen at higher altitudes, which causes higher emissions of carbon monoxide and other pollutants. Intense sunlight results in more smog.

Since the mid-1990s, Mexican leaders have attempted to address the problem. The government required that gasoline be reformulated to remove lead. Polluting refineries and factories were encouraged to clean up their emissions and move away from the urban center. Public transportation was expanded to encourage people to drive less.

Change has been gradual, but the steps taken to address Mexico City's pollution problems have paid off. The presence of lead in the air is just one-tenth of what it was in 1990. Dust, soot, chemicals, and other suspended particles have been cut by 70 percent. There are still gains to be made, however, and the government continues to look for ways to reduce pollution. Much of these involve greener solutions to transportation, including the expansion of the low-emissions bus system, the addition of hybrid buses, and a new suburban train system.

6. Based on this excerpt, how does Mexico City's location contribute to its pollution problem?
   a. Its high altitude leads to less oxygen and greater emissions of pollutants.
   b. Its tropical location leads to hotter air temperatures and greater smog.
   c. Its proximity to the United States means that it deals with excess pollution from the north.
   d. Its dry climate leads to more dust particles in the air.

7. According to the passage, which of the following events occurred first?
   a. Mexico City was named the most polluted city in the world.
   b. The lake basin on which Mexico City is located was drained.
   c. Dust, soot, and chemicals have been reduced in Mexico City's air by 70%.
   d. The Mexican government expanded public transportation to encourage people to drive less.

8. Which of the following best supports the idea that Mexico's policies have made a difference in its pollution levels?
   a. Polluting refineries were encouraged to clean up their emissions.
   b. There are lower levels of oxygen at Mexico City's high altitudes.
   c. The presence of lead in the air dropped to one-tenth of 1990 levels.
   d. The government plans to build a new suburban train system.

Use the following to answer questions 9–11.

In 1904, Udo J. Keppler published the following political cartoon in *Puck* magazine. Look at the cartoon and answer the questions that follow.

9. Based on the cartoon, the artist most likely has a very _____ opinion of Standard Oil.
   a. positive
   b. negative

10. Which of the following is most likely the intended audience for this cartoon?
    a. working-class readers
    b. oil industrialists
    c. politicians
    d. marine biologists

11. Which of the following historical circumstances seems most likely to have informed the artist's point of view in this cartoon?
    a. the expansion of American corporations into foreign markets
    b. the dramatic increase in petroleum extraction and production in the nineteenth century
    c. the spread of powerful corporate monopolies in the late nineteenth century
    d. the territorial disputes between Spain and the United States that led to the Spanish-American War

Use the following to answer question 12.

King County (Washington) Single-Family Home Sales

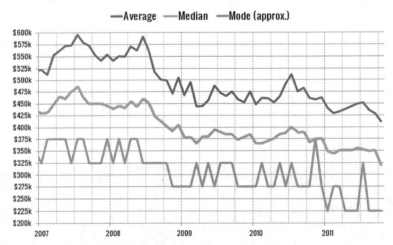

Source: http://seattlebubble.com/blog/2011/11/22/king-co-average-price-30-off-peak-mode-down-40/.

GLOBAL FINANCIAL CRISIS

In 2008, a global financial crisis threatened the stability of countries around the world. Many, including the United States, fell into deep recessions. The crisis was triggered by the bursting of a housing bubble in the United States. In economic terms, a bubble is a rapid increase in the price of some commodity that is not related to the actual change in its value. When a bubble bursts, prices fall rapidly. In the United States, when the housing bubble burst, high real estate prices dropped. Because the mortgages, or home loans, on these pieces of real estate were tied to financial markets around the world, the sharp fall in real estate prices triggered a financial panic and severe strain on banks and government budgets. Though some countries had yet to recover fully from the crisis as of 2014, the United States had recovered substantially from the economic crisis by 2010. Despite this, the real estate markets in many urban areas continue to suffer.

12. Which of the following would be the most accurate indicator of the effects of the global economic crisis on the Seattle, WA, housing market?
   a. average
   b. mode
   c. median
   d. range

Use the following to answer question 13.

Read the Preamble to the U.S. Constitution.

EXCERPT

We the People of the United States, in Order to form a more perfect Union, establish Justice, insure domestic Tranquility, provide for the common defence, promote the general Welfare, and secure the Blessings of Liberty to ourselves and our Posterity, do ordain and establish this Constitution for the United States of America.

13. What is the main purpose of the Preamble?
   a. to tell why the Constitution is needed
   b. to present an outline of the document
   c. to describe the new system of government
   d. to review the reasons for breaking from England

Use the following chart to answer questions 14–16.

Reasons for Not Voting, 2012

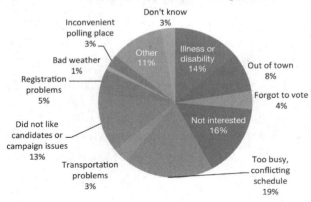

14. What is the biggest reason that people did not vote in 2012?
    a. illness or disability
    b. lack of interest
    c. too busy, conflicting schedule
    d. not liking candidates or campaign issues

15. Which change would likely have the greatest impact on voting rates?
    a. relocating polling places
    b. extending the polling hours or days
    c. sending reminders to registered voters
    d. changing the voter registration process

16. Consider the following opinion.
    Americans are apathetic about politics and do not appreciate the right to vote.
    What evidence from the chart could be used to support this opinion?
    a. Of Americans who did not vote, 16% said it was because they were not interested.
    b. Of Americans who did not vote, 5% said it was because they had registration problems.
    c. The most often-cited reason for not voting was that people were too busy.
    d. Of those who did not vote, 13% did not like the candidates or campaign issues.

Answers and Explanations

Chapter Practice

1. d. This question is asking you to figure out from the details when Washington made this speech. Nothing in the speech says specifically where or when it occurs, so you need to look for clues—the facts or details from which you can make an inference. Return to the passage to explore how the details might give you the clues you need to figure this out. The first clue is that Washington is addressing *Friends and Citizens.* This suggests that it is a speech to a larger group of people than the Continental Army (choice **a**) or the Constitutional Convention (choice **b**). From the first sentence, you learn that *The period for a new election . . . [is] not far distant.* You need to apply your knowledge of social studies to understand that Washington is talking about a presidential election. At the end of the paragraph, he says he wants *to decline* the nomination. Only choices **c** and **d** have to do with presidential elections, and as you probably know well, Washington was the first U.S. president. That means he did accept a nomination at some point, but at the time he is giving the speech, he does not want the nomination. So the only answer choice that makes sense by logical inference is choice **d**.

2. When Christopher Columbus landed in the New World, he brought with him horses, cattle, and seeds for planting. Over the next decades, European explorers and settlers brought to the New World other domesticated animals and plants. Wheat and other grains soon became a staple crop in North America. Meanwhile, from the New World to the Old went corn, squash, turkeys, tomatoes, and the ever-important potato. <u>This transfer of plants, animals, and diseases, known as the Columbian Exchange, transformed the diets and lifestyles of people on both sides of the Atlantic.</u>

3. b. The organization will hold its 45th annual *convention* in June. The annual convention is a **formal assembly or gathering**.

4. a. The military government clashed with the *conventions* of the native peoples. The native conventions are **customary ways of doing things**.

5. c. One of the reasons it can be difficult to read historical documents is that they follow different *conventions* from those used today. The historical conventions are **familiar or preferred writing styles of the times**.

6. *Answers will vary:*
The purpose of this passage is to **convince listeners that women do not want to be dominated by men.**

7. Fact.

8. Opinion.

9. Fact.

10. c. This is the only hypothesis that is supported by evidence from the passage. Columbus's discovery led to the Spanish conquest of the New World and the decline of the Incan empire.

11. *Answers will vary:*
Jim Blanchard is an **environmentalist**. He is concerned about **the use of nonrenewable natural resources**.
All the details in the passage describe a person who is most likely an environmentalist. The very first sentence of the passage states that Blanchard "is looking for ways to reduce his carbon footprint," and the remaining sentences describe his concern about use of plastic and nonrenewable natural resources such as gasoline.

12. *Answers will vary:*
Cattle ranches are the leading cause of deforestation of the Amazon rain forest. When you look at the pie chart, the biggest slice—cattle ranches—should grab your attention. At 60%, it is twice as large as the next leading cause of deforestation.

13. *Answers will vary:*
Beef exports are projected to significantly increase worldwide by 2015, but especially in Brazil and the United States. Looking at the bar chart, the darker bar (denoting the 2015 projections) is significantly taller than the lighter bar (denoting beef exports in 2006) for overall worldwide beef exports. Of the individual nations, the difference is most stark for Brazil and the United States, indicating that both nations make up a big chunk of that worldwide projection.

14. c. We can confidently predict, based on these charts, that a growing beef export industry in Brazil will put increasing pressure on the Amazon rain forest and lead to more deforestation.

15. 1. The bill is introduced to Congress.
2. The House and the Senate pass different versions of the bill.
3. The differences are ironed out in a Conference Committee.
4. The bill returns to Congress, where it must be passed through both houses.
5. The bill is then presented to the president.
6. The president signs the bill.

16. c. South Carolina complained that the Northern states had encouraged slaves to run away and fueled *servile insurrection*, or slave revolts.

17. a. The Republican Party would be most likely to cut the food stamp program in order to reduce the deficit.

18. *Answers will vary:*
The author has expressed a bias in favor of unemployed and poor Americans and believes that helping them should be a responsibility of the wealthy. This bias is evident when the author uses prescriptive words like *should*. When someone says we *should* do something, he or she is usually about to express an idea that reveals bias. The final sentence of the passage also shows clear bias. Strong language such as *The best way—perhaps the only way* is also prescriptive and should alert you that the writer is about to express a strong opinion that will give you a hint about his or her bias.

19. women. The depiction of the woman rolling up her sleeves to do work and the "We Can Do It!" in the poster's title indicate that the target audience was women. More specifically, the audience was women in the United States during World War II, while many of the men were overseas fighting in the war.

20. *Answers will vary:*

The goal of the poster was to **keep production up during wartime by boosting the morale of women workers.** This poster was created in 1942 by an artist named J. Howard Miller. It was a part of the Westinghouse Company's War Production Coordinating Committee's series of posters for the war effort.

21. b. In the speech, Truth describes her life, stressing that her strength and abilities are equal to those of men. By asking "Ain't I a woman?" she is calling on the audience to recognize that equality.

22. a. The graph shows a steady increase in the price of SuperSport Sneakers, so you would expect this trend to continue. Note that while there are many variables that could influence this, the question is asking you only to use the information that has been provided.

23. c. The passage states that 60 million soldiers were deployed in the war. Millions of men from each country were deployed. If the men of a country are away from their families or are killed, they clearly cannot father children. Although the question does not ask about this, note that an even deeper dip in the birth rate occurred in the 1930s and early 1940s—the years of the Great Depression and World War II.

Social Studies Practices Review

1. c. The other paragraphs support Churchill's plea for supporting the war *whatever the cost and the agony may be.* Choice **a** is incorrect because although Churchill gives an update on the war, this is not the main reason he gives the speech. Choice **b** is incorrect because Churchill speaks of his allies, but the address is to the people of Britain; this is shown in the first sentence, when he speaks of *our country.* Choice **d** is incorrect because although the tone is indeed solemn and respectful of those fighting for freedom, this is not the purpose of the speech.

2. c. Germany has broken through France's defenses and taken over Holland. Churchill expresses his fears and expectation that Germany will continue its advance toward Britain. Choice **a** is incorrect because Churchill suggests that Germany is a formidable enemy, but he stresses that Britain will be able to defeat it. Choice **b** is incorrect because Holland has indeed been invaded by Germany, but there is nothing that indicates that it has allied itself with Germany; on the contrary, Churchill equates Holland's experience with ruin and slavery. Choice **d** is incorrect because although Churchill mentions the alliance with France, he is poised for Britain to act alone.

3. b. Churchill is expressing growing confidence. He admits that fighting has been fierce but states that the British position is much stronger than it used to be. Choices **a**, **c**, and **d** are incorrect because these sentences support the main idea but do not express the main idea.

4. World War II. This can be discerned by the date of the speech—1940. If you did not know the specific dates of the war, you should be able to apply more general knowledge of the war and its battles to be able to correctly identify the context of this speech.

5. Nazi Germany. Using context clues should be able to help you discern that this term refers to the German army and tank brigade.

6. a. The excerpt points out that the location of Mexico City at a high altitude has contributed to its air pollution problems. Choice **b** is incorrect because although the passage mentions smog, it does not claim that the city's tropical location is responsible. Choice **c** is incorrect because the passage does not mention excess pollution from the United States. Choice **d** is incorrect because the passage does not mention the dry climate as an important factor in pollution.

7. b. The second paragraph states that Mexico City is located on a lake basin that was originally drained in the 1600s. Choice **a** is incorrect because the first paragraph of the passage says that in 1992, Mexico City was named the most polluted city in the world. Choices **c** and **d** are incorrect because they were steps the Mexican government took to reduce pollution in response to the pollution problem.

8. c. The drop in lead pollution levels is evidence that the new policies have made a difference. Choice **a** is incorrect because encouraging refineries to clean up their emissions would not be evidence that new policies have been effective. Choice **b** is incorrect because lower levels of oxygen at Mexico City's high altitudes are not the result of antipollution policies. Choice **d** is incorrect because future plans do not indicate evidence that existing policies have made a difference.

9. b. Based on the cartoon, the artist most likely has a very **negative** opinion of Standard Oil. The cartoon suggests that Standard Oil is a monster seizing control of the land, the government, and the people.

10. a. The cartoon is aimed at working-class readers in an attempt to arouse public sentiments against Standard Oil. Choice **b** in incorrect because the cartoon portrays Standard Oil in a negative light and therefore would not be aimed at oil industrialists. Choice **c** is incorrect because the cartoon suggests that politicians are already under the control of Standard Oil, and therefore politicians would not be swayed by the cartoon's message. Choice **d** is incorrect because although the cartoon depicts Standard Oil as an octopus, its message is not intended for marine biologists.

11. c. The cartoon depicts Standard Oil as a corporation that has seized massive power and control, as did several corporate monopolies in the late nineteenth century. Choice **a** is incorrect because the cartoon does not make reference to the expansion of American corporations into foreign markets. Choice **b** is incorrect because although petroleum extraction and production increased in the nineteenth century, the cartoon is aimed specifically at Standard Oil rather than the industry as a whole. Choice **d** is incorrect because the cartoon does not make reference to territorial disputes between the United States and Spain.

12. c. The median is the middle house price at any given time, which gives the clearest picture of a general trend. Choice **a** is incorrect because the mean, or average, housing price could be pulled sharply up or down by an unusually low or high sales price, so it isn't a reliable indicator of the overall state of the housing market. Choice **b** is incorrect because the mode is more or less irrelevant to the question, since it doesn't show an overall trend. Choice **d** is incorrect because the range of housing prices would not be indicative of a trend.

13. a. The Preamble lists six reasons that a new governing document is needed. Choice **b** is incorrect because although the Preamble is at the beginning of the Constitution, it does not provide an outline of the document. Choice **c** is incorrect because although the Constitution describes the new system of government, the Preamble does not. Choice **d** is incorrect because although the causes for separating from England were very much in the minds of the authors of the Constitution, the Preamble does not review these.

14. c. To find the most common reason given, look for the biggest slice of the pie, or the item with the highest percentage. The most common reason given was being too busy or having a conflicting schedule, which is 19%. The next biggest reasons given were: not interested (16%), illness or disability (14%), and did not like candidates or campaign issues (13%).

15. b. Being too busy was cited by more nonvoters than any other reason. Providing longer polling hours might enable busy people to get to the polls. Choice **a** is incorrect because although this might encourage some people, only 3% of respondents suggested that they had not voted because the polling place was inconvenient. It is not the most influential factor on the list. Choice **c** is incorrect because although some people may benefit from a reminder, only 4% of respondents suggested that they had forgotten to vote; it is not the most influential factor on the list. Choice **d** is incorrect because although people have to register in order to vote, the registration process is not intended to be a barrier. Only 5% of respondents said they had registration problems, so it is not the most influential factor on the list.

16. a. *Apathy* is defined as a lack of interest or enthusiasm. The fact that, according to the chart, 16% of Americans did not vote simply because they were not interested supports this opinion. You cannot assume that a person who is too busy to vote is apathetic about politics or unappreciative of his or her right to vote.

CHAPTER 4

CIVICS AND GOVERNMENT

The study of civics and government is a core component of social studies literacy. All citizens and residents should understand how local, state, and federal governments affect their lives. This lesson will help build your

- familiarity with the types of governments throughout history and around the world
- understanding of the historical and philosophical basis of the U.S. government and how it operates
- knowledge of how the U.S. political system functions and shapes policy

Types of Modern and Historical Governments

Government is the overall structure by which nations, states, and cities carry out their political, economic, and social agendas. Many kinds of governments throughout history have shaped the types of governments that exist today.

Democracy

Throughout most of history, political power has been reserved for kings, dictators, and wealthy landowners. The history of democracy is the history of power being transferred from wealthy rulers to everyday people, regardless of social status, gender, race, or creed. Democracy is truly, as Abraham Lincoln stated in his Gettysburg Address, "government of the people, by the people, and for the people."

There are four types of democracy: direct democracy, representative (or indirect) democracy, parliamentary democracy, and presidential democracy.

Direct Democracy

In a **direct democracy**, or pure democracy, citizens hold ultimate political power. The term "direct democracy" usually means that citizens have significant involvement in determining laws and public policy on their own without having representatives and legislatures. This involvement can take place in a democratic assembly or group meeting or through voting processes such as initiatives and referendums. In these types of processes, citizens vote directly on issues instead of for candidates or parties. In the United States today, the classic example of this is the New England town meeting, where any citizen of the town who wants to discuss, debate, and vote on town policy is allowed to do so. This system eliminates the layer of elected representatives from the political process, giving citizens a much greater voice in and closer connection to making laws and implementing other public policy.

By 500 BCE, the city-state of Athens became the first direct democracy, although slaves, women, and foreigners could not vote. The system in Athens had three separate parts: the *ekklesia* was a sovereign governing body that created laws and developed foreign policy, the *boule* was a council of representatives from the ten Athenian tribes, and the *dikasteria* made up the court system, where cases were argued before

juries of citizens who had been randomly selected by lottery. Although Athenian democracy would survive for only two centuries, this invention was one of ancient Greece's most enduring contributions to the modern world.

Later, these types of direct democracy assemblies were used in small governing bodies called cantons in Switzerland, as well as in town meetings in some American colonies and states. Today, Switzerland is the only example of direct democracy, and then only at the local level.

Discussions about the strengths and weaknesses of direct democratic governments focus on several issues. Proponents of direct democracy argue that it promotes the democratic principles of popular sovereignty, political equality, and the idea that all citizens should have the right not only to elect representatives but also to vote on policy issues in referendums.

Opponents claim that direct democracy contains some dangers. For example, during a referendum process, citizens usually have very few choices and little input into what those choices are. This can create voter apathy, opponents argue, especially if the choices are not popular. Some also believe that the people who create and write referendum questions hold too much power, because they can present the questions and choices in such a manner that might help shape the outcome of the vote.

Representative Democracy

Because most societies grow and become more complex, a direct democracy system is extremely difficult or impossible in practice. Many modern democratic societies have abandoned direct democracy and replaced it with representative democracy, or **indirect democracy**. In this system, voters elect a group of political representatives who work on behalf of the citizens to make decisions and lead the government. Interestingly, some people believe that this new trend might be reversed because of new breakthroughs in communication technologies that might create some form of "electronic direct democracy."

In a representative democracy, citizens vote to elect officials who then create public policy, write laws, and appoint other governmental officials, such as judges. Most modern democracies today are representative democracies. The concept of representative democracy can trace its roots to ideas and institutions that emerged during the European Middle Ages, the Enlightenment, and most significantly during the American and French Revolutions. Modern democracies such as the United States, the United Kingdom, and Germany are representative democracies.

Since Ancient Greece, and Aristotle in particular, political philosophers generally agree that no political system is going to be perfect and live up to its expectations. Some democratic systems can maintain strong democratic principles and institutions in practice; usually, however, few are perfect or represent ideal democracy.

In order to achieve the best and most effective form of representative democracy, governments today rely on strong, reliable, and stable political institutions and processes. These include the following:

- **Open, impartial, and frequent elections.** Citizens can participate in elections as voters and as candidates, although governments can place some restrictions on them.
- **Freedom of speech and expression.** Citizens can express themselves publicly in a variety of methods on almost all political subjects without fear of punishment.
- **Freedom of association.** Citizens have the right and are protected by law to meet with others and to form groups, such as interest groups and political parties, without government interference.
- **Free press.** Citizens have access to all kinds of political information that is not published or controlled by government agencies. Also, laws

protect citizens' right to publish or spread relevant political information. All citizens are encouraged and have the right to look for and use these sources of information.

Parliamentary Democracy

Parliamentary democracy is similar to representative democracy because in both forms of government, the people elect officials to represent them. The parliamentary system is the most common form of democratic government in the world today. A few examples among the many parliamentary democracies are Canada, Great Britain, Italy, Japan, Latvia, the Netherlands, and New Zealand. However, this system is often also a constitutional monarchy, as in the United Kingdom and Japan, where the monarch—a king, queen, or emperor—is a figurehead without true political power. In this case, the head of state (a queen, for example) is different from the head of government.

A defining characteristic of the parliamentary system is that the legislative branch holds significant power in relation to the executive, legislative, and judicial branches of government. Another feature is that parliamentary democracies merge executive and legislative duties and responsibilities. Usually, the lawmaking or legislative process takes place in either a one- or two-bodied chamber system. A one-body legislature is called unicameral, while a two-body chamber system is called bicameral. In both types, the members are always accountable to the people they represent. In most parliamentary systems, a **prime minister** is the head of the executive branch. He or she appoints officials called ministers to perform the duties of the executive branch. Ministers are the leaders of the government departments or agencies within the executive branch.

Another key feature of a parliamentary democracy is that the prime minister may be removed from power whenever he or she loses the confidence of a majority of the ruling party or of the parliament as a whole. A *no confidence* vote from parliament against the prime minister means that government can be dissolved. When this happens, an election may be asked for immediately so that new members to parliament can be voted into office. Once new members are in office, they can then repeat the process of selecting a new prime minister and cabinet of ministers.

Presidential Democracy

Some representative and constitutional democracies, like the United States, have a **presidential system** of government. This system of government is usually made up of three independent and equal branches of government. These branches are the legislative, the executive, and the judicial. The most important feature of this system is that each branch is separate from the others, unlike the parliamentary system, in which the legislative and executive branches are entwined. In addition, governmental powers are shared among the three branches. In a presidential democracy, the president is the head of state and also the head of government. The president therefore has the authority to appoint and nominate government officials. Presidents are elected by the citizens of the country and are independent of the congress or legislature. The presidential system originated in the United States and is the most famous example of this system. Other democracies that use the presidential system include Argentina, Brazil, Mexico, and France.

Differences between Parliamentary and Presidential Democracies

One of the biggest differences between a parliamentary democracy and the U.S. system of presidential democracy is that the leaders of the government are chosen by the elected representatives in the parliament, and not by citizens in an election. The political party that has won the greatest support from voters is rewarded with more representation in the parliament or legislature. Often, the ruling government is formed by several political parties to create a governing coalition of parties. The leader of the majority party or coalition is appointed the head of government, who is often titled the prime minister or chancellor. Parliamentary democracies are often noted for the regular and vocal challenges of minority parties in opposition to the majority.

Another significant difference between a parliamentary form of democracy and a presidential system is that the presidential system usually gives more power to the head of government. The U.S. president can have great influence and power in determining foreign and domestic policy. Although in many presidential systems of representative democracy that have constitutions and give the chief executive significant authority, most also have built-in limits that provide the other branches opportunities to check and balance executive powers.

Presidential and parliamentary systems also differ in how legislators are elected. The United States uses single-member district, winner-take-all style of elections. Americans elect members of their legislatures one at a time in small districts. The candidate with the most votes is the winner. Parliamentary systems use variations of **proportional representation** elections.

The basic principle upon which proportional representation elections are built is that all voters deserve representation, not just those who voted for the winner. This system also reinforces the idea that all political groups or parties should be represented in the legislatures in proportion to their popularity or strength among the voting public. This emphasizes the concept of the right to fair representation.

In order to achieve fair representation, all proportional representation systems have some common characteristics. Most notably, they all use multi-member districts. Unlike in the U.S. where only one candidate is elected to represent a district, proportional representation allows for several candidates to be elected. The number of elected candidates varies based on the size of the district. Some individual districts may have ten or more representatives while others might have only four or five.

Another characteristic of all proportional representation systems is that they award, or apportion, the seats in multi-member districts based on the proportion of votes received in the district for each party or group with candidates on the ballot. For example, if the candidates of a political party win 60 percent of the vote in a 10-member district, they receive six of the ten seats, or 60 percent of the seats. Another party's candidates might win 30 percent of the vote, and consequently win three seats.

Supporters of a parliamentary system argue that it is more efficient than a presidential system because it does not have limitations, such as checks and balances, to slow or even stop the legislative process. Checks and balances and the sharing of power between the three branches of government can often slow down the operations of government and create gridlock. Gridlock occurs when legislation grinds to a halt and nothing is accomplished.

Democratic Socialism

Democratic socialism combines the political philosophy of democracy with the economic philosophy of socialism. Democratic socialism is characterized by having a socialist economy, in which the means of production are collectively owned or controlled, operating within a politically democratic system of government.

Socialism is a social and economic philosophy that supports the public rather than private ownership or control of property, natural resources, and the means of production. This is often called common ownership. This type of system can emerge under different types of governments, including democratic and totalitarian states. Many people add the term *democratic* to this style of socialism to distinguish it from the Marxist–Leninist style of socialism that governed the Soviet Union. Most political scientists would agree that the Soviet Union was nondemocratic in practice.

According to socialists, individuals in a society should live cooperatively with one another. Everything that society produces should be considered a social product. Since common citizens all played a part in producing these social goods, they should earn a share in it. The underlying concept here and in most socialist thinking is that society as a whole should own or control property for the benefit of all citizens.

The goal of common ownership and ultimately a classless society is present in socialist theories. However, democratic socialism and other forms differ in how they think they can accomplish these goals. For example, democratic socialists do not support a resort to authoritarian governance. They also generally resist the idea of central planning of the economy. Perhaps the greatest contrast is that democratic socialism promotes its ideals and policies, social changes, and governmental progress through fair elections and the voting process.

Although no country has fully instituted democratic socialism, many countries have applied democratic socialist ideas, such as the literacy program in Nicaragua, the national healthcare system in Canada, the nationwide childcare program in France, and the community health centers created by the U.S. government in the 1960s.

Practice

1. Andover, Massachusetts, claims to be the largest community in the world to be governed by an annual Town Meeting. All registered voters are eligible to attend and vote at Town Meeting. Citizens have the opportunity to stand up and be counted on issues such as the town and school budgets and special projects and issues, such as new sidewalks and changes in the zoning laws. The type of government in Andover is best described as
   a. presidential democracy.
   b. democratic socialism.
   c. parliamentary democracy.
   d. direct democracy.

2. Which of the following practices best reflects the principle of representative government?
   a. voting for a state senator
   b. fulfilling obligatory jury duty
   c. paying taxes
   d. working as an election judge

3. Which of the following features of parliamentary democracy is most different from the presidential democracy of the United States?
   a. the powers of the judicial branch of government
   b. the method of electing members to the chief legislative body
   c. the method of electing the head of the executive branch
   d. the powers of the legislative branch of government

4. Which of the following is most associated with proportional representation?
   a. presidential elections
   b. direct democracy systems
   c. winner-take-all elections
   d. multiparty coalition governments

5. Identify the basic tenets of democratic socialism. Select all answers that apply.
   a. Promotes complete government control of all aspects of social life.
   b. The means of production are socially and collectively owned or controlled.
   c. Advocates for free and fair elections
   d. Follows the socialist political structures.

Monarchy

A **monarchy** is a form of government that has a single person known as a monarch as its leader. Monarchs are often called king, queen, emperor, or empress. Monarchies were one of the most common types of governments throughout early societies. Today, however, they are rare.

Monarchies have been around since the first civilizations emerged. The ancient Egyptians, for example, granted their monarchs godlike status, or in some cases even revered them as actual gods. Beginning in the 1500s, some European monarchs argued that their power and right to govern came directly from God. This idea was called the **divine right of kings**.

In most monarchies, the monarch gains his or her power either through military victories or through inheritance. Most likely, monarchies grew out of the practice of early human societies to base their power structures around a family or a tribe. These groups often had power struggles because it was common for one individual to exert more authority over the others. Monarchs usually used their power for their own benefit and at the expense of others.

A common monarchy is a class-based system. People born into so-called higher classes were considered to be more intelligent and superior than the people from outside that class. Supporting this view was the prevailing belief within monarchies that the so-called common people live their lives to serve the monarch. This is quite different from modern democratic governments, in which government leaders are called on to serve the common citizens.

There are two types of monarchies. An **absolute monarchy**, also called a **despotic monarchy**, is a form of government in which a ruler or despot inherits power for life. The despot's power is absolute and not limited by laws or by a constitution. For example, ancient Roman despots could put any citizen to death for any reason or for no reason at all. The despot's opinion was law.

In a **constitutional monarchy**, the monarch's power is limited by a constitution and by the law. This kind of government is often associated with parliamentary democracy, in which the king or queen has no real power and only serves as a ceremonial figurehead based on tradition.

By the 1700s, more and more people around the world living under monarchies began to see leaders not as divine rulers but as tyrants. The citizens of the British colonies in North America rebelled against the British monarchy. Other people in many other countries throughout the world also rebelled and broke away from monarchies in order to gain their independence. It is interesting to note that most of governments formed after these rebellions were democratic governments and not monarchies.

In the world today, notable constitutional monarchies govern in the United Kingdom, Spain, Sweden, The Netherlands, Morocco, Jordan, and Japan. The monarchies in some nations, such as Saudi Arabia and Swaziland, exercise much greater control and power.

Oligarchy

In an **oligarchy**, a small group of people controls the government. These people are often royalty, part of the wealthy class or the military, or members of the predominant religion. Many oligarchies are controlled by politically powerful families that are usually considered to be part of the elite class. A notable feature of these families is that the children are raised and educated to be heirs within the oligarchy. In the past, these elites have tended to use power to protect and promote their own interests and those of their own class. Historically, oligarchies maintained their power by creating controlling governments that oppressed citizens and made them feel hopeless.

There are four types of oligarchies, each with its own type of ruling class.

1. In an **aristocracy**, political power is in the hands of the nobility, who bear hereditary titles such as baron, duke, or count. Historically, this ruling class has been wealthy landowners entitled to education denied to the lower classes. The American Revolution was a rebellion against the privilege of English aristocracy and the aristocratic system.

2. A **military junta** is government by military leaders. Some South American countries, including Colombia and Brazil, have been governed by juntas, although juntas are not limited to that continent. This type of government is often subject to a military coup d'état, often just called a coup, in which one military force overthrows another to gain power.

3. A **plutocracy** (from the Greek word *ploutos*, meaning wealth) is a government system in which wealth is the principal basis of power. The influence of money in politics and in governance is sometimes exhibited by wealthy citizens who actually hold leadership positions. More often, however, wealthy individuals, groups, or classes use their money to control and influence the government. The wealthy can influence governments by supporting them with financial contributions. Sometimes they can gain more influence by refusing to give the government financial support. Because the wealthy often own or control vital industrial or financial businesses, they can put pressure on governments by refusing to pay taxes or threat-

ening to move their operations to other locations.

Plutocracy and aristocracy are often linked because historically wealth and nobility have been closely associated. Today, the term *plutocrat* is considered to be an insult.

Examples of plutocracies include the Roman Republic, some city-states in Ancient Greece, the civilization of Carthage, the Italian city-states/merchant republics of Venice, Florence, and Genoa, and the pre-World War II Empire of Japan.

Many social scientists have described the Gilded Age (1870–1900) in the United States as a plutocratic era because robber-baron industrialists, such as John Jacob Astor and Andrew Carnegie, wielded political power through the great wealth they had amassed in business.

4. In a **stratocracy**, the government is run by military leaders. It is different from a junta government because in a stratocracy, the military and the government are considered as one by a military constitution. Stratocracy need not be autocratic in order to preserve its right to rule. Myanmar (Burma) is the only modern example of this form of oligarchy.

Practice

6. Which of the following is a plutocrat?
   a. duke
   b. robber baron
   c. elected official
   d. military general

7. The American Revolution
   a. was a coup.
   b. opposed oligarchy.
   c. supported oligarchy.
   d. made way for a military constitution.

8. Which of the following political systems allows citizens the most opportunities to participate in the political process?
   a. democracy
   b. aristocracy
   c. monarchy
   d. oligarchy

9. A military overthrow of the government is called a _____.
   a. plutocratic revolt
   b. coup d'état
   c. monarchial inheritance
   d. revolution

Authoritarianism

An **authoritarian** government is ruled by a single, absolute dictator or a small group of despots whose word is law. Under authoritarianism, citizens have no freedom except what is allowed by the ruler. This ruler is often cruel and arbitrary because, as the saying goes, "Power corrupts, and absolute power corrupts absolutely."

It is not uncommon for authoritarian governments to hold elections, but citizens usually have no input into how they are governed once leaders assume power. In addition, authoritarian leaders rarely allow citizens much freedom or many choices. Most authoritarian governments suppress the freedoms of speech and the press, as well as tolerating very little religious activity. Historically, authoritarian leaders have often emerged from a small class or group, such as top military officers, or from a small class of aristocratic families.

One form of authoritarianism is an **autocracy**, in which one person is the absolute ruler of the government. As discussed earlier, an absolute monarch is an autocratic leader, whose power is unlimited. The basic premise of an autocracy is that the leader is never challenged politically by citizens of the state. In addition, the autocratic leader is so powerful that other government institutions or agencies, such as courts of law, legislative branches, or electoral processes, are unable to limit the leader's authority.

There have been many autocratic states of different types and in all parts of the world, including in Nazi Germany under Adolf Hitler and in the Soviet Union under Joseph Stalin. In the modern world, for example, North Korean dictator Kim Jong-un has eliminated people he perceives as political enemies by having them sentenced to death and executed without trial.

Despotism and **dictatorship** are two other forms of autocracy. In this type of government, the people are ruled either by a single individual or by a small group of despots or dictators. The ancient Egyptian pharaohs were despots and treated their peoples like slaves.

The English word *dictator* comes from the Latin *dictator*. In the Roman Republic, a dictator was an official who was given temporary significant authority during times of crises. This allowed for quick, decisive decisionmaking. But history has shown that modern dictators have acted more like tyrants than like the Roman dictators.

Unlike their Roman predecessors, modern dictators acquire power through undemocratic methods, often relying on force and terror to gain political prominence. Once they have gained power, they and their regimes usually try to suppress basic civil liberties while using propaganda to build and maintain public support.

Totalitarianism is similar to autocracy in that power is controlled by a single, absolute ruler or party intolerant of dissent. In the early 1920s, Italian dictator Benito Mussolini popularized the term *totalitario* to describe the new fascist state of Italy: "All within the state, none outside the state, none against the state."

A key distinction between a totalitarian government and an authoritarian government is that a totalitarian state tries to control nearly every aspect of people's public and private lives whereas, historically, authoritarian states have mostly been concerned with maintaining and holding onto political power. Usually, if the citizens do not represent a challenge to political power, an authoritarian government will give them some degree of freedom.

Traditionally, totalitarian leaders have tended to view themselves as all-powerful, believing that their authority is unlimited. Many totalitarian governments throughout history have been controlled by very charismatic leaders. Government agencies then work to build a cult-like status around this leader. To maintain this position and to project this crafted image of the leader, totalitarian governments use force and fear to develop and strengthen citizens' loyalty to the leader.

A common characteristic of totalitarian states is that they try to destroy the important traditional social, legal, and political institutions of the country. Once they accomplish that, they install new institutions, usually based on the regime's guiding principles. It is also common for a totalitarian state to have a fundamental or primary goal. This goal can be military conquest, or the development or expansion of industries within the country. These goals often become the overriding focus of the government, which can lead to ignoring other state issues. This drive to reach the state goal often leads to the emergence of a unique **ideology**, or system of ideas and ideals.

As mentioned earlier, because dictatorships or autocratic states are mostly interested in staying in power, they usually have no issue with giving citizens some freedoms. The freedoms are usually protected unless citizens challenge the government's political power. A totalitarian government, on the other hand, tries to keep all citizens involved in and focused on the state's driving ideology and its fundamental goal.

A totalitarian state will utilize all means to promote the official state ideology, including controlling free expression. For example, art is normally an instrument of free expression, but the German Nazis and Soviet communists dictated that the techniques and subjects of art reflect their politics and ideologies. Thus they controlled free expression and turned art into political propaganda in favor of their totalitarian goals.

Practice

10. Based on the definitions covered so far in this chapter, a(n) _____ government would be the most likely to support freedom of expression.
   a. democratic
   b. autocratic
   c. Nazi
   d. despotic

11. Which of the following is a characteristic of most totalitarian governments?
   a. an elected head of state who holds absolute power
   b. a ruling class of wealthy landowners who wield power
   c. a charismatic leader with a cult-like following
   d. a tradition-based state that suppresses new ideologies

12. Which of the following best describes a dictatorship?
   a. a constitution-based government led by a monarch
   b. a government run by the nation's nobility
   c. a government by non-elected, self-appointed rulers
   d. a government run by military leaders

Other Types of Government

Political and religious philosophies throughout history have shaped other forms of government besides the types covered earlier in this chapter. Each philosophy provides supporting reasons for the existence of the type of government it justifies.

Anarchism is not a form of government but rather the absence of government and laws. Anar-chists believe that every form of government is corrupt because people should be free to do as they please without pressure from an authority or rules and laws. Anarchists (those who advocate anarchy) believe that government is both harmful and unnecessary. Revolutions and civil wars, such as the French Revolution and the Russian Civil War, are popularly described as states of anarchy.

The term *anarchism* comes from the Greek *anarchos*, which means *without ruler*. The term had a positive meaning and described a distinct political belief. Over time, however, the word *anarchy* has come to be most often used negatively to describe a state of disorder or chaos.

There are three general types of anarchism: philosophical anarchism, individualist (or libertarian) anarchism, and social anarchism.

Philosophical anarchism argues not only that it is not possible for governments to have moral legitimacy but that citizens are not obligated to follow government laws or rules. Furthermore, most followers of philosophical anarchism argue that a government can never have the authority to command or control its citizens. It is important to note that followers of philosophical anarchism do not advocate a revolution to overthrow the government. Instead, they think that society and governments should change slowly over time to eventually reach a point where governments wield very little, if any, control over their citizens.

Individualist anarchism, also called **libertarian anarchism**, is the view that individuals pursuing their self-interest is the most important aspect of society. Followers of this philosophy argue that all individual pursuits should be free from government or social restrictions. Many who follow this philosophy believe that the principle of majority rule inherent in some aspects of democratic governance can become oppressive to those in the minority.

Social anarchism promotes the ideals of community, cooperative help, and social equality. Because of its social emphasis, this type of anarchism often conflicts with the ideas of individualist anarchism. It is similar to other philosophies, such as **libertarian socialism**, in that its ultimate goal would be to create a society that is not segmented by political, economic, or social hierarchies.

In a **meritocracy**, individuals gain power and advance socially based on intellectual ability and talent. For example, civil service exams are used to measure a person's eligibility for employment and promotion. These tests, graded on merit, were first administered by the Chinese during the Han Dynasty in 200 BCE. Today, in countries worldwide, people take civil service exams for jobs ranging from doctor to dog catcher.

A **republic** is similar to a representative democracy in that power is held by the people through their elected officials and not by a monarch such as a king or queen. Rome established the first republican empire in 753 BCE. The term *republic* comes from the Latin phrase *res publica*, which means *matter* or *thing of the people*. The common definition usually describes any political order that is not ruled by a monarch. In theory, a republic is made up of citizens who hold ultimate authority and who can elect political officials and representatives accountable to the people. The concept of liberty—freedom from unjust or undue governmental control—is often associated with the self-governing principles found in a republic form of government. The United States is the most successful example of a modern republic.

Justifying governance by divine guidance, a **theocracy** is a system in which religion or faith plays the dominant role. A theocratic state, therefore, is controlled by elected, selected, or other special officials who interpret and carry out laws in a deity's name. The word *theocracy* comes from the Greek word *theokratia*. The basic parts of the word are *theos*, which means *god*, and *kratein*, which means *to rule*. Thus, theocracy literally means *rule by god*.

Some of the oldest governments in history were theocracies. For example, the ancient peoples of Egypt and Tibet established theocracies. Many early American Indian civilizations also followed theocratic principles. Vatican City, Iran, and Brunei are modern examples of theocracies.

Finally, the term **puppet government** describes a government that has little power of its own because it needs financial or military support from a larger or more powerful government. Puppet governments mostly serve such a subordinate role in order to guarantee their survival. Although controlled by a foreign government, a puppet government and its citizens tend to try to maintain their national or cultural identity by keeping their flags, music or specific songs, and other cultural traditions and institutions.

Because puppet governments depend on outside powers to support them, major world governing bodies consider them illegitimate, so the term *puppet state* has negative or condescending connotations. Examples of puppet states include Albania, Monaco, and Vichy France, which was controlled by Germany and Italy during World War II.

Practice

13. Which form of government rewards talent?
   a. puppet state
   b. republic
   c. theocracy
   d. meritocracy

14. While Iran does have an elected president and legislature, it also has a supreme leader, the Islamic cleric Ayatollah Sayyed Ali Khamenei, who was elected by the Islamic Assembly of Experts and has ruled Iran since 1989. The Supreme Leader is the highest-ranking political and religious authority in the Islamic Republic of Iran. The type of government in Iran is best described as a(n)
   a. theocracy.
   b. oligarchy.
   c. dictatorship.
   d. democracy.

15. Sovereignty is the power or authority of a government. At one time, people believed that governments ruled by divine right, with power granted by God. Today's democratic governments receive their sovereignty from the people. By what means do the people demonstrate sovereignty in a democracy?

a. crowning a king

b. serving in the armed forces

c. voting on issues

d. obeying the law

The Principles of American Constitutional Democracy

Government is the process through which a society provides the necessary political, economic, and social requirements to sustain itself. The key responsibilities of governments include maintaining order, providing security, providing public services, and creating and implementing public policies that strengthen the society or community. Types of governments vary from society to society and are usually based on a number of factors, including how large a society is and even the special traditions of its peoples. Who governs and how they govern also changes over time as societies grow and change. Ultimately, the citizens of a nation or community must establish a process for choosing leaders, as well as determining how much authority those leaders will have and how they can use it.

Historically, governments have been created and maintained on the basis of the following ideas: divine right, brute force, and natural rights.

Divine right, discussed earlier, claims that a god or deity confers on an individual the right to rule. Because it is a god-given right, this ruler generally does not think he or she is accountable to the people but only to that god. Some monarchies and most theocracies are based on the concept of divine right.

Brute force is governance by physical power and control. This type of power is not viewed as legitimate by those who are being controlled. Dictators, warlords, criminal gangs, and terrorists often depend on this type of governance to maintain their position of power.

The concept of **natural rights** is the belief that people are born with inalienable rights (rights that are not to be taken from them). In other words, power comes from the people. Most democracies are based on the principle of natural rights.

Perhaps the greatest responsibility of all governments—past and present—is to provide for the safety and welfare of their citizens. Because no society can ever create the perfect world in which citizens never have disputes, it is the government's job to help resolve these disputes fairly and without violence. This is most effectively accomplished by creating a justice system.

This section describes the seven key principles that helped establish and shape American democracy.

Compared to other countries throughout the world, the United States is relatively young, but it is the oldest representative democracy in the world. The ideas that helped form American constitutional democracy, however, were developed more than 2,500 years ago. The founders of the United States built some of the key concepts of their government on the ideas of ancient Greece and Rome. Centuries later, European thinkers from the 1700s and 1800s also helped shape American democracy.

Many of the rights that American citizens exercise today grew out of the political and legal traditions of England and the ideas of a cultural and intellectual movement called the **Enlightenment**, which emerged in eighteenth-century Europe. Enlightenment thinkers developed concepts that revolved around the belief that the natural laws in the universe can and should be applied to political, social, and economic situations. Enlightened thinkers believed that the best way to learn about and understand these situations was through the use of reason, and by applying logic and evidence-based methods learned through the scientific method. This emphasis on reasoning, science, and logic was known as **rationalism**.

The English colonists who came to North America in the 1600s had some, even if very little, knowledge of limited representative government. As the new European Enlightenment ideas spread to the colonies, they motivated the colonists to question their relationship with and standing within the English monarchy.

Natural Rights

One Enlightenment thinker, the English political philosopher John Locke, who lived mostly in the seventeenth century, argued that all people are born free, equal, and independent. Each individual possesses rights, called natural rights. Locke's natural rights were the right to life, liberty, and property. He also argued that no government can take away these natural rights.

In the U.S. Declaration of Independence, Thomas Jefferson put Locke's idea into practice but replaced the word *property* with the phrase *pursuit of happiness*. Jefferson did not explain his reason for this change, but the phrase has been widely interpreted as a call for freedom of opportunity and not just the right to accumulate material goods.

In his *Essay on Human Understanding*, Locke presented an argument that ran counter to the traditional Christian philosophy of original sin. In fact, he insisted that individuals are not born sinful but that their young minds are blank and can be molded and influenced by education and society. Ultimately, Locke believed, these forces would help produce better and more productive citizens. Locke's ideas of natural rights and the improvement of society have long been considered cornerstones of American democracy.

Individual Rights

Before the American Revolution, many American colonists advocated for and embraced Locke's idea of the protection of natural and individual rights. Some early colonial governments even had bills of rights that defined and protected some individual rights. Individual rights include the natural rights of life, liberty, and the pursuit of happiness laid out in the Declaration of Independence and the Bill of Rights.

When the colonies finally decided to rebel, colonial leaders took this a step further and created constitutions that protected these freedoms and rights even more. The first ten amendments to the Constitution, known as the **Bill of Rights**, are the best-known enshrinement of the importance of protecting individual rights. The Bill of Rights was added as soon as the new government took office in 1789.

Unlike the rest of the Constitution, which is primarily concerned with the structure and organization of the government, the Bill of Rights covers rights and protections afforded to individuals, including

- freedom of expression
- the right to a trial by jury
- freedom from unreasonable searches and seizures
- the right of an individual to practice his or her religion

Rule of Law

Rule of law is the concept that states that each individual in a society must follow and practice the legal codes and processes established by the society and its institutions. Without rule of law, a democracy would not be able to function successfully. Among other features, rule of law requires

- clear, publicized laws
- a fair and transparent legislative process
- accountability of officials and leaders to the citizens
- open and frequent elections
- a free press that is not restricted by government authority

Without rule of law, citizens are subject to unwarranted and unauthorized actions by government officials.

Majority Rule

Majority rule is the concept that the authority to make political or vital social decisions should be based on what most (the majority) of the people think is appropriate. Majority rule is a fundamental requirement of a functioning democracy, and indeed plays a large role in key aspects of the American political process. In elections at all levels, the candidates who win a majority of votes are declared the winners. In addition, members of Congress must work to gain support of the majority of their colleagues before a bill can become a law.

It is crucial to note, however, that majority rule does not mean unlimited power. The protection of **minority rights** is equally important. In democratic governments, the rights of those in the minority are protected even if it means that the decisions of the majority are overturned. In addition, those in the minority still have the right to free expression and can disagree with and speak out against the majority. All individual rights apply equally to those in the minority. Supporters of protecting the rights of the minority, including the English philosopher John Stuart Mill, have argued that without minority rights, majority rule would grow into *tyranny of the majority*, in which the majority would suppress the rights of the minority.

Practice

16. The application of science and reason to understanding the world resulted in the 1700s being known for the
   a. Progressive Movement.
   b. New Deal.
   c. Enlightenment.
   d. Reformation.

17. John Locke's ideas about _____ had a profound influence on the framers of the Constitution.
   a. minority rights
   b. rule of law
   c. divine right
   d. natural rights

Constitutionalism

Constitutionalism is the foundation of the government and laws of the United States. It is the set of basic principles that guide our country's constitutional government.

The U.S. Constitution is one of the oldest as well as one of the shortest written constitutions in effect today. It acts as the framework of the national government and the source of American citizens' individual rights. Simply, it is the most important document in the United States.

The constitutional framers were well aware of the problems of establishing and maintaining a representative government. In the Constitution, they put forth their best ideas on how to solve those problems. As discussed earlier, the United States is a *representative democracy*. It can also be called a republic. Most Americans today use the terms *representative democracy* and *republic* interchangeably. Both describe a government system in which the people are the final source of authority.

The framers of the Constitution emphasized a core principle of American democracy—**popular sovereignty**—through the opening words of the Constitution: "We the people." Popular sovereignty means *authority of the people*. In practice, through the process of voting, American citizens are sovereign. Although elected representatives are given political and decisionmaking authority, the people always retain ultimate power in a republican system of government. To strengthen this concept, the framers made sure to explain and describe how the American people consent to be governed and how that consent can be taken away. The Constitution also describes the powers and rules that the people grant the government to use in governing.

Another key aspect of American constitutionalism is the idea of **limited government**. Although most of the framers thought that the nation needed a stronger central authority, many feared the abuse or misuse of power, as they had experienced living under the United Kingdom's Parliament. The framers worked to create a system that would prevent the government from using its power to give one group advantages over other groups or even to limit or suppress the rights of other groups. The Constitution restricts and defines the specific powers or responsibilities that have been granted to the government by the people of the nation.

Constitutions can be written or oral. Great Britain, with a very strong democracy, has only an oral constitution. Parts of the written U.S. Constitution are very precise about the powers granted to the federal government. In other parts, however, the language is vague. Nonetheless, by producing a written constitution, the framers laid out as best they could what they intended to accomplish. Whether constitutions are long or short, written or not, they outline the accepted standards to which people and bodies of government must conform.

Practice

18. The notion that a legitimate government can only function with the consent of the governed is known as popular sovereignty. Which of the following slogans from the American Revolutionary period most directly supports the notion of popular sovereignty?
   a. Don't tread on me.
   b. A man's house is his castle.
   c. No taxation without representation.
   d. Join or die.

Read the following advantages and disadvantages of a written constitution. After each item, write whether it is an advantage or a disadvantage.

19. It is open to multiple interpretations. _____

20. It is slow to respond to social, political, and technological changes. _____

21. Laws might not align to standards of justice and human rights. _____

22. The basic structure of the government, as well as the basic responsibilities of each component, is spelled out. _____

23. Individual rights are spelled out and guaranteed. _____

24. The basis of laws is spelled out, providing security and predictability. _____

25. Rule of law protects individuals and organizations. _____

The Separation of Powers and Checks and Balances

The U.S. Constitution calls for the **separation of powers** between the three branches of the federal government. The concept of separation of powers was developed and advocated by the eighteenth-century French social and political philosopher Baron Montesquieu. In 1748, Montesquieu wrote *Spirit of the Laws*, a major work in political science, and one that influenced many of the leaders who crafted the Constitution. Montesquieu argued that there are three kinds of political power: executive, legislative, and judicial. He also believed that the best way to promote liberty and protect citizens from an unjust government was to make these three powers distinct and independent from the others. A common characteristic of separation of powers is the division of government responsibilities into distinct branches to limit any one branch from handling the key responsibilities of another branch.

In the United States, the two houses of Congress make up the **legislative branch** of government. It is responsible for writing laws. The **executive branch**, headed by the president, makes sure that the laws go into effect and that citizens follow them. The **judicial branch** is the system of federal courts, which is responsible for interpreting federal laws and making decisions in cases involving those laws. It is important to note that no one serving in one branch of government can serve in any other branch at the same time.

In addition to separating the powers of the government into three branches, the framers of the Constitution created a system of **checks and balances** through which each branch of government can check, or limit, the power of the other branches. This system helps balance the power of the three branches and prevents one branch of the government from becoming more powerful than other branches.

Practice

Describe the checks and balances taking place in each question by writing **legislative**, **executive**, *or* **judicial** *in the spaces provided. Each of the three choices can be used more than once.*

26. The president nominates judges to the federal court system, including the Court of Appeals and the Supreme Court. The _____ branch checks the _____ branch.

27. The Supreme Court can declare laws unconstitutional. The _____ branch checks the _____ branch.

28. Congress has the power to impeach and remove federal judges. The _____ branch checks the _____ branch.

29. Judges who are appointed for life are protected from being controlled by special interests or by another branch of government. The _____ branch checks the _____ branch.

30. An Executive Order is a statement, having the force of law, made by the president to an executive branch agency. Which foundational American democratic principle might a Senator argue is being violated by the president issuing an Executive Order?
a. individual rights
b. federalism
c. limited government
d. separation of powers

Read the passage and answer questions 31 and 32.

The U.S. Constitution gives the president the power to veto, or reject, a bill passed by Congress. The president typically states his objections to the bill when he announces the veto. Because it takes a two-thirds vote from both the House of Representatives and the Senate to override a veto, Congress often changes the bill to make it more acceptable to the president. Sometimes Congress adds provisions to a bill that the president strongly favors. The president does not have the power of line-item veto, in which lines or parts of a bill can be rejected individually. The president must accept or reject the bill as Congress has written it.

31. Which of the following statements can you infer from the passage?
   a. Congress is more powerful than the president.
   b. Congress tries to get the president to accept its bill by attaching provisions to it that the president supports.
   c. A president is more effective when members of the same political party are the majority in Congress.
   d. If a president vetoes a bill, there is no way to get it passed into law.

32. Which of the following conclusions can you make based on the passage?
   a. It is easier to rewrite and make a bill more acceptable to the president than it is to override a veto.
   b. It is easier to override a veto than it is to rewrite and make a bill more acceptable to the president.
   c. The U.S. Constitution gives the president the power to edit the bills he receives from Congress.
   d. The system of checks and balances ensures that the president has no influence over the lawmaking branch of government.

Federalism

Federalism is a form of government that consists of a central government as well as other smaller, more localized governments. Although the Constitution created a much stronger central government than had been in place with the Articles of Confederation, it did not take away all the powers of the states. By ratifying the Constitution, the states gave up some their powers to the national government while holding onto others. This principle of shared power is a feature of federalism. For example, the Constitution does not allow states to print their own money.

In many ways, federalism reinforces the idea of limited government. For example, the federal government provides opportunities for the people of each state to deal with their needs and problems in their own way without interference. Conversely, in many situations the federal government encourages and pushes the states to act collaboratively to address issues that affect all Americans.

In the United States, federalism involves

- a national government, often referred to as the federal government, which is responsible for issues of national importance.
- state and local governments that deal with local issues, such as the funding of public schools and fines for speeding tickets.

The line between federal government and state government is not precise, and changes over time.

Practice

33. In federalism, governmental power and authority is
   a. concentrated with local governments.
   b. shared between governments.
   c. nonexistent.
   d. concentrated with the federal government.

The Structure and Design of the U.S. Government

As mentioned earlier in this chapter, the Constitution is the most important document in the United States. First, it is the supreme law of the United States. Second, it describes from where and how the government gets its powers. Third, it restricts what the government can do, thus helping to protect the fundamental rights of American citizens. Finally, it outlines the basic structure of the U.S. government, detailing the powers and responsibilities of the three branches of government.

The Legislative Branch

Established by Article I of the Constitution, the **legislative branch** consists of the House of Representatives and the Senate. Together they make up the U.S. Congress. Congress's two primary roles are to make the nation's laws and to decide how to spend the government's money. The Constitution also clearly states that Congress is the only government group that can declare war against a foreign country.

An important responsibility of Congress is to monitor the executive branch and investigate possible misuse of power or illegal activity. Because these types of responsibilities can potentially have great political significance, the Constitution lays out how the process is conducted. It is the responsibility of the House of Representatives to impeach, or bring formal charges against, any federal official it thinks has committed wrongdoings or acted in an unlawful manner. If the House does impeach an official, the Senate then acts as a court and tries the accused official. Officials who are found guilty can be removed from office.

The House of Representatives

The House of Representatives is made up of 435 elected members. The total number of representatives is divided among the 50 states in proportion to their total populations. In addition, there are six more representatives who are elected from the District of Columbia, the Commonwealth of Puerto Rico, and four other U.S. possessions. These six representatives, however, are non-voting members.

The leader of the House of Representatives is the **Speaker of the House**, who is chosen by the members of the House. The speaker is third in the line of succession to the presidency. Members of the House are elected every two years and must be at least 25 years old, must have been a U.S. citizen for at least seven years, and must be a resident of the state they represent. They do not, however, necessarily have to reside in the district they represent.

The Constitution describes several specific powers and responsibilities of the House. These include the power to initiate revenue bills for spending government money, the authority to impeach federal officials, and the duty to elect the president in case of a tie in the Electoral College.

The Senate

The Senate is made up of a hundred senators, two for each state. Senators serve six-year terms, the terms being staggered among the senators. This means that about one-third of the Senate is up for reelection every two years. Until the ratification of the Seventeenth Amendment in 1913, Senators were chosen by state legislatures, not by citizens through popular vote. Since then, they have been elected by the people of each state. Senators must be at least 30 years of age, must have been a U.S. citizen for at least nine years, and must be a resident of the state they represent.

The vice president of the United States serves as President of the Senate and may cast the deciding vote if the Senate ends up in a tie.

Like the House, the Senate is also granted specific powers and responsibilities by the Constitution. These include the power to approve treaties with foreign countries before they are ratified and the responsibility to confirm presidential appointments of cabinet secretaries, federal judges, executive branch officials, some military officers, and ambassadors. As mentioned above, the Senate also tries impeachment cases for federal officials referred to it by the House.

Committee Structure

The most important job of members of Congress is to represent their constituents, who are the people of their home states and districts. Senators and representatives do this mostly through writing or supporting legislation that becomes law. Thousands of bills, or proposed laws, are introduced in Congress each year. It would be impossible for an individual member of Congress to study all of these bills carefully. To help members of Congress get their jobs done, both chambers use committees of selected members to study proposed legislation.

Standing committees are permanent committees in both the House and Senate that specialize in a particular topic, such as foreign relations, armed services, or finance. These committees are then usually divided into subcommittees that focus on a particular aspect of an issue. Currently the House and Senate have some 20 standing committees.

Both the House and Senate also organize temporary **select committees** that address issues requiring special attention. Select committees meet until that specific issue is solved. Some committees also have oversight responsibilities. This might include monitoring government agencies, programs, or activities.

Joint committees are made up of members from both the House and Senate. These committees meet to consider specific issues. A **conference committee** performs an important duty. When the House and the Senate pass different versions of the same bill, a conference committee is organized to reach a compromise bill that both chambers can agree on.

Membership in congressional committees follows a traditional process. Party leaders decide how many Republicans and how many Democrats should be on each committee and what the proportion should be. The ratio of Republicans to Democrats in each committee is approximately the same as the ratio between the majority party and the minority party members in the full chamber. Each party is allowed to choose which members will serve on the committees. Once membership is established, each committee is responsible for assigning its members to subcommittees, if appropriate.

In the Senate, the leader of each committee and the majority of members come from the majority party, which gives them control over the committee's agenda.

Practice

Use the following two excerpts from the U.S. Constitution to answer questions 34 and 35.

> The Senate of the United States shall be composed of two Senators from each state, chosen by the legislature thereof, for six years, and each Senator shall have one vote.
> —U.S. Constitution, Article I, Section 3

> The Senate of the United States shall be composed of two Senators from each state, elected by the people thereof, for six years; and each Senator shall have one vote. The electors in each state shall have the qualifications requisite for electors of the most numerous branch of the state legislatures.
> —U.S. Constitution, Seventeenth Amendment

34. Which statement is true based on the given information?
   a. U.S. Senators have always been elected by popular vote.
   b. A state's two senators can cast only one unified vote on any law.
   c. The framework of the U.S. government can be altered by amendment.
   d. Senators can serve only one six-year term.

35. What nonlegislative power resides in the House of Representatives?
   a. approving presidential nominees
   b. introducing revenue bills
   c. impeaching federal judges
   d. trying public officials

The Executive Branch

The **executive branch** includes the president, the vice president, and many different executive offices, departments, and agencies. The executive branch executes, or carries out, the laws that Congress passes.

As discussed earlier, the head of the executive branch is the **president**. Presidential elections are held every four years. There are only three qualifications for the president listed in the Constitution: the president must be at least 35 years of age, be a natural-born citizen, and have lived in the United States for at least 14 years. Today, the president and his or her family live in the White House in Washington, D.C., which also houses the president's business office—the Oval Office. The president's senior staff also works at the White House. When the president travels by plane, it is identified as *Air Force One*.

Although millions of Americans vote in presidential elections every four years, they are not directly electing the president. Instead, on the first Tuesday in November of every fourth year, American voters elect members to the **Electoral College**. Each state gets as many Electoral College members as it has members of Congress. Electoral College members are usually selected by the candidate's political party, but the laws covering this vary from state to state. These electors then cast the votes for president. There are currently 538 electors in the Electoral College. It takes 270 Electoral College votes to be elected president.

The president performs three key duties. As **chief executive**, the president is in charge of making sure that the laws Congress passes are implemented. As the nation's **chief diplomat**, the president develops and carries out foreign policy, appoints ambassadors, and negotiates treaties with foreign countries. As **commander in chief** of the U.S. military, the president has the authority to direct military forces in times of war or emergency. The president is the highest-ranking commander of all U.S. armed forces during wartime.

Working with the president is the **vice president**. The main job of the vice president is to be ready to take over the presidency if the president is unable to perform his or her duties. This can be because of the president's death, resignation, or temporary inability to handle the responsibilities. In addition, the vice president can take over the presidency if he or she and a majority of the president's cabinet decide that the president cannot perform the duties of the office.

The vice president has an office in the West Wing of the White House, as well as in the nearby Eisenhower Executive Office Building. Like the president, the vice president also has an official home. This is located at the United States Naval Observatory in Washington, D.C.

It is interesting to note that the vice president plays a role in two government branches. As was just discussed, the vice president's executive branch duties include taking over for the president if necessary. In the legislative branch, the vice president heads the Senate. In this position, the vice president can cast a vote only in case of a tie in voting processes in the Senate. However, this situation is quite rare. In practice, members of the majority party select a senator from their party each day to run the Senate.

To handle and coordinate the responsibilities of the executive branch, the president relies on 15 executive offices, departments, and independent agencies. Each department is responsible for a different area of government. The leaders of these offices and departments are also members of the president's **cabinet**. The cabinet advises the president and helps make decisions. Members of the cabinet are usually trusted allies and some of the president's closest advisors. The president is responsible for nominating officials to cabinet positions. Once nominated, the Senate either approves or rejects the nominations.

Currently, all the members of the cabinet take the title of Secretary, except the head of the Justice Department, who is called the Attorney General. Following is a list of the 15 executive departments constituting the cabinet, along with their official published mission statements.

1. The **Department of Agriculture** (USDA) develops and executes policy on farming, agriculture, and food.

2. The **Department of Commerce** (DOC) is tasked with improving living standards for all Americans by promoting economic development and technological innovation.

3. The **Department of Defense** (DOD) provides the military forces needed to deter war and to protect the security of our country. The department is headquartered at the Pentagon.

4. The **Department of Education** (ED) promotes student achievement and preparation for competition in a global economy by fostering educational excellence and ensuring equal access to educational opportunity.

5. The **Department of Energy** (DOE) advances the national, economic, and energy security of the United States.

6. The **Department of Health and Human Services** (HHS) works to protect the health of all Americans and provide essential services, especially for those who are least able to help themselves.

7. The **Department of Homeland Security** (DHS) works to prevent and disrupt terrorist attacks; protect the American people, critical infrastructure, and key resources; and respond to and recover from incidents that do occur.

8. The **Department of Housing and Urban Development** (HUD) is responsible for national policies and programs that address America's housing needs, that improve and develop the nation's communities, and that enforce fair housing laws.

9. The **Department of the Interior** (DOI) is the nation's principal conservation agency. It protects America's natural resources, offers recreation opportunities, and conducts scientific research. The DOI also works with American Indians, Alaskan Natives, and the government's responsibilities to its island communities.

10. The **Department of Justice** (DOJ) enforces the law and ensures public safety against foreign and domestic threats. The DOJ also provides federal leadership in preventing and controlling crime.

11. The **Department of Labor** (DOL) oversees federal programs for ensuring a strong American workforce.

12. The **Department of State** (DOS) plays the lead role in developing and implementing the president's foreign policy.

13. The **Department of Transportation** (DOT) ensures a fast, safe, efficient, accessible, and convenient transportation system that meets vital national interests and enhances the quality of life of the American people.

14. The **Department of the Treasury** (TREAS) is responsible for promoting economic prosperity and ensuring the soundness and security of the U.S. and international financial systems.

15. The **Department of Veterans Affairs** (VA) is responsible for administering benefit programs for veterans, their families, and their survivors.

Practice

36. How do the president and Congress share wartime power?
a. Only Congress can declare war, but the president commands the armed forces.
b. The president can declare war, but Congress must authorize funds for the military.
c. Congress and the president work together to command the armed forces and negotiate peace treaties.
d. Congress declares war, but only the president can write laws after a war is declared.

The Law-Making Process

Although the idea of writing laws seems rather straightforward, the legislative process is often incredibly complex and time-consuming.

The entire legislative process begins with the introduction of a bill to Congress. Legally, anyone can write a bill, but only members of Congress can introduce one as legislation. Historically, some bills have been introduced because the president requests it. This is traditionally the case with the annual federal budget. From the time a bill is introduced and goes through the legislative process, it can undergo significant changes, usually because so many people are involved.

After being introduced, a bill is sent out for analysis and evaluation by the appropriate congressional committee. As discussed earlier, congressional committees are responsible for specific areas of policy. Subcommittees existing within the committee structure are even more specialized. This ensures that legislation is carefully examined before it moves ahead. If the subcommittee reaches consensus on a bill, it sends its report back to the full committee. Then the full committee holds a vote to either approve or reject the bill. If the full committee approves the bill, it then goes to the full House or Senate. The leadership of the majority political party decides when to present the bill for debate and, eventually, a full vote.

After these debates and discussions, the bill may be passed, rejected, or returned to the original committee to rework it and make changes so it stands a better chance of being passed.

The Constitution specifically outlines the process for signing legislation into law. It even states that related bills passed by the House and Senate must have the exact same wording. This, however, does not happen much in practice. To make sure that a bill from the House and the Senate are as similar as possible, congressional leaders create a conference committee. This is a committee made up of members from both the House and the Senate. These members write a conference report, which acts as the final version of the bill. Each chamber then votes again to approve the conference report.

Once a bill passes both houses of Congress by majority vote, the president has the option of either signing it into law or vetoing (rejecting) it. If the president vetoes a bill, Congress may override the veto by passing the bill again in each chamber with at least two-thirds of each body voting in favor. If the president approves the bill and signs it, the bill becomes law.

Presidential Veto Power

As just mentioned, when a bill is presented to the president, he or she can sign it into law or veto it. By law, if the president decides to neither sign nor veto the bill, the bill becomes law regardless. If Congress adjourns within ten days, or is not in session during this time, the bill does *not* become law. This is called a pocket veto. The chart below shows the total number of vetoes in U.S. history.

TOTAL VETOES	REGULAR VETOES	POCKET VETOES	VETOES OVERRIDDEN	PERCENTAGE OF POCKET VETOES OVERRIDDEN	PERCENTAGE OF REGULAR VETOES OVERRIDDEN
2,564	1,497	1,067	110	4%	7%

Practice

37. How is a pocket veto different from a regular veto?

  a. A pocket veto is done in secret.

  b. The president does not take any action.

  c. Congress cannot overturn a pocket veto.

  d. A pocket veto can involve just one part of a bill.

38. The role of a conference committee in Congress is to

  a. hold hearings on proposed legislation.

  b. oversee the actions of the executive branch of the government.

  c. reconcile differences in bills passed by the House and the Senate.

  d. conduct hearings that make information available to the public.

The Judicial Branch

The U.S. **judicial branch** is made up of three different levels of courts. These courts review and evaluate laws, and can even interpret parts of the Constitution. Article III of the Constitution established the judicial branch, but does not provide much guidance on how it should be structured or how it should operate. In fact, the U.S. Supreme Court is the only federal court mentioned in the Constitution, but the framers did give Congress the power to build the federal court system as it sees fit.

The head of the judicial branch is the **chief justice** of the **Supreme Court**. All justices of the Supreme Court are nominated by the president and approved by the Senate. The constitutional framers were very aware of the power of the court system and how it might be corrupted by political issues. Therefore, no term limits are placed on federal judges and justices; they can serve until their death or retirement. On the other hand, federal judges can be removed through impeachment by the House of Representatives and conviction in the Senate. This might happen in cases of unlawful activity or behavior.

The **Supreme Court** of the United States is the highest court in the land and the only part of the judicial branch required by the Constitution. In addition, the Constitution does not even state how many justices should serve on the Court. Instead, as in other issues of the judicial branch, Congress has the power to determine the number. Historically, the Court has had as few as six sitting justices. But since 1869, nine justices have been on the Court.

By law, the U.S. Supreme Court is the final authority in the federal court system. Because there are more lower federal courts, the vast majority of the Supreme Court's cases originate from lower federal court decisions. Only cases that involve foreign ambassadors or disputes between states can begin in the Supreme Court.

As briefly mentioned earlier, although the Constitution does not describe the role of the judicial branch in detail, this does not mean that the judicial branch has not played an important role in the country's history. Although some sections of the Constitution are quite detailed regarding the structure and responsibilities of government agencies, other sections are very vague. It is within these vague, or undetermined, areas that the role of the courts, and the Supreme Court in particular, has grown. In 1803, for example, Supreme Court Chief Justice John Marshall expanded the power of the Court by striking down an act of Congress in the case of *Marbury* v. *Madison*. The Marshall Court basically ruled that an act of Congress was unconstitutional. This decision gave rise to the principle of judicial review, which gives the judicial branch the power to review and decide whether the actions of the executive or legislative branches are consistent with the Constitution. Although not mentioned in the Constitution, the concept of judicial review has given the judicial branch significant power by making the Supreme Court the ultimate authority in interpreting the meaning of the Constitution.

Below the Supreme Court are the district and the appellate courts. U.S. **district courts** are the lowest level of the federal court system. District courts hear criminal and civil cases covered by federal laws. Because federal district courts have original jurisdiction (the authority to hear cases for the first time), all federal cases must begin in a district court. District courts are responsible for bringing out and discovering the facts of a case, operating as the trial courts for both criminal and civil federal cases. A key characteristic of federal district courts is that they are the only federal courts where witnesses testify and juries hear cases and reach verdicts.

The **appellate courts** are the middle level of courts in the federal judicial system. Appellate courts are also known as appeals courts. Such courts take over cases from district courts in which the losing side has asked for a review of the decision. A federal appeals court can overturn a verdict or order the retrial of a case if it disagrees with the lower court's decision. Currently, there are 14 appeals courts in the United States, one for each of the 12 federal districts, a military appeals court, and an appellate court for the federal circuit.

Just as a person who loses a district court case can appeal to a federal appellate court, a litigant who loses in a federal court of appeals, or in the highest court of a state, may file a petition for a *writ of certiorari*. This is an official document that asks the Supreme Court to review the case, giving the person another opportunity to have the case decided. The Supreme Court, however, does not have to accept these cases. Most often, the Court only agrees to hear a case when it involves a new or important legal principle, or when several appellate courts have disagreed in their rulings.

Practice

Read the following passage and answer questions 39–41.

The U.S. Constitution does not explicitly give the power of judicial review to the Supreme Court. In fact, the Court did not use this power—which gives it the authority to invalidate laws and executive actions if they conflict with the Constitution—until the 1803 case of *Marbury* v. *Madison*. In that case, Chief Justice John Marshall ruled that a statute was unconstitutional. He argued that judicial review was necessary if the Court was to fulfill its duty of upholding the Constitution. Without it, he felt that the legislature would have a "real and practical omnipotence." Moreover, several of the Constitution's framers expected the Court to act in this way. Alexander Hamilton and James Madison emphasized the importance of judicial review in the *Federalist Papers*, a series of essays promoting the adoption of the Constitution. The power of judicial review continues to be controversial because it allows the justices—who are appointed rather than elected—to overturn laws made by Congress and state lawmaking bodies.

39. Which of the following statements is an implication of judicial review?
   a. The Constitution is a historic document with little influence over how the government operates today.
   b. The Constitution must explicitly state which branch of government is to have what authority.
   c. The framers never meant for the Supreme Court to have this power.
   d. The Constitution is a living document that continues to be interpreted.

40. Which of the following best describes the process of judicial review?
   a. to declare a law unconstitutional
   b. to follow public opinion polls
   c. to determine the country's changing needs
   d. to propose new laws

41. In which federal courts do juries try cases?
   a. all levels of federal courts
   b. the Supreme Court
   c. district courts
   d. appellate courts

Federal versus State Government

As described earlier, the Constitution took away some powers that states traditionally held and gave them to the national government. The Constitution also protected and strengthened some state powers. This principle of shared power is called federalism.

The Constitution describes three types of government powers. The first are the powers that belong only to the federal government. These are called **enumerated powers**. Among the enumerated powers defined in the Constitution are the power to print or coin money, to raise and maintain the nation's military, to establish federal courts, and to regulate interstate and foreign trade.

The second kind of powers are those that have been granted to the states. These are called **reserved powers**. The Constitution does not specifically list these powers. Instead, the Tenth Amendment declares that all powers not directly given to the federal government "are reserved to the States, or to the people." Over time, reserved powers have evolved to include the authority to regulate trade within a state, establish schools, and pass marriage and divorce laws.

The third type of powers outlined in the Constitution are **concurrent powers**. These are powers the federal and state governments share. Both federal and state governments share authority in imposing taxes on citizens, borrowing money, maintaining criminal and civil court systems, and providing for the well-being of all citizens.

If there are disagreements between a federal law and a state law, the case must be settled in a federal court. Article VI of the Constitution declares that federal laws have authority over state laws. This has come to be known as the **supremacy clause**. Ultimately, the Constitution declares that it is "the supreme Law of the Land."

Practice

42. One of the powers that is shared by the federal and state governments is the power to raise revenue. What was the most likely reason that led to this power being shared?
   a. The federal and state governments both need money to operate effectively.
   b. The federal government would be too weak without the power to raise revenue.
   c. The federal government would be too strong with the power to raise revenue.
   d. It helps maintain the balance of power between the two levels of government.

*Write either **federal** or **state** on the line next to each of these scenarios:*

43. A family opens a restaurant and wants to incorporate the business to gain tax advantages. The business applies for corporate papers from which level of government? _____

44. A bank with headquarters in New York City has branches in New Jersey, Connecticut, and Massachusetts. The bank is subject to regulation by which level of government?

_____

45. The employees of a post office in rural Mississippi are paid their salaries by what level of government? _____

Individual Rights and Civic Responsibilities

For a democratic government to be strong, effective, and durable, its citizens must fulfill their civic duties and responsibilities. All American citizens have certain basic rights, but they also have responsibilities that should be fulfilled. The American democratic system is based on the idea of self-government, and the notion that in the end, citizens are responsible for maintaining an effective and just government and making sure government actions are in line with society's ideals and principles.

There were many different and often heated debates during the time when Americans were deciding whether to adopt the Constitution. Many who opposed ratifying the Constitution argued that it might provide opportunities for the federal government to oppress Americans. They recalled British violations of civil rights before and during the Revolution. Those who were fearful of a tyrannical federal government wanted a bill of rights included in the Constitution. A bill of rights would explain how the rights of individual citizens would be protected.

The U.S. **Bill of Rights** makes up the first ten amendments to the Constitution. A member of the Constitutional Convention, James Madison, was the chief architect of the Bill of Rights. Madison was very familiar with the important legal documents in English history and tradition. To help him craft the Bill of Rights, Madison turned to documents such as the Magna Carta, the English Bill of Rights, the Virginia Declaration of Rights, and the Virginia Statute of Religious Freedom. All these documents were designed to protect individual rights and freedoms from oppressive and tyrannical governments.

In broad terms, the rights of Americans fall into three basic categories. One category covers the right to be protected from unfair actions of the government. Another protects and promotes the right of all Americans to be treated the same under the law. The third helps Americans keep and exercise their certain basic freedoms.

Parts of the Constitution and certain amendments in the Bill of Rights protect Americans from unjust government actions. For example, citizens are guaranteed the right to be represented by a lawyer if accused of a crime. In addition, if accused, the citizen is guaranteed the right to have a trial by jury. Citizens are also protected from unreasonable searches and seizures. This means that police or other law enforcement agencies must have a court order before searching a citizen's home for potential criminal evidence.

A core principle in American democracy and in the U.S. legal system is the concept of **due process**. This means that the government must follow established legal procedures guaranteed by the Constitution, and treat all people equally. In practice, it means that all American citizens regardless of race, religion, gender, or political beliefs have the right to be treated the same under the law.

As briefly touched upon above, citizens hold ultimate power when living in a democracy. Therefore, citizens must be informed about what is happening in the world around them. And therefore they must have opportunities and the ability to exchange ideas and information without restrictions, especially any imposed by the government. The rights to exchange information freely are described in the First Amendment. These include freedom of speech, freedom of religion, freedom of the press, freedom of assembly, and the right to petition the government. With these protections, Americans are allowed to criticize the government without fear of punishment. Citizens also have rights that are not specifically detailed in the Constitution or the Bill of Rights. The Ninth Amendment states that the rights of citizens are not limited to those listed in the Constitution. Over the years, Americans have claimed additional basic rights that have either been upheld by legal rulings or have been guaranteed through additional amendments to the Constitution.

The Bill of Rights

- The **First Amendment** protects freedom of speech, press, religion, peaceable assembly, and the right to petition the government.
- The **Second Amendment** protects the right of the people to keep and bear arms to maintain a well-regulated militia.
- The **Third Amendment** protects against quartering, or housing, of troops in citizens' homes.
- The **Fourth Amendment** protects against unreasonable search and seizure.
- The **Fifth Amendment** protects the right to due process and private property and protects against double jeopardy (being tried twice for the same crime) and self-incrimination.
- The **Sixth Amendment** protects the right to criminal trial by jury and other rights of the accused.
- The **Seventh Amendment** protects the right to civil trial by jury.
- The **Eighth Amendment** prohibits excessive bail and cruel and unusual punishment.
- The **Ninth Amendment** protects the rights of individuals not described in the Constitution, including the Bill of Rights.
- The **Tenth Amendment** reserves powers not explicitly granted to the federal government to the states and people.

Practice

Read the following passage and answer questions 46 and 47.

The Sixth Amendment to the U.S. Constitution states, "In all criminal prosecutions, the accused shall enjoy the right to a speedy and public trial, by an impartial jury of the State and district wherein the crime shall have been committed, which district shall have been previously ascertained by law, and to be informed of the nature and cause of the accusation; to be confronted with the witnesses against him; to have compulsory process for obtaining witnesses in his favor, and to have the Assistance of Counsel for his defence [sic]."

46. Which of the following instances is NOT protected by the Sixth Amendment?
    a. a person accused of a crime silently prays before his or her trial begins
    b. a person accused of drug trafficking hires a lawyer to defend him or her
    c. a trial is moved to another area because no jurors could be found who had not heard of the crime and had an opinion about who committed it
    d. a lawyer informs an accused person of his or her charges

47. The _____ is the first ten amendments to the Constitution.
    a. Preamble
    b. Declaration of Rights
    c. Bill of Rights
    d. Magna Carta

Civic Duties

Being a U.S. citizen means fulfilling certain duties and responsibilities. **Duties** are actions required by law. **Responsibilities** are voluntary actions. By performing these duties and responsibilities, each citizen participates and helps to make sure that everyone's rights are protected and that the government is looking out for the well-being of all Americans.

Local, state, and federal laws make sure that citizens perform certain duties. Citizens who do not fulfill their duties can face fines or even be imprisoned. Many foreign countries require their citizens to perform extraordinary duties compared to the United States. For example, citizens of some countries are required to serve in the military for a certain amount of time. The duties the U.S. government requires its citizens to perform include the following:

- **Obey the law.** Obeying the various layers of government laws is perhaps the most important civic duty of Americans. Laws help protect the safety, health, and property of all citizens. Because American citizens hold ultimate authority, they have opportunities and processes that allow them to change laws they think are wrong or ineffective.
- **Pay taxes.** In order to operate, governments must raise revenues, usually through taxes. Governments use this tax money to equip the military, to build roads and bridges, and to provide support for citizens in need.
- **Perform jury duty.** The Constitution guarantees all Americans the right to a trial by a jury of their peers. This requires citizens to serve on a jury if called. Because Americans are guaranteed the right to a fair and speedy trial, the judicial system needs a constant flow of potential jurors to accommodate every case.
- **Defend the nation.** All American males aged 18 or older are required to register with the government in case they are needed for military service.
- **Attend school.** Most states have laws that require citizens to go to school until a specific age. The knowledge, skills, and abilities vital to supporting a democratic government are taught in most schools.

Civic Responsibilities

Civic responsibilities are not written down in laws or in constitutions. Although they are not as clear cut as civic duties, civic responsibilities are just as important because they help maintain an effective government and order in society. Civic responsibilities include the following:

- **Respecting the rights of others.** American citizens should respect the rights of other Americans, including those with whom they disagree. The U.S. citizenry is comprised of people who represent a tremendous range of backgrounds, ethnicities, religions, and other cultures. Respecting and accepting others, regardless of their differences, is called tolerance. Tolerance of differences is essential in a democracy because it promotes unity and equality.
- **Being informed.** American citizens need to know what is happening not only in their communities but in their states, the nation, and the world. Knowing and understanding what the government is doing and being vocal about it helps make the government more accountable and can lead to changes that better reflect the interests of the citizens.
- **Being involved.** Responsible citizens look after the well-being of their neighbors and fellow citizens as well as themselves. Strong communities seek out ways to protect and promote the health and welfare of every person. These communities also rely on their citizens to contribute to the common good and to volunteer their labor, time, and money to make their communities better places in which to live.
- **Voting.** Perhaps the most important responsibility of an American citizen is to vote. Most American citizens 18 years of age and older have the right to vote. By voting, citizens are actively involved in the political process and can help shape the future of their communities, their states, and their country. Responsible citizens do more than simply cast a ballot: they learn about the candidates and the issues before voting so they can make better-informed decisions. In addition, the voting process does not end as soon as the elections are over. Responsible citizens also monitor the actions of those who have been elected to public office. If an official does not

seem to be representing the interests of his or her constituency, voters can choose another candidate in the next election.

All citizens must keep in mind that government decisions affect their lives.

Practice

48. How old must citizens be to vote for president?
  a. 25
  b. 18
  c. 16
  d. 21

49. Which of the following is the most important civic duty of American citizens?
  a. attend school
  b. pay taxes
  c. serve on a jury
  d. obey laws

Political Parties, Campaigns, and Elections in American Politics

Politics and creating public policy in the United States are organized generally through the major political parties and the campaign and election process. A **political party** is made up of individuals who share similar political views. The key tasks of a party are to win elections, operate various levels of government, and work to influence public policy.

The Constitution makes no mention of political parties, but the first parties formed during the early years of the nation. Currently, the United States has several political parties, but two parties dominate American politics: the Democratic and Republican parties.

The Two-Party System

For much of its political history, the United States has had two major political parties. Today, however, these two parties are very different from their predecessors 200 years ago. In addition, there have been numerous attempts to establish third, or independent, parties, but they have not been very successful to date in influencing elections.

Political parties, and especially parties in competition with each other, have evolved into an important part of American democratic government. First and foremost, political parties provide a link between citizens and their elected officials. Political parties also give voters choices when electing officials or voting on ideas.

When evaluating political parties, one way to identify the differences between them is to read the party **platforms** that are produced every four years at presidential nominating conventions. The platform is a series of statements that explains the party's principles, beliefs, and positions on important election and political issues. Each individual part of the platform is called a **plank**. Simply put, the platform tells voters what the party and its candidates will try to do if they win.

The Purpose of Parties

When functioning properly, political parties can identify and define important issues in American society. Through the party's organizational structure and its members, it can translate these problems into topics that can be debated and, ideally, resolved through the political or government process. Because membership in the major political parties reaches millions of people, parties can also create strong political alliances that have the power to influence and shape policy and political action.

The people who perform the work of political parties play an important role in the American system of government. These people help select candidates for public office and then work to get them elected. It is important to note that political parties are the only organizations that select and present candidates for public office. They do this through the nomination process. The major parties in all the states nominate candidates for most levels of government.

Political Primaries

The most common method of nominating candidates is the **direct primary**. This is an election in which voters choose candidates to represent each party in a future general election. There are two main forms of the direct primary: open and closed. Most state primaries are **closed primaries**, in which only declared members of a party are allowed to vote for that party's nominees. For example, only Democrats can vote in the Democratic Party's primary. The method for declaring a party preference is different throughout the states. This is mainly because the states are granted constitutional authority to manage elections. Some states require voters to declare a party when registering to vote. Others allow voters to declare just before actually voting.

Some states hold **open primaries**. These are elections in which voters do not have to state a party preference in order to vote for the party's nominees. In most open primary states, voters privately choose a party in the voting booth.

The Roles of Political Parties

Political parties also play an important role in helping Americans practice self-government. Parties can help citizens communicate with their government leaders. They also help monitor and ensure that government remains accountable and responsive to the interests of the people. And they help inform voters about their ideas and views on public issues. This mostly occurs during election campaigns. Party candidates make speeches and publish and distribute information in various formats. The most common methods include print ads in newspapers and magazines and commercials or ads broadcast on television, radio, and Internet sites.

Another key role of political parties is hiring workers for government jobs. This is because Congress and state legislatures are structurally organized primarily on the basis of party affiliation.

Many civil service and government jobs are earned on the basis of merit, experience, and abilities. However, some leaders—such as the president, governors, and other office holders—can hire trusted and loyal party supporters to high-level positions.

Another key role of political parties is to link the different levels and branches of government and help them work better together. Government leaders from the same political party are likely to have similar policy ideas and goals. These similarities can often lead to greater cooperation to solve mutual problems. In addition, when the majority party in the legislature and the chief executive are members of the same party, cooperation between the two branches is likely to be more effective than if they belong to opposing parties.

Political parties also act as government overseers, sometimes called *watchdogs*. The minority party in Congress or in a state legislature monitors the party in power, mainly for mistakes or misuse of power. Opposition parties publicize government problems or leadership issues and then offer solutions. This is one way they can attract more people to the party and perhaps win future elections.

Major Political Parties Today

For more than 150 years, the two major political parties have been the Democratic Party and the Republican Party.

The Democratic Party

The **Democratic Party** is not only the largest and oldest political party in the United States, it is one of the oldest political parties in the world. The Democratic Party traces its roots to 1792 and Thomas Jefferson and his supporters. By the early 1800s, the party called itself the Democratic Republicans, and by the time Andrew Jackson was elected president in 1828, it had become known simply as the Democratic Party. A donkey is the symbol of the Democratic Party.

The Democratic Party is considered to be liberal, and on the left of the political spectrum. This means that the party advocates positions that are generally open to ideas of reform or progress. Liberals tend to pursue positions that are not tied to traditional values or attitudes.

Although initially shaped by Thomas Jefferson, who supported the idea of a smaller and less powerful federal government, the modern Democratic Party has evolved into a party that generally supports a stronger government. Today, the party advocates for a government with the power to regulate business and industry when it is in the public's interest. The Democratic Party is also a supporter of social services and benefits for the poor, the unemployed, the elderly, and other disadvantaged groups, often by using federal money. Democrats have generally been staunch supporters for the protection of civil rights.

Many Democrats advocate for a strong separation of church and state, while also opposing government regulation of the personal lives of Americans. In addition, Democratic leaders have steered the country's foreign policy toward more open relations throughout the world and have supported formal international organizations. A good example would be the party's strong support of international institutions like the United Nations.

Famous Democratic presidents include Andrew Jackson, Franklin D. Roosevelt, and Barack Obama.

The Republican Party

The other major political party in the United States is the **Republican Party**. The Republican Party is nicknamed the GOP, which stands for Grand Old Party. An elephant is the symbol of the party. The Republican Party is considered to be conservative, and on the right of the political spectrum. This means that the party promotes and supports a political philosophy and policies that are based on tradition and social stability. Republicans prefer gradual developments and changes rather than quick or abrupt changes. Republicans in the past have historically supported and promoted the established democratic institutions in the U.S.

The Republican Party traces its history to a protest meeting in Ripon, Wisconsin, in 1854. At this meeting, a group of antislavery activists, known as Free Soilers, organized a new grassroots movement. The Republican Party continued this antislavery philosophy through the 1800s. Republicans fought the expansion of slavery into new territories while many also worked to abolish slavery once and for all.

Like the Democratic Party, the Republican Party has evolved and changed over the years. For example, many early Republicans fought against recognizing the right of states and territories to allow slavery. The modern Republican Party, however, generally supports states' rights and has worked to diminish the power of the federal government. In addition, during the twentieth and twenty-first centuries, the Republican Party has promoted laissez-faire capitalism and low taxes, and has pushed to implement conservative social policies.

Today's Republican Party also strongly opposes regulations imposed by the federal government or its attempts to control what have long been state and local matters, such as education and law enforcement.

Famous Republican presidents include Abraham Lincoln, Theodore Roosevelt, and Ronald Reagan.

Practice

50. A political party's belief, position, or principle on an election issue is called a(n)

_____

a. plank

b. ideology

c. platform

d. idea

51. Which of the following is most likely to be supported by a political liberal?
   a. Privatizing social security
   b. Expanding social welfare programs
   c. Shrinking the size of the bureaucracy
   d. Engaging in a conflict abroad

Voting

Perhaps two of the key aspects of American democracy are the election process and citizens' right to vote. Voting provides a method of active participation while giving citizens a chance to influence their government. Voting is a basic political right of all citizens in a democracy who meet certain qualifications set by law.

Although restrictions vary by state, most citizens are qualified to vote if they have not been convicted of a felony or have a diagnosed mental condition. In addition,

- a voter must be a citizen of the United States
- a voter must be at least 18 years old
- most states also require a voter to be a resident of the state for a specific period of time and to be registered to vote

Citizens of the United States who are registered can vote in all local, state, and federal elections. The Constitution gives states the power to control and regulate elections and the voting process. That is why registration requirements vary from state to state. Some requirements are commonly found in many states. For example, first-time voters must show proof that they are legal citizens, of voting age, and have a valid home address within the district where they are voting. When registering, people can use many forms of identification that have been approved by the state. Voters are then assigned to an election district.

Over the years, the federal government has tried to make the registration and voting process easier for Americans. For example, the 1993 National Voter Registration Act, also called the Motor Voter Act, requires states to allow people to register to vote when renewing their driver's license. People receiving government support through welfare or for disabilities are also covered under this law.

On election day, voters cast their ballots at a polling place within their home precinct, or voting district. Because election methods are left to the states, the kinds of voting machines used vary widely. The two most common types of voting machines are the punch-card machine and the lever machine. Citizens who cannot get to a polling place on election day are allowed the option of voting by absentee ballot through the mail.

Elections

All elections in the United States political system go through a two-part process. The first part is the nomination of candidates in a primary election, described earlier. Primary elections help to narrow the field of candidates. Following the primaries, a general election is held. Federal general elections always take place on the first Tuesday after the first Monday in November. All seats in the U.S. House of Representatives and about one-third of the seats in the Senate are at stake in general elections.

For all elections except the presidential election, the candidate who wins the majority of the popular vote is elected to office. This is the winner-take-all system. In a presidential race, the voters are actually electing people called electors, who hold electoral votes and are part of the Electoral College system. Article II, Section 1, of the Constitution established the Electoral College. Some of the framers of the Constitution wanted the American people to have direct power over the federal government. Others were afraid of wide swings in popular opinions that might create havoc within the government. These framers wanted Congress to have the power to elect the president. The Electoral College, therefore, was a compromise measure. The framers decided to have the legislatures in each state choose presidential electors who are directly chosen by the voters in each state.

Other types of elections include the initiative, the referendum, and the recall.

- The **initiative** is a process in which citizens can propose new laws or state constitutional amendments.
- The **referendum** is a way for citizens to approve or reject a state or local law. Only about half of the states provide the referendum to their citizens.
- The **recall** is a special election in which citizens in some states can vote to remove a public official from office.

Election Campaigns

Elected officials in the United States are governed by laws that limit the amount of time that they can serve, and so candidates for offices at the local, state, and federal levels must periodically run for office. Typically, candidates run for office by establishing a campaign that promotes them and tries to convince citizens to vote for them. A primary activity of political campaigns is publicizing the candidates' positions on issues. The most common way that local candidates do this is to reach out and meet voters directly. Candidates for national offices, who usually have access to greater campaign funding, take advantage of the mass media to promote themselves and their positions.

Practice

52. Which of the following statements describes the significance of the Motor Voter Act, the nickname for the National Voter Registration Act of 1993?
- **a.** It creates a federal identification system for all eligible voters.
- **b.** It provides funding for online voting for people who frequently travel.
- **c.** It directs states to test people when registering to vote at driver's license facilities.
- **d.** It requires states to provide voter registration opportunities when applying for a driver's license.

53. _____ is/are responsible for certifying electors to the Electoral College.
- **a.** Political parties
- **b.** The Supreme Court
- **c.** Congress
- **d.** State legislatures

54. A(n) _____ is an election process through which voters can remove an elected official from office.
- **a.** redaction
- **b.** recall
- **c.** initiative
- **d.** referendum

Contemporary Public Policy

In order to function, modern governments develop many policies and procedures in addition to laws. If a policy seems reasonable and is generally accepted, it rarely receives any public attention. However, many public policies are subject to vigorous public debate. Areas of controversy can arise at any time.

The beginning of the policymaking process is the recognition that a problem exists and needs a solution. Policymaking experts generally describe five basic steps in the creating of public policy.

1. **Building an agenda.** The first step is to identify the problem. This leads to the appropriate people having discussions about how best to tackle the problem. From there, they can create an agenda with a rough plan for addressing the issue.
2. **Formulating policy.** With an agenda, policymakers can start looking at and evaluating possible solutions or policies and deciding the best way forward.
3. **Adopting and budgeting for the policy.** If the policymakers can agree on a solution and get it authorized, they can request resources and money. This is part of the budgeting process.
4. **Implementing the policy.** Once the policymakers have completed their job, the people in charge of putting policies into action take over and work to implement the policy.
5. **Evaluating the policy.** This final step involves many people who are impacted by the new policy. These people look to see whether the policy is working. This stage can also involve making recommendations or adjustments to improve results.

Some ongoing topics of public policy that are generally contentious include the following:

- **tax policy,** including simplifying the tax code, whether to raise or to cut revenues, and who should be impacted by these changes. Americans pay a variety of different taxes. Individuals and corporations facing high taxes have strong incentives to find or create loopholes to the tax laws.
- **budget policy,** including deciding how large a deficit can be tolerated, spending and taxing priorities, and the role and obligations of the government
- **trade policy**, including encouraging or discouraging imports and exports and using trade as a component of foreign policy

- **defense policy**, including the deployment and equipping of armed forces, defining missions, and determining the objectives and exit strategy of military operations
- **environmental policy**, including interventions to address pollution, energy, and development
- **foreign policy**, which affects not only Americans but also people around the world. Every foreign policy decision or action by the president or Congress is open to extensive scrutiny and criticism throughout the country and from abroad. And because the United States is a democracy that guarantees freedom of speech, foreign policy disputes will continue to be a major component of the national conversation.

Civics and Government Summary

The concepts of self-rule and representative democracy have shaped the United States from its early history. Colonists brought European ideas about government, such as natural rights, to America. The U.S. government took shape based on core principles, including constitutionalism, rule of law, checks and balances, and federalism.

The Constitution of the United States of America is the manifestation of those principles. It outlines the relationship between the federal government and the states, the three branches of government, and the method of representative democracy that has shaped public policy from the country's founding to today.

Practice Answers and Explanations

1. d. Town Meeting, in which every registered voter can participate, is considered to be a direct democracy. A presidential democracy (choice **a**) is a government system based on the separation and sharing of powers between three independent and equal branches of government: legislative, executive, and judicial. Democratic socialism (choice **b**) combines a socialist economy with a politically democratic system of government. Andover's economy, however, is not socialistic. A parliamentary democracy (choice **c**) is quite different from Andover's democracy because rather than voting for representatives to address their concerns, they represent themselves.

2. a. Casting a ballot in an election is an example of the principle of representative government in action. Serving on a jury (choice **b**) is a legal duty many citizens around the world must perform and does not affect how they are politically represented. Paying taxes (choice **c**) is one way citizens contribute to maintaining various governments. It is not, however, a principle of representative government. Working as an election judge (choice **d**) is a display of political and civic involvement. It is not, however, a principle of representative government.

3. c. In the United States, the president is elected by American citizens and through the process of the Electoral College. In a parliamentary government, the prime minister is chosen from members of the legislature who make up the majority party or coalition of parties. The judicial branches (choice **a**) in both forms of government operate as a separate and independent branch of government. Members of Congress in the United States and members of parliaments or key legislative bodies (choice **b**) are all elected by popular vote in established districts, although the number of elected officials may be different. The legislative branches (choice **d**) in both systems have sole responsibility for introducing new laws and for actively maintaining the work of government.

4. d. Coalition governments are common in countries whose parliaments are elected by proportional representation, with several or many organized political parties often represented. This usually happens because an individual party on its own cannot win a majority in the parliament. Presidential elections (choice **a**) involve the election of a single candidate for head of government and do not involve proportional representation. Direct democracy systems (choice **b**) do not use any kinds of representational government. Winner-take-all elections (choice **c**) appoint the candidate who wins the most votes in an election, rather than several candidates who represent various groups within a district.

5. b and c. Democratic socialism is the merging of a socialist economy with a democratic system of government. A socialist economy is one in which the means of production are collectively owned by the citizens or by the state. Democratic socialism also promotes political change and progress through traditional methods, such as the voting process. Government control of all social life (choice **a**) is a feature of totalitarian regimes. Democratic socialism follows the political principles of democracy, not of socialism (choice **d**).

6. b. A plutocrat is an individual whose power is based on wealth. Although a duke (choice **a**) is part of the privileged class in an aristocracy, the term plutocrat refers to wealthy individuals without aristocratic titles. An elected official (choice **c**) is selected by a democratic process, ideally unrelated to wealth or social status. A military general (choice **d**) does not usually rule government except in the case of a military junta or in a stratocracy, although military leaders can also run for elected office.

7. b. The American Revolution was a rebellion against the privilege of English aristocracy and the aristocratic system. Although it was won by militia, the battle was against the British king and his aristocracy, not one junta against another (choice **a**). The system of government that eventually emerged in the United States after the Revolution was based on the principles of democracy, and was not an oligarchy (choice **c**) in any way, nor was it based on a military constitution (choice **d**).

8. a. Democratic governments are built on the idea that citizens should control the government. This would provide opportunities for all citizens to engage in the political process. Aristocracies (choice **b**) are a form of government that places power in the hands of a small, privileged ruling class. This limits the role most citizens can play. Monarchies (choice **c**) are a system of government in which one person reigns, usually a king or queen. This limits the role of the majority of citizens in the political process. Oligarchies (choice **d**) are a form of government in which all power is concentrated in a few persons or in a powerful class or group. It is government by the few.

9. b. A military coup d'état, often just called a coup, occurs when one military force overthrows another to gain power. A plutocratic revolt (choice **a**) often may result in social unrest and economic problems. Plutocracies, however, usually do not control the military, so it is unlikely to lead to a military takeover of the government. Monarchial inheritance (choice **c**) is the most common way that power is passed from one monarch to the next. A revolution (choice **d**) is an overthrow of an established government or political system by the citizens of the nation, and usually has great social significance as well as military involvement.

10. a. In a democratic society, power rests in the free thought and expression of individuals. Authoritarian forms of government suppress personal freedoms and expression. An autocratic government (choice **b**) is led by a ruler with absolute power that is unchecked. This would allow the leader to wield enormous power and most likely restrict free expression. The German Nazi government (choice **c**) controlled free expression through coercion, fear, and brutality. A despotic regime (choice **d**) uses terror and intimidation to suppress basic civil liberties like free expression.

11. c. Most totalitarian governments are led by charismatic leaders whose image and power has been carefully crafted and developed to elicit adoration, as in a cult. Totalitarian governments usually do not arise through free elections (choice **a**). A ruling class of wealthy landowners (choice **b**) is a characteristic of aristocratic governments, not of a totalitarian one. Totalitarian states usually suppress or try to dissolve traditional political and cultural institutions (choice **d**), and replace them with new ones.

12. c. Dictatorships are governments in which the people are ruled by either a single individual or a small group of despots or dictators. A government led by a monarch and a constitution (choice **a**) is a constitutional monarchy, not a dictatorship. A government led by the nation's nobility (choice **b**) is an aristocracy, not a dictatorship. A government run by military leaders (choice **d**) is a stratocracy, not a dictatorship.

13. d. A meritocracy is based on merit, intelligence, and talent, and civil testing leads to social promotion. A puppet state (choice **a**) is a nation or government that is controlled by another nation and acts in subordination to the other power in exchange for its own survival. A republic (choice **b**) is a government in which supreme power is held by the people and their elected representatives, and has an elected or nominated president rather than a monarch. A theocracy (choice **c**) is a government run by direct divine guidance or by officials who are regarded as divinely guided.

14. a. While having an elected parliament and a president is considered to be evidence of democracy, any democratically elected individual can be overruled by a religious authority. A government in which the final say is given to a religious leader is a theocracy. An oligarchy (choice **b**) is a form of government in which all power is vested in a few persons or in a dominant class or clique, not in religious clergy. A dictatorship (choice **c**) is a government in which the people are ruled either by a single individual or by a small group of despots or dictators, who may or may not be religiously guided. In a democracy (choice **d**), power is held by the people, who rule either directly or through freely elected representatives. This is different from a theocracy.

15. c. In a democracy, only by voting do people choose those who will represent them in government. Crowning a king (choice **a**) is associated with nations that have a monarchy. Although some democracies have retained monarchy, these are usually constitutional monarchies in which the monarch has only ceremonial powers. Crowning a king would not affect sovereignty. Military service (choice **b**) may be either voluntary or forced, as through a draft. Neither method, however, nor military service itself, involves the concept of sovereignty. Obeying the law (choice **d**) is a legal requirement for citizens. It does not demonstrate how power is exercised or by whom.

16. c. The Enlightenment was a philosophical movement in Europe in the seventeenth and eighteenth centuries. Enlightened thinkers advocated the use of reason to discuss and solve political, religious, and social issues. The Progressive Movement (choice **a**) describes the era from the 1890s to 1920s in the United States that was characterized by social activism and political reforms. The New Deal (choice **b**) was a series of government programs and policies implemented by President Franklin D. Roosevelt in the 1930s to improve conditions for Americans suffering in the Great Depression. The Reformation (choice **d**) was a sixteenth-century movement for the reform of the Roman Catholic Church. The Reformation ended in the establishment of the Reformed and Protestant Churches.

17. d. Locke believed that all people are born free, equal, and independent and that everyone possesses natural rights to life, liberty, and property that no government could take away. Minority rights (choice **a**) are protected by the Constitution, but not because of Locke's influence. Although Locke discussed and advocated for the rule of law (choice **b**), the concept dates back to ancient civilizations and had been supported by many other thinkers. Locke's concept of natural rights was a complete rejection of the idea of divine right (choice **c**).

18. c. This saying best expresses the notion of popular sovereignty. The colonists claimed that the right to collect taxes depended on the consent of the colonists. "Don't tread on me" (choice **a**) was a saying used mainly to reinforce the colonists' defense of their individual rights and liberties, not as a statement to describe how governments gain power. "A man's house is his castle" (choice **b**) is most closely tied to Locke's concept of an individual's natural right to property. "Join or die" (choice **d**) was a cartoon drawn by Benjamin Franklin urging American colonists to unite against the British. It supports the idea of independence rather than being a direct call for popular sovereignty.

19. disadvantage
20. disadvantage
21. disadvantage
22. advantage
23. advantage
24. advantage
25. advantage
26. The **executive** branch checks the **judicial** branch.
27. The **judicial** branch checks the **legislative** branch.

28. The **legislative** branch checks the **judicial** branch.

29. The **judicial** branch checks the **executive** branch.

30. d. Article I, Section 1, of the Constitution states that all legislative powers are granted to Congress. Because an Executive Order has the power of law, a senator might think that the president is exercising a power that is not granted by the Constitution, and therefore is violating the principle of separation of powers. In this situation, no one's individual rights (choice **a**) are being violated. Federalism (choice **b**) is the division of power between the federal government and state governments. This situation does not involve state governments, nor does it involve the concept of limited government (choice **c**).

31. b. Because the president cannot reject single items within a bill, he or she must accept them in order for the favored provisions to become law. Through the system of checks and balances, the legislative and executive branches are theoretically equal in power (choice **a**). Although a president might be more effective when his or her party has a majority in Congress (choice **c**), there is nothing in the passage to support this claim. Congress can override a presidential veto and pass a law (choice **d**) with a two-thirds vote from both the House of Representatives and the Senate.

32. a. Because Congress would rather rewrite a bill than try to override a veto (choice **b**), you can conclude that it is easier to do so. The passage clearly states that the president does not have the Constitutional authority to rewrite or edit legislation (choice **c**). The president can state objections to bills as a means of influencing Congress and its work (choice **d**).

33. b. Federalism is the principle of shared power. The Constitution grants the federal government certain powers and responsibilities. Powers not granted to the federal government are given to the states. Power and authority are not concentrated either with local governments (choice **a**) or with the federal government (choice **d**). Choice **c**, nonexistent, is factually incorrect.

34. c. In 1913, the Seventeenth Amendment to the U.S. Constitution took the power to elect U.S. senators from the state legislatures and gave it to the people. When the Constitution was written, senators were elected by state legislatures, which is different from how they are elected today (choice **a**). The Seventeenth Amendment clearly states that each senator shall have one vote, not one unified voted (choice **b**). The statement in choice **d** is not relevant to the passages. Neither passage mentions term limits.

35. c. The Constitution grants the House the power to impeach federal officials. Impeached officials are then tried in the Senate (choice **d**), not the House. Approving presidential nominees (choice **a**) is a power granted to the Senate, not the House. The Constitution states that all revenue bills (choice **b**) must be introduced in the House, but this is a legislative power.

36. a. Congress has the authority to declare war, while the president serves as commander in chief of the military. The Constitution clearly states that only Congress can declare war, not the president (choice **b**). The Constitution explicitly states that the president, not Congress, is in command of the armed forces (choice **c**). Although Congress does have the power to declare war, the president does not have the power to write laws (choice **d**).

37. b. The president does not take any action in a pocket veto. The pocket veto occurs when Congress adjourns, not because of secret actions (choice **a**). If Congress adjourns within ten days and the president takes no action, the bill dies and Congress may not vote to override. Congress can, when it comes back into session, take up the bill again and go through the normal legislative process (choice **c**). This is a line-item veto, not a pocket veto (choice **d**).

38. c. The Constitution requires that related bills written in the House and the Senate have the exact wording when finalized and presented to the president. A conference committee works to align the two bills. Many different committees hold hearings (choice **a**) in both the Senate and the House. A conference committee meets once legislation has been written. Both the House and the Senate have separate and independent committees that oversee the executive branch and other governmental functions (choice **b**) and do not involve conference committees. Conference committees are not involved in making decisions of this sort (choice **d**).

39. d. Through judicial review, the Supreme Court is continually interpreting the limits set by the Constitution. Far from having little influence (choice **a**), the Constitution continues to be the foundation for how the U.S. government operates. The Constitution does explicitly outline some powers and which branch or level of government can exercise them. However, many powers are left unexpressed (choice **b**). Several of the framers did support the concept of judicial review. As the passage points out, Alexander Hamilton and James Madison emphasized the importance of judicial review in the *Federalist Papers* (choice **c**).

40. a. According to the passage, judicial review is "the authority to invalidate laws and executive actions if they conflict with the Constitution." Choice **a** is a good paraphrase of the excerpt from the passage. Public opinion polls (choice **b**) are not associated with judicial review. Determining the country's changing needs (choice **c**) does not fall under the scope or authority of the Supreme Court. Proposing new laws (choice **d**) is the responsibility of Congress, not the judicial branch.

41. c. District courts are responsible for determining the facts of a case; they are the trial courts for both criminal and civil federal cases. District courts are the only federal courts in which witnesses testify and juries hear cases and reach verdicts. Only district courts have juries; appellate courts and the Supreme Court do not (choice **a**). The Supreme Court (choice **b**) does not have juries. Appellate courts (choice **d**) do not have juries.

42. d. Sharing the power to raise revenue helps keep both levels of government strong and independent and maintains a balance of power. Choices **a**, **b**, and **c** are incorrect.

43. state. State governments have the power to grant corporate status to businesses.

44. federal. The federal government regulates interstate commerce, including banks that have headquarters and branches in different states.

45. federal. The federal government runs the U.S. Postal Service and therefore pays local post office employees, even in rural areas.

46. a. Prayer is protected by the First Amendment, which involves the freedom of religion. Anyone charged with a crime has the right to legal representation (choice **b**). The Sixth Amendment guarantees people charged with a crime the right to a trial by jury (choice **c**). The Sixth Amendment requires that people charged with a crime be informed of the charges (choice **d**).

47. c. The first ten amendments are called the Bill of Rights. A preamble (choice **a**) is an introductory statement that explains the purpose of a formal document, such as the Declaration of Independence or the U.S. Constitution. A declaration of rights (choice **b**) can refer to other documents that describe basic civil rights, but it is not the name of the first ten amendments. The Magna Carta (choice **d**), issued by the English King John in 1215, was an important English political document that protected civil liberties.

48. b. The Twenty-Sixth Amendment to the Constitution, passed in 1971, lowered the voting age to 18 in both federal and state elections. Twenty-five (choice **a**) is the minimum age a person needs to be to get elected to the House of Representatives. Sixteen (choice **c**) is factually wrong. Twenty-one (choice **d**) was the minimum voting age until 1971.

49. d. Obeying laws is the most important civic duty Americans perform. Choices **a**, **b**, and **c**, because they are duties and legal requirements, all fall under obeying the law.

50. a. A plank is a political party's stand or view on a single issue. An ideology (choice **b**) is a broad statement of beliefs, not a position on a single issue. A political platform (choice **c**) is the statement of a political party's combined positions and beliefs on a wide range of issues. An idea (choice **d**) is a general term and does not relate to the specific political nature of the question.

51. b. Expanding social welfare is an important component of liberal ideology. The other options (choices **a**, **c**, and **d**) all represent actions that would more likely be supported by a person with a conservative ideology.

52. d. This law made it easier for Americans to register and vote. It requires states to offer voter registration opportunities to people who apply for or get a new driver's license. The Act only accumulates individual data (choice **a**) for those people registering to vote when applying for a driver's license or receiving social assistance. At the time of the Act's passage, the Internet (choice **b**) was just developing, and so a platform for online voting would not have been available. Any type of test (choice **c**), including a literacy test, was ruled unconstitutional in the 1960s.

53. d. The Constitution specifies that state legislatures certify the electors to the Electoral College. Although political parties (choice **a**) can influence who the electors are, they are not responsible for certifying them. The Supreme Court (choice **b**) is not involved in certifying electors to the Electoral College. Congress (choice **c**) is not involved in certifying electors to the Electoral College.

54. b. A recall is a procedure that allows citizens to remove and replace a public official before his or her term is up. Redaction (choice **a**) is the editing of a document in such a way that confidential and secret information is protected. It is not a political process for removing elected officials. An initiative (choice **c**) enables citizens to propose statutes and, in some states, constitutional amendments on a ballot. It does not involve removing an elected official from office. A referendum (choice **d**) is a way for citizens to approve or reject a state or local law. It does not involve removing an elected official from office.

5  UNITED STATES HISTORY

An understanding of United States history is important to all U.S. citizens and residents. Understanding the historical roots of the country's political system and government, as well as major trends and events in its history, provides insight into what values have motivated the American people, their government, and their businesses. Understanding American history helps shed light on how we got where we are today and helps us make sense of current events and political groups.

Key Historical Documents

A descendant of the English system of government, American constitutional government has been influenced by ideas set forth in several important documents in the history of Western Europe and the United States.

The Magna Carta

The Magna Carta, or Great Charter, was written in 1215 in England. It was the most important document during the medieval period and limited the absolute power and authority of the king of England. Essentially, the

Magna Carta established for the first time the idea that everybody, including the king, was to be treated equally under the law. Primarily an agreement between the king and the nobility, its key provisions, among others, concerned

- rights of landholders and tenants
- freedom of the church from the influence of the king
- reform of law, and the fair, nonarbitrary execution of justice

Here is an excerpt from the document.

> No free man shall be arrested or imprisoned or disseised or outlawed or exiled or in any way victimised, neither will we attack him or send anyone to attack him, except by the lawful judgment of his peers or by the law of the land.

Revised in the centuries that followed, the Magna Carta is considered the foundation of Great Britain's constitutional democracy. As well, it contains the ideals of self-rule and limitation of power that are enshrined in the founding documents of the United States.

Practice
1. In the Magna Carta, the word *we* refers to

_____.

The Mayflower Compact
The Mayflower Compact was the first governmental document written and implemented in a territory that would become part of the United States. The 41 male English colonists on the *Mayflower*, which carried approximately 102 colonists to New England,

signed the document on November 11, 1620, and agreed to

> . . . covenant and combine ourselves together into a civil Body Politick . . . And by Virtue hereof to enact, constitute, and frame, such just and equal Laws, Ordinances, Acts, Constitutions, and Officers, from time to time, as shall be thought most meet and convenient for the general Good of the Colony; unto which we promise all due Submission and Obedience.

The Mayflower Compact proved to be effective; John Carver, who had helped organize the *Mayflower's* voyage, was chosen as the first governor of the colony.

Practice
2. Reread the excerpt above and summarize in one or two sentences what the colonists agreed to in the Mayflower Compact.

_____

_____

_____

_____

The Declaration of Independence
In the spring of 1776, following a year of fighting the British, many American colonists were not prepared to break away from Great Britain. Even many of the colonial leaders in the Second Continental Congress did not want to separate completely from the British Empire. Most, however, did support the right to govern themselves. With no end of the war in sight, however, most colonial leaders realized that the time had come to declare their independence.

In January 1776, English-born writer Thomas Paine published the pamphlet *Common Sense*, in which he outlined his argument for American independence. Within three months, *Common Sense* had sold 100,000 copies. Paine's pamphlet had great influence in gathering support for the vote for independence.

In early July, a committee in the Continental Congress that included Benjamin Franklin, Robert Livingston, John Adams, Roger Sherman, and Thomas Jefferson submitted a document that the committee had been tasked to create. Jefferson, with input from the others, was the chief writer. This document explained the reasons for the call for independence.

On July 4, 1776, the Continental Congress issued this Declaration of Independence.

Probably more than any other document, the Preamble of the Declaration of Independence encapsulates the United States' most idealistic aspirations.

Here is an excerpt from the document.

> We hold these truths to be self-evident, that all men are created equal, that they are endowed by their Creator with certain unalienable rights, that among these are Life, Liberty and the Pursuit of Happiness.

The Declaration of Independence is divided into four general sections.

- The Preamble explains why the Continental Congress drafted the Declaration.
- The Declaration of Natural Rights states that people have certain basic rights and that government should protect those rights.
- The List of Grievances lists the colonists' complaints against the British government.

- The Resolution of Independence declares that the colonies are "Free and Independent States" with the power to make war, to form alliances, and to trade with other nations.

The Declaration of Independence was an important document in world political history. The American colonists were the first people to create a written document that explained precisely the political, moral, and legal reasons why they declared themselves to be independent of Great Britain. Colonies throughout the world would use the Declaration of Independence as a model and inspiration for declaring their own independence from their ruling nations. Additionally, some groups in the United States, including minorities and those fighting for women's rights, would use the language and concepts of the Declaration in their arguments.

Practice

3. What was the purpose of the Declaration of Independence?
   a. To allow the United States to become the most powerful nation on Earth.
   b. To justify a revolution against the rule of Great Britain.
   c. To establish democracy throughout the world.
   d. To help create the conditions for the Industrial Revolution.

4. The chief author of the Declaration of Independence was _____
   a. Thomas Paine.
   b. John Adams.
   c. Thomas Jefferson
   d. Benjamin Franklin

Use this excerpt from the Declaration of Independence to answer questions 5 and 6.

IN CONGRESS, July 4, 1776.

The unanimous Declaration of the thirteen united States of America, When in the Course of human events, it becomes necessary for one people to dissolve the political bands which have connected them with another . . . a decent respect to the opinions of mankind requires that they should declare the causes which impel them to the separation.

We hold these truths to be self-evident, that all men are created equal, that they are endowed by their Creator with certain unalienable Rights, that among these are Life, Liberty and the pursuit of Happiness. . . . That whenever any Form of Government becomes destructive of these ends, it is the Right of the People to alter or to abolish it, and to institute new Government. . . . Prudence, indeed, will dictate that Governments long established should not be changed for light and transient causes; and accordingly all experience hath shewn, that mankind are more disposed to suffer, while evils are sufferable, than to right themselves by abolishing the forms to which they are accustomed. But when a long train of abuses and usurpations, pursuing invariably the same Object evinces a design to reduce them under absolute Despotism, it is their right, it is their duty, to throw off such Government, and to provide new Guards for their future security. . . .

5. Which best states the meaning of *unalienable* in the excerpt?
   a. absolute
   b. historical
   c. resolute
   d. governmental

6. Based on the excerpt, which type of government are people generally least likely to move forward to "throw off"?
   a. an oppressive government that is new to the people
   b. a government that has been governing unfairly for a long time
   c. an undemocratic government with self-serving motives
   d. a recently formed government that commits multiple offenses against the people

The Constitution of the United States of America

The Constitution serves as the framework of national government and the source of American citizens' basic rights. It is the most important document in the United States. It lays out the duties and responsibilities of the three branches of government and provides for a system of checks and balances.

Written in 1787, the Constitution was the second attempt by the 13 independent colonies to create a United States of America. In November 1777, during the Revolutionary War, the Continental Congress created the Articles of Confederation as a way to hold together the colonies under a central government. The Articles of Confederation became the first national constitution of the United States. However, with the war ended and the new nation facing massive war debts, the Articles proved to be too weak and ineffective. The Articles that Congress had created made the government so weak that it could not even tax the states without their permission.

In the summer of 1787, delegates from all the states except Rhode Island met in Philadelphia at the Constitutional Convention. The initial goal was to revise the Articles of Confederation. Instead, the delegates proposed creating a new constitution.

Major Issues at the Convention

As the delegates worked to hammer out the details of the new Constitution, they found themselves divided, mostly based on regional, population, and geographic differences. Delegates from the small states wanted changes that would protect them from the voting power of the big states. Also troubling were the arguments between Northern and Southern states over how to treat slavery in the new constitution.

The convention leadership organized a special committee to devise a compromise. Benjamin Franklin headed this committee. The committee returned with a plan developed by Roger Sherman of Connecticut. This plan is often called the **Connecticut Compromise** or the Great Compromise. Sherman's plan called for two chambers in the Congress. In one house, the House of Representatives, states would be represented according to the size of their populations. In the other house, the Senate, each state would have equal representation. Citizens in each state would vote to elect the members of the House. Senators, however, would be chosen by the state legislatures.

The slavery issue was settled with a compromise that has come to be known as the **Three-Fifths Compromise**. Southern states argued that they should be allowed to count enslaved people when determining their number of representatives. Delegates from the North argued that because the enslaved people could not vote, they should not be counted. The Three-Fifths Compromise stated that every five enslaved people would count as three free people for determining both representation and taxes.

Structure of the U.S. Constitution

The Constitution is made up of three main parts. The first part is called the **Preamble**. The second part contains seven **articles**. Each article describes a certain part of the government. For example, Articles I, II, and III describe the three branches of the national government: the legislative, executive, and judicial branches. The third part contains the **Bill of Rights** and additional changes to the Constitution, called **amendments**.

The Preamble to the Constitution establishes the purpose of the U.S. government. In this short passage, the framers clearly state that the power of the U.S. government comes from the people. The rest of the Preamble outlines six key purposes of the government.

> We the People of the United States, in Order to form a more perfect Union, establish Justice, insure domestic Tranquility, provide for the common defence, promote the general Welfare, and secure the Blessings of Liberty to ourselves and our Posterity, do ordain and establish this Constitution for the United States of America.

The second part of the Constitution is divided into seven sections called articles. Each article is identified by a Roman numeral. Articles I–III describe the powers and responsibilities of each branch of government.

Article I addresses the **legislative branch**, balancing the needs of large and small states by creating a two-house Congress composed of the following:

- House of Representatives, with membership based on population, giving more power to more populous states
- Senate, composed of two members from each state, giving equal power to less populous states. The intent of this solution was to limit the power of the majority by encouraging compromise and protecting minority rights.

- The legislative article details the lawmaking abilities of the Congress as well as the roles of the president and vice president.
- The impeachment process is also described, with the House of Representatives having the responsibility of impeaching, or charging, a government official, and the Senate having the responsibility of conducting the impeachment trial.

This section of the Constitution also stipulates that the Congress has the power to declare war.

Article II creates and describes the **executive branch**, which includes the president. The executive branch makes sure that the nation's laws are carried out.

- The first executive section declares that the president is the head of the executive branch.
- It describes the election of the president, with each state appointing electors equal in number to the total of its members of the House and Senate—a system referred to as the Electoral College.

Each state can decide how its electors are selected. Most states have a system in which the presidential nominee who wins the most votes in the state gets all the electoral votes; however, that is not always the case. Three times in American history, the candidate who lost the popular vote, which is the total vote count, won the electoral vote and became president.

- The remaining executive powers include being commander in chief of the armed forces, appointing executive officials and judges with the advice and consent of the Senate, entering into treaties with the advice and consent of the Senate, and overseeing the executive branch.

Article III establishes the **judicial branch**. This is the part of government that makes sure that laws are interpreted fairly. The judicial branch is also in charge of hearing cases in courts of law.

- This section provides for a Supreme Court and gives Congress the power to create lower courts.
- It also details the scope of the federal judiciary.

Articles IV through VII describe how the national government and the states work together. These articles also describe the relationships between the national government and the states.

- These include the requirement that each state and the federal government respect the laws, records, and judicial proceedings of any other state; the process of admitting new states; and the federal commitment to protect states from attack.

Finally, there are articles that lay out procedures for amending the Constitution and that commit the United States to repay all debts incurred before the ratification of the Constitution. For the Constitution to go into effect, only nine states were required to sign, but all thirteen states signed. As part of that agreement, Congress and the states approved the first ten amendments to the Constitution, known collectively as the Bill of Rights. In the more than 200 years since then, there have been only 17 additional amendments.

Ratification and the Bill of Rights

With a new Constitution written and the Constitutional Convention over, the delegates and other Americans turned to working toward getting the document ratified. Each state elected delegates and organized conventions where the new system of government would be either ratified or rejected. The framers stipulated that nine of the thirteen states had to ratify the Constitution in order for it to be implemented.

Supporters of the new Constitution called themselves **Federalists**. The Federalists believed that power should be divided between a central government and regional governments. Prominent Federalists included James Madison, Alexander Hamilton, and John Jay, who all wrote essays in support of ratification in an influential publication called *The Federalist*.

Opponents of the Constitution were known as Anti-Federalists. Anti-Federalists did not oppose the system of federalism, but rather were concerned that the central government would become much more powerful than the state governments. Prominent Anti-Federalists included John Hancock, Patrick Henry, and Samuel Adams.

Another chief concern of the Anti-Federalists was the lack of a bill of rights in the Constitution. Federalists quickly addressed these concerns by promising to attach a bill of rights to the Constitution once it was ratified. They also agreed to support an amendment that would reserve for the states all powers not specifically granted to the federal government.

The compromises and concessions made by the Federalists eventually persuaded enough state delegates to support ratification. On June 21, 1788, New Hampshire became the ninth state to ratify the document, and it was subsequently agreed that government under the U.S. Constitution would begin on March 4, 1789.

Practice

7. What was a main difference between the U.S. Constitution and the Articles of Confederation?
  a. The U.S. Constitution created new state boundaries.
  b. The U.S. Constitution established a representational government.
  c. The U.S. Constitution encouraged states to work together in times of war.
  d. The U.S. Constitution strengthened the power of the central government.

8. What is the main purpose of the Preamble to the U.S. Constitution?
  a. to tell why the Constitution is needed
  b. to present an outline of the document
  c. to describe the new system of government
  d. to review the reasons for breaking from England

9. What was a chief problem that confronted the framers of the Constitution?
  a. How to deal with the problem of the western territories
  b. How to balance the interests of small states with the interests of the large states
  c. How to make the president into an "uncrowned king"
  d. How to create a government too weak to threaten individual rights

10. Many Anti-Federalist fears were laid to rest when the Federalists agreed to add a _____ to the Constitution
  a. second chamber in the Congress
  b. supreme court
  c. bill of rights
  d. preamble

The Emancipation Proclamation and Reconstruction Amendments

As mentioned earlier, in the more than 200 years since the ratification of the Constitution and the addition of the Bill of Rights, there have been only 17 additional amendments. Perhaps the most important amendments are those that came in the wake of the American Civil War.

The Civil War was the cauldron through which the United States addressed the most pressing issue of its early history: slavery. The **Emancipation Proclamation** and the Thirteenth, Fourteenth, and Fifteenth Amendments to the U.S. Constitution (known as the Reconstruction Amendments) addressed slavery and would begin to heal the injustice of slavery in the United States.

The Emancipation Proclamation, which freed the slaves who lived in the Confederacy, was issued by President Abraham Lincoln on January 1, 1863. It referred to a preliminary version issued in September 1862, which stated

That on the first day of January, in the year of our Lord one thousand eight hundred and sixty-three, all persons held as slaves within any State or designated part of a State, the people whereof shall then be in rebellion against the United States, shall be then, thenceforward, and forever free; and the Executive Government of the United States, including the military and naval authority thereof, will recognize and maintain the freedom of such persons, and will do no act or acts to repress such persons, or any of them, in any efforts they may make for their actual freedom.

After listing the states and parts of states still considered to be in rebellion and repeating the announcement of the abolition of slavery in rebellious areas, the Proclamation continued,

And I hereby enjoin upon the people so declared to be free to abstain from all violence, unless in necessary self-defence; and I recommend to them that, in all cases when allowed, they labor faithfully for reasonable wages.

And I further declare and make known, that such persons of suitable condition, will be received into the armed service of the United States to garrison forts, positions, stations, and other places, and to man vessels of all sorts in said service.

And upon this act, sincerely believed to be an act of justice, warranted by the Constitution, upon military necessity, I invoke the considerate judgment of mankind, and the gracious favor of Almighty God.

At the conclusion of the Civil War, amendments were ratified that resolved the conflict over slavery, including

- the Thirteenth Amendment, which abolished slavery in the United States
- the Fourteenth Amendment, which guaranteed the rights of citizens, due process, and equal protection under the law for all people
- the Fifteenth Amendment, which guaranteed citizens the right to vote, regardless of "race, color, or previous condition of servitude"

Despite the passage of these amendments, it would take decades before the children of the formerly enslaved would gain access to equal rights.

Prehistory to Revolutionary and Early Republic Periods

The history of the United States can be traced to the earliest inhabitants of the country, but conflict with early settlers and disease introduced by them decimated Native American populations. By the time the United States was established, colonists faced their own conflicts over freedom and civil liberties with Great Britain, which ruled much of the eastern seaboard of North America. After the American Revolution, the new nation gradually established its political identity and economic independence, fueled largely by the early growth of the Industrial Revolution.

The Native Americans

The original inhabitants of North America populated the entire continent before European settlement began. The ancestors of the original inhabitants of the Americas arrived from Asia. Their arrival date has not been exactly determined, but estimates range from about 40,000 to 20,000 years ago. Native American, or Indian, peoples settled North America and formed societies and nations in many regions. The culture and lifestyles of Native Americans varied greatly across the continent. Many Native Americans lived as nomadic hunters while others lived in large, complex cities. Key Native American societies include

- Iroquois and Algonquian in the Northeast
- Creek, Cherokee, and Seminole in the Southeast
- Arapaho, Blackfoot, Sioux, Cheyenne, and Comanche on the Plains
- Hopi, Zuni, and Yuna in the Southwest
- Paiute and Shoshone in the Great Basin
- Hupa, Shasta, and Salina in California
- Chinook, Nez Perce, and Tlingit on the Northwest coast and plateau

These nations and tribes are only a small portion of the many Native American societies settlers encountered after Columbus arrived in the New World in 1492.

The encounters between Native Americans and early colonists shaped the formation of the early United States. Native Americans, who passed on their understanding of the environment and resources to the colonists, numbered approximately 25 million people, according to Howard Zinn in *A People's History of the United States*. These numbers would dwindle as contact with European settlers, disease, and conflict took their toll. In addition, nearly all Native Americans were driven from their lands as Europeans colonized the continent and established control from the Atlantic to the Pacific.

The Colonization of North America

Christopher Columbus's first voyage to the Americas in 1492 led to an era of European exploration and colonization in the New World. Europeans looked to this new world for exploration, discovery, and potential wealth through new trade opportunities and plunder. However, not all Europeans who came to North America were searching for wealth. Many came simply to build new lives for themselves in a new land.

Spain founded the first European colonies in the Americas. Spanish explorers and settlers established colonies in California and Florida, as well as in Mexico, Central America, and South America. Other European powers—England, Holland, and France—also explored North America, but did not establish permanent colonies until the 1600s.

France began explorations in North America in 1525 with a voyage along the Atlantic coast in search of the Northwest Passage. This was a northern water route through North America to the Pacific Ocean. Eventually, the French built fur trading posts and established mutually beneficial trading relationships with Native American trappers in present-day Canada and the Great Lakes regions. The French continued to explore the vast interior of North America.

These explorations led to the finding of the Mississippi River and the claiming of a huge territory known as Louisiana.

In 1609, the Dutch East India Company hired Henry Hudson to search for a river route through the North American continent. Instead, Hudson located what today is called the Hudson River. Following Hudson's voyages, the Dutch settled in the region and named it New Netherland. They established a settlement on the island of Manhattan and named it New Amsterdam. Although New Amsterdam became a busy and prosperous port, England eventually forced the Dutch out of North America and took over the colony. New Amsterdam was renamed New York.

In 1497, John Cabot commanded the first English expedition to North America. However, the English explorations stopped, and their colonization efforts were put on hold for nearly 80 years. In the late 1500s, religious, economic, and political changes in England motivated the founding of the first English colonies in North America. The Jamestown settlement was established in present-day Virginia in 1607. This colony struggled for several years as settlers faced starvation and harsh winter weather that they were unaccustomed to. The leadership of Captain John Smith and periodic supplies from England saved the colony.

In 1620, the Puritans, also known as Separatists, became another group of English colonists who sailed to North America after forming their own religious congregations. Later known as Pilgrims, these immigrants were searching for religious freedom. They founded Plymouth Colony in present-day Massachusetts. This colony survived and provided inspiration for the building of other English settlements along the Atlantic coast.

Practice

11. The _____ established a network of fur trading with Native Americans that accounted for its primary economic activity.
   a. English
   b. Dutch
   c. French
   d. Spanish

12. The Columbian Exchange refers to the vast movement of peoples, plants, animals, and microbes between the Old and New Worlds. A significant negative effect of the Columbian Exchange on Native Americans was

   _____
   a. the acquiring of new foods from the Old World, which dramatically impacted Native American diets.
   b. the introduction of the horse, which tremendously altered many Native Americans' lifestyles.
   c. the introduction of diseases to which Native Americans were not immune, devastating populations.
   d. the introduction of gunpowder and muskets, which altered tribal relationships.

Read the following passage and answer question 13.

When European settlers arrived on the North American continent at the end of the fifteenth century, they encountered diverse American Indian cultures—as many as 900,000 inhabitants with over 300 different languages. These people, whose ancestors crossed the land bridge from Asia in what may be considered the first North American immigration, were virtually destroyed by the subsequent immigration that created the United States. This tragedy is the direct result of treaties, written and broken by foreign governments, of warfare, and of forced assimilation. *Source: The Library of Congress, American Memory.*

13. What does the author of this passage believe?
   a. The U.S. government was faithful to its treaties with American Indians.
   b. American Indians made up a homogeneous group.
   c. The European settlers were responsible for the decimation of native people.
   d. Native cultures were unsophisticated.

The Founding of the Original Colonies

Increasing numbers of immigrants in the 1600s helped lead to the creation of the thirteen original English colonies. These colonies were grouped into three general geographic groups:

- The **New England Colonies** (Massachusetts, Connecticut, Rhode Island, and New Hampshire) occupied land that was rocky and had poor soil. The Atlantic Ocean provided alternatives to farming. Fishing and whaling soon became important economic activities. Shipbuilding and supplying materials for the fishing industries also grew.
- The **Middle Colonies** (New York, New Jersey, Pennsylvania, and Delaware) had a moderate climate and fertile soils, which allowed farmers to produce surpluses. The rise of large cities also attracted immigrants from many different countries and backgrounds, leading to a more diverse society.
- The **Southern Colonies** (Maryland, Virginia, North Carolina, South Carolina, and Georgia) had a warm climate and fertile soil, leading to an economy and culture based on growing crops for export, along with bringing in more and more enslaved Africans to work the crops on the region's large plantations.

Practice

14. The New England Colonies were different from the Middle and Southern cColonies in that
   a. agriculture was not the primary economic activity.
   b. they occupied regions in warm climates.
   c. they were much more ethnically diverse.
   d. they did not use slave labor for their large plantations.

The Causes of the American Revolutionary War

While a number of European nations were involved in colonizing the Americas, the area that would become the United States in 1783 was under the control of Great Britain after the end of the French and Indian War, which was part of the larger Seven Years' War fought in Europe from 1754 to 1763.

Victory in the French and Indian War left the British government with overwhelming debt. In the 1760s, the English imposed several unpopular taxes on the American colonies to help pay off the debt. King George III of England also imposed several laws that the colonists thought restricted their freedoms. Many colonists started to resist.

Among the acts implemented by the British were the following:

- The Proclamation of 1763 prohibited settlement west of the Appalachian Mountains.
- The 1764 Currency Act attempted to stop the colonies from printing their own currency.
- The 1764 Sugar Act taxed sugar.
- The 1765 Stamp Act required tax stamps on many documents.
- The 1765 Quartering Act forced homeowners to let British soldiers stay in their homes.
- The 1767 Townshend Revenue Act increased taxes on glass, paper, and tea.
- The 1773 Tea Act enforced taxes on tea and the British East India Company's monopoly on its sale.

These measures were fiercely opposed by the Committees of Correspondence, which were local groups of legislators who began organizing in 1764. By 1772, the Committees had become an established method of coordinated action among colonies when Samuel Adams organized the Boston Committee of Correspondence.

The Boston Tea Party in 1773 was one of the most important protests against the British measures. Colonial patriots called the Sons of Liberty boarded a merchant ship loaded with tea and dumped it into Boston Harbor. In response, the British enacted what came to be known as the 1774 Intolerable Acts, which attempted to punish the colonists by banning town meetings and closing Boston Harbor.

Instead of intimidating the colonists, these actions angered the colonial leadership from Great Britain and led to the outbreak of hostilities, which started with the following events:

- the "shot heard round the world" at the Battle of Lexington and Concord on April 19, 1775, between the British and the Massachusetts Minutemen
- the Battle of Bunker Hill on June 17, 1775, considered the beginning of the American War for Independence
- the British evacuation of Boston in March 1776

The Committees of Correspondence had established the Continental Congress to act on behalf of all colonists in 1774. In 1775, The Second Continental Congress appointed George Washington as commander of the Continental Army. The Continental Congress remained the government of the United States until the U.S. Constitution was implemented in 1789. The Declaration of Independence, written by Thomas Jefferson and approved by the Continental Congress, was adopted in 1776.

Practice

15. In 1770, outside the State House in Boston, Massachusetts, British soldiers shot and killed five colonists in an event still known as the Boston Massacre. When the soldiers were brought to trial, their lawyer was the colonist patriot John Adams. Which of the following foundational principles was most likely the key reason Adams took on this case?
   a. defending the underdog
   b. individual rights
   c. right to bear arms
   d. rule of law

George Washington and Independence

George Washington led the colonists in the War for Independence against Great Britain (1775–1783). Facing the most highly trained and equipped army in the world, Washington's Continental Army suffered defeat after defeat in the early years of the war. Several times, Washington relied on tactical maneuvers to allow for safe retreats to save his army from complete defeat. Not until the Battle of Saratoga in 1777 did the Continental Army claim its first significant victory. Following the victory at Saratoga, France began providing aid to the Americans, which proved to be crucial to the successes of the Continental Army.

In 1781, fighting moved south when British General Charles Cornwallis invaded Virginia. A French naval fleet surprised Cornwallis and drove off the British fleet providing supplies to the British land forces. Washington and French troops then marched to Virginia and surrounded Cornwallis's army. The fighting ended. The Treaty of Paris, signed in 1783, brought the war to an end.

The first president of the United States, Washington was the rare national leader who, after a period of great service to his nation, voluntarily gave up power. Washington voluntarily retired twice, first as commander in chief of the Continental Army after the military victory in the War for Independence, and later after serving two terms as president.

The tradition that he created was so strong that only one president in U.S. history—Franklin Delano Roosevelt in the twentieth century—has served more than two terms, a limitation that was formalized in 1951 as the Twenty-Second Amendment to the United States Constitution.

Practice

16. Which of the following statements about the Revolutionary War is correct?
   a. The war began with the British victory at Saratoga.
   b. The Continental Army had more men and war supplies than the British.
   c. France joined the war on the American side after the defeat at Bunker Hill.
   d. The fighting ended with Cornwallis's surrender at Yorktown.

17. The outbreak of war was caused primarily by the British
   a. demanding that town hall meetings publish their activities.
   b. forcing colonists to relocate west of the Appalachian Mountains.
   c. prohibiting American ships from sailing out of Boston Harbor.
   d. implementing the Intolerable Acts.

The Louisiana Purchase

The Treaty of Paris, signed in 1783, established the borders of the United States. The country now stretched from Canada in the north to the Gulf of Mexico and Florida in the south. In addition, lands stretching west of the Mississippi River were ceded to the young country through the terms of the treaty. Spain controlled Louisiana in 1799, but in 1800 it agreed to give it to France, which was ruled by Napoleon Bonaparte. Napoleon was convinced that war with Great Britain was coming and that France could not defend the vast Louisiana Territory from the British who might invade from Canada. The French then offered to sell the entire territory to the United States.

In 1803, President Thomas Jefferson bought the Louisiana Territory from France in what is known as the **Louisiana Purchase**. The Louisiana Territory included more than 800,000 square miles of territory west of the Mississippi River, effectively handing complete control of this important waterway to the United States.

To explore and learn about this vast new territory, Jefferson sent Meriwether Lewis and William Clark on an expedition to find a route to the Pacific Ocean. This Corps of Discovery traveled nearly 8,000 miles on its three-year expedition. As a bonus, Lewis and Clark also claimed parts of the Oregon territory along the Pacific coast for the United States.

The War of 1812

War between England and France in 1812 also pulled the United States into the conflict. The **War of 1812** became the second war between the United States and Britain in North America.

In an attempt to thwart France's war efforts, the British navy began intercepting American ships that were engaging in trade with France. Once stopped, the British often captured American sailors and forced them to serve on British ships. This practice is known as impressment. Many Americans were angered by these acts. To them it was an attack on the nation's sovereignty. Another concern that pushed the country to war was the continuing clashes between Native Americans and settlers living on the western frontier. Many Americans blamed the English for inciting the conflicts between these groups.

These issues with the British led a group of congressmen, mainly from the South and the West, to push for war. They became known as *War Hawks* for their strong beliefs.

During the war, the United States unsuccessfully tried to invade Canada. But only after the defeat of Napoleon were the British able to attack the United States, which they did in 1814, burning Washington, D.C. Other British attacks all failed, most memorably the unsuccessful assault on Baltimore, which inspired the national anthem, "The Star-Spangled Banner."

Because of vast distances and limitations on communications at the time, the final battle of the war, the Battle of New Orleans on January 8, 1815, was actually fought after the signing of the peace treaty ending the war.

The War of 1812 lasted only 18 months. The Treaty of Ghent officially ended the war, but left the borders of the United States and Great Britain the same. The treaty did not even address the causes of the war. The war did have several important effects, however. The United States established its rights on the open seas, and in the process earned the respect of foreign nations. At home, the war helped spark a new spirit of patriotism and the building of national unity.

Manifest Destiny

Following the War of 1812, the United States entered a period described as the *Era of Good Feelings*. Americans took great national pride in their efforts in the War of 1812, and started looking to the vast, unsettled western territories with hope and optimism. And even though these western regions were claimed by other countries, many Americans believed that they should be part of the United States.

American leaders were still concerned about persistent European interests in much of the western continent, as well as Latin and South America. To protect these valued lands, President James Monroe issued a proclamation in 1823 that stated that European nations must not interfere with any nations in the Western Hemisphere or try to acquire new territory there. This policy is now known as the **Monroe Doctrine**, and has been a foundation of U.S. foreign policy ever since.

In the 1820s, American settlers began moving in large numbers across the Great Plains to western regions. Many also headed south to Texas and even farther west to Oregon, Utah, and California. In addition, victory in the Mexican-American War in 1848 gave much of the Southwest to the United States.

Americans throughout the country defended their views of westward expansion with the concept of **Manifest Destiny**. This is the idea that the United States would eventually control the North American continent and that it was inevitable. According to the concept of Manifest Destiny, Americans had the duty to bring democracy and progress to the Western Hemisphere.

Practice

18. During the War of 1812,
  a. the British burned Washington, D.C.
  b. the United States successfully occupied Canada.
  c. the British captured Baltimore, Maryland.
  d. the United States claimed the Louisiana Territory from the British.

19. The concept of *Manifest Destiny* describes the idea that
  a. the United States would become the most powerful nation on Earth.
  b. the United States had the moral obligation to settle European conflicts.
  c. the United States should and eventually would control all of North America.
  d. the United States was the greatest country.

20. The _____ established the long-term U.S. policy of opposing European intervention in the Western Hemisphere.
  a. Treaty of Paris
  b. Monroe Doctrine
  c. Louisiana Purchase
  d. Treaty of Ghent

The Reform Movements

In the early 1700s, many Americans were swept up in a revival of religious feelings and actions that is known as the **Great Awakening**. Another revival of religious energy, called the **Second Great Awakening**, moved across the country beginning in the early 1800s and lasted for nearly half the century. This religious-inspired era created an environment in which many Americans set out to reform the country in many areas. These reformers were motivated by the belief that common individuals have the power to improve society and themselves. Subsequently, reform movements emerged throughout the country, attracting members from all levels of society. Many of these movements were characterized by the influential presence of women.

One of the significant reform efforts in the 1800s was the **Temperance Movement**. Supporters of temperance, or moderation in the consumption of alcohol, worked to spread information about the dangers of alcohol and in some cases to ban the sale of it altogether. Other movements worked to improve the prison system and the conditions in which prisoners were held. Many Americans also saw problems with the country's education system and worked to provide more and better education opportunities.

The Abolitionist Movement

Soon, reformers also set out to help the most exploited people of all: enslaved African Americans in the South. Beginning in the early 1800s, a small but increasing number of people who opposed slavery began to make their position public. Because they wanted slavery abolished, or ended, they became known as abolitionists. The great reform movement they forged and pushed forward was the **Abolitionist Movement**.

One of the most influential abolitionists was William Lloyd Garrison. Garrison published *The Liberator*, a strong antislavery newspaper. He also helped found the Anti-Slavery Society, serving as its president for 23 years.

Another well-known abolitionist, and arguably the most effective, was Frederick Douglass, a former enslaved African American. His oratory skills and vivid stories about the difficulty of his life as a slave attracted large crowds, helping to spread the abolitionist cause. His autobiography, *Narrative of the Life of Frederick Douglass*, influenced many Americans. During the Civil War, Douglass worked as an adviser to President Lincoln. Douglass also became a strong supporter of the women's movement.

Although the abolition movement remained small and mostly confined to the North, it continued to grow steadily and provided a voice against the practice of slavery.

The issue of slavery, and the heated debates it ignited, deeply divided the country. The issue exposed the great regional and cultural differences between the urban and industrialized North and the rural and agricultural South.

The Early Women's Rights Movement

The fight for women's rights stretches back through U.S. history. The struggle for the right to vote, for instance, began to crystallize in the middle of the nineteenth century, and equal pay for equal work is still an issue being fought on many fronts.

The struggle for **women's suffrage**, or right to vote, began in the middle of the nineteenth century and would stretch into the second decade of the next century. In 1848, Elizabeth Cady Stanton and Lucretia Mott organized the first women's rights convention in American history, the Seneca Falls Convention, in Seneca Falls, New York.

Written by Elizabeth Cady Stanton and signed by 100 delegates of the convention, the Declaration of Sentiments, presented at the conference, closed with the following remarks:

> Now, in view of this entire disfranchisement of one-half the people of this country, their social and religious degradation—in view of the unjust laws above mentioned, and because women do feel themselves aggrieved, oppressed, and fraudulently deprived of their most sacred rights, we insist that they have immediate admission to all the rights and privileges which belong to them as citizens of these United States.

A few years later, Susan B. Anthony emerged as another major leader of the suffrage movement. Anthony joined forces with Stanton and other suffrage leaders in forming the National Women's Suffrage Association (NWSA) in 1869.

In 1890, the NWSA merged with the more moderate American Women Suffrage Association, creating a wider political umbrella that would lead the struggle for voting rights to all states of the union.

By the end of the nineteenth century, some western states, as well as some countries around the world, had given women the right to vote. The pace of the spread of suffrage increased in the early twentieth century.

In the United States, the final triumph of the suffrage movement occurred in 1920 when the Nineteenth Amendment guaranteed women the right to vote. Women and supporters of women's rights continue to work for complete parity of women with men—economically, politically, and socially—and while full equality has not been achieved, great strides have been made.

Practice

Use the following photograph and passage to answer questions 21 and 22.

After 72 years of campaigning and protest, women were granted the right to vote in 1920. Passed by Congress and ratified by 36 of the then 48 states, the Nineteenth Amendment of the U.S. Constitution states: "The right of citizens of the United States to vote shall not be denied or abridged by the United States or by any State on account of sex."

Source: National Archives and Record Administration.

21. Whom are the women in this photograph addressing?
    a. other women who say they don't want the right to vote
    b. President Woodrow Wilson
    c. abolitionists
    d. suffragettes

22. With which of the following statements would the photographer most likely agree?
    a. Women should behave in a dignified and orderly manner even if they are protesting.
    b. Women stand outside the gates of governmental power.
    c. The suffragettes would be more effective if they had more powerful slogans.
    d. Demonstrations are the most effective ways to influence lawmaking.

The Industrial Revolution

During the Revolutionary War and the early republic periods, another revolution was gathering momentum. The **Industrial Revolution**, which began in Great Britain, was spreading to the United States by the late 1700s and was beginning to fundamentally change the lives of virtually all Americans.

A key change was in how the production of manufactured goods shifted from the use of hand tools to the reliance on large, complex machines. Because of the shift, skilled artisans and craftspeople were replaced with unskilled workers who were often assigned few or highly specific tasks. During this period, factories also emerged, with some housing hundreds of machines and workers. These large factories eventually replaced home-based workshops, which had provided work and income for large numbers of Americans. There were other significant changes, such as in transportation, where the locomotive and the steamship allowed manufacturers to sell their products locally, nationwide, or even to foreign lands.

The key to this industrial revolution was a spirit of innovation and experimentation that helped transform industrial sectors. For example, in 1814, Francis Lowell revolutionized the American textile industry by opening a series of mills in Massachusetts. Lowell's mills introduced the mass production of cotton cloth to the United States. Lowell and other industrialists also applied these new mass-production processes to produce other goods, such as leather, lumber, wagons, and even shoes.

Although most famous for inventing the cotton gin, Eli Whitney popularized the concept of interchangeable parts. Whitney changed gun making from a single step-by-step process into a factory process. Whitney's factory machines produced large numbers of identical pieces that workers then assembled. Again, the use of interchangeable parts was utilized in other industries as well.

While key inventions such as the power loom and the railroad were developed in Great Britain, the United States was also a center of innovation. Because early American industrialization focused on water-powered textile factories in the Northeast, early American inventions included the cotton gin, the fire hydrant, and the steamship.

The list of new processes and products accelerated through the mid-nineteenth century. Morse code and the telegraph transformed communication, while the steamship and the railroad transformed transportation. By the end of the nineteenth century, many of the components of modern life were already in place, including these inventions:

telephone	paper bag
electric lightbulb	typewriter
automobile	phonograph
steel	photography
vacuum cleaner	skyscraper
escalator	

And there were thousands of other technological innovations as well.

The era of these material advances in the United States and Western Europe coincided with the development of democratic rule and the capitalist system of production and distribution. While the Industrial Revolution led to the greatest increase in wealth in recorded history, inequality and exploitation of workers were constant challenges.

Practice

23. The system of _____ transformed how factories produced complex products.
   a. interchangeable parts
   b. free enterprise
   c. home-based workshops
   d. water-driven machines

The Civil War and Reconstruction

The greatest challenge and trauma ever to face the United States was the Civil War. It was rooted in slavery and the reliance of Southern states on plantation agriculture. In addition to wrenching the nation apart, the Civil War was also one of the first major wars of the industrial age. The new weapons created for this war, including rifle-barrel shotguns and repeating firearms, in addition to the mass production of war materials and equipment, introduced an unprecedented level of carnage. The deep-seated animosity between the North and South, the loss of life, and the devastation of land and economic livelihoods would affect the country for decades.

Economic Causes of the Civil War

During the late 1700s and early 1800s, the United States expanded its territory. In 1803, President Thomas Jefferson doubled the size of the country by buying land from France through the Louisiana Purchase. Under President James Monroe, westward expansion continued. Despite this growth and the country's increased wealth, economic and cultural differences among regions developed.

Sectional disputes over slavery and its spread westward soured the era of good feelings following the War of 1812. **Sectionalism** is the practice of regions of a country supporting their own self-interests instead of the nation's interest as a whole. For example, the Northeast relied on an industrial economy while the South had an agricultural economy supported by slave labor. Both regions fought for and supported policies or goals that served these specific interests at the expense of the other region.

As the country expanded and new states entered the union, the central sectional debate focused on whether new states would become free states or allow slavery. Admitting new slave states or free states would upset the balance of power between Northern states and Southern states in the national government.

In 1819, this balance of power issue created a crisis with Missouri's admission to the Union as a new state. At that time, the country had an equal number of slave states and free states—which meant equal regional power in the United States Senate. If Missouri entered the Union as a slave state, it would tip the balance in favor of the South. This possibility alarmed northern congressmen. A New York congressman proposed banning slavery in Missouri as a price for joining the Union. This proposal outraged southern leaders, who then claimed a right to expand slavery westward.

In 1820, after a long and bitter debate, Henry Clay crafted the **Missouri Compromise**. The northern district of Massachusetts would enter the Union as the free state of Maine to balance the admission of Missouri as a slave state. To prevent future problems over state admissions, the compromise also established a slavery line, which determined where slavery could exist. This line ran across the continent from the southwestern corner of Missouri to the western boundary. Territories south of that line would enter as slave states. Those north of the line would become free states.

The Missouri Compromise solved the short-term crisis. But it also exposed and highlighted the growing division between the North and the South over the expansion of slavery.

Practice

24. Which of the following conclusions do the data in the following table support?

Free African Americans in the North and South, 1820 to 1860			
	1820	**1840**	**1860**
United States	233,504	386,303	488,070
North	99,281 (83.9%)	170,728 (99.3%)	226,152 (100%)
South	134,223 (8.1%)	215,575 (8.0%)	261,918 (6.2%)

Percentages in parentheses represent percentage of total African American population.

   a. By 1820, there were no more slaves in the North.
   b. Between 1820 and 1860, millions of freed slaves emigrated from the South to the North.
   c. Prior to the Civil War, there were no free African Americans in the South.
   d. Between 1820 and 1860, there were many more African Americans in the South than in the North.

Slavery and States' Rights

Cotton was a very labor-intensive crop. Southern plantations dealt with their labor needs by using slaves, who were originally from sub-Saharan West Africa. Opposition to slavery came from several sources.

While the Southern economy depended on slave labor, slavery had become a moral issue in Europe as well as in the United States. Slavery was abolished in Great Britain and most of the British Empire in 1833, and by the end of the following decade, Britain abolished slavery throughout the rest of its empire.

In the United States, the Abolitionist Movement against slavery on both moral and practical grounds spread across the Northern states, all of which had abolished slavery by the middle of the nineteenth century. At the end of the previous century, more than 90 percent of slaves in the United States had lived in the South. The Southern states increasingly perceived their influence waning and their way of life threatened.

To protect that way of life, states' rights became a focus of the South's opposition to the federal government and the North's rising opposition to slavery. Southern politicians advocated for the right of individual states to overrule federal law or ultimately to secede from the Union.

Practice

25. The Missouri Compromise maintained a balance of power between the North and the South in the Senate by
  a. allowing slavery in no regions of the Louisiana Territory.
  b. splitting Massachusetts into two free states.
  c. adding a slave state and a free state to the Union simultaneously.
  d. allowing slavery in all new states that joined the Union.

The Civil War

In the lead-up to the 1860 presidential election, the slavery issue split the Democratic Party. The election evolved into a four-way race, with the Republican Party candidate Abraham Lincoln, a lawyer from Illinois, winning. Many southerners believed that Lincoln's goal was to take away their right to govern themselves, abolish slavery, and destroy the Southern economy.

Some southern leaders believed that they could no longer be a part of the United States. Shortly after the 1860 election, South Carolina seceded, or withdrew, from the Union. By February 1861, Georgia, Florida, Alabama, Mississippi, Texas, and Louisiana seceded as well. These states created the Confederate States of America.

On April 12, 1861, Confederate forces opened fire on Fort Sumter in Charleston, South Carolina, and the Civil War began. Virginia, North Carolina, Tennessee, and Arkansas soon joined the Confederacy. Maryland, Delaware, Kentucky, and Missouri, which were all slave states, remained in the Union as the Border States.

As both sides prepared for war, the North's advantage became obvious. The population of the Union was more than 22 million. The Confederacy numbered around 9 million. The Union also held a large advantage in the number of factories that could produce war materials and in transportation networks, including more railroads.

The Fighting Begins

Confederate forces won several key victories in the first two years of the war. Southern generals proved to be remarkably adept at exploiting the Union's weaknesses. Lincoln, on the other hand, could not find a Union general capable of matching the Confederate commanders. Finally, in 1863, Ulysses S. Grant emerged as the fighter Lincoln was looking for and needed.

In early July 1863, the Union won two significant battles. At the Battle of Gettysburg, Union forces defeated Robert E. Lee's Army of Northern Virginia in southern Pennsylvania. On the same day, a Union army under Grant forced the surrender of Confederate forces in the Mississippi River town of Vicksburg, Mississippi. Grant's victory gave the Union control of the entire Mississippi River, cutting off crucial Confederate supply lines.

Lee's defeat at Gettysburg halted the Confederates' invasion of the North and significantly reduced the size and effectiveness of his army for the remainder of the war. In addition, the Union victory convinced Great Britain to remain neutral in the war. These factors played a huge role in helping to restore Union morale.

In November 1863, President Lincoln traveled to Gettysburg to dedicate part of the battlefield as a cemetery. His speech, now known as the **Gettysburg Address**, has become one of the best-known speeches in American history.

Practice

Use the following excerpt from Abraham Lincoln's Gettysburg Address to answer question 26.

> Four score and seven years ago our fathers brought forth, upon this continent, a new nation, conceived in liberty, and dedicated to the proposition that "all men are created equal." Now we are engaged in a great civil war, testing whether that nation, or any nation so conceived, and so dedicated, can long endure. We

are met on a great battle field of that war. We have come to dedicate a portion of it, as a final resting place for those who died here, that the nation might live. This we may, in all propriety do. But, in a larger sense, we can not dedicate—we can not consecrate—we can not hallow, this ground—The brave men, living and dead, who struggled here, have hallowed it, far above our poor power to add or detract. The world will little note, nor long remember what we say here; while it can never forget what they did here. . . .

26. Abraham Lincoln begins the Gettysburg Address by referencing 1776, a pivotal year in American history, with the words *four score and seven years ago*. The word *score* means a group or set of how many years?

   a. 5
   b. 10
   c. 15
   d. 20

Now in command of all Union forces, Grant used his superior numbers and resources to pursue and wear down Confederate forces. As Grant chased Robert E. Lee in Virginia, Union General William T. Sherman attacked Confederate armies farther south, eventually capturing and destroying much of Atlanta on his army's March to the Sea. Sherman then turned his army east through Georgia to the Atlantic coast, destroying anything that might help the Confederate war effort.

Unable to slip away from the pursuing Grant, and with supplies running out, Lee surrendered to Grant at Appomattox Courthouse, Virginia, on April 9, 1865, ending the war.

At least 750,000 people were killed in the American Civil War, according to some recent estimates. This was the highest number of Americans ever killed in one conflict and the largest and bloodiest war between the defeat of Napoleon and the beginning of World War I. The American Civil War remains the largest conflict ever fought in the Western Hemisphere.

Postwar Reconstruction

Four million slaves were freed during the period of Reconstruction that followed the war. Five days after the Northern victory, President Lincoln was assassinated by Confederate sympathizer John Wilkes Booth. Resentment and division between the South and the North were not resolved for decades after the war's end.

The majority of fighting during the Civil War took place on Southern soil, causing massive destruction there. The period after the war, in which the nation started to rebuild and attempted to reunite the country, was called **Reconstruction**.

Led by a group of Republican congressmen called the Radical Republicans, Congress forcefully pushed ahead with a plan to assimilate the formerly enslaved people into American society and to grant them the same rights as other Americans. Ratification of the Thirteenth Amendment ended slavery forever, and the Fourteenth Amendment granted freed slaves full rights of citizenship.

At first, it appeared that Southern states would adjust to the end of slavery, and former black slaves would be integrated into all aspects of civil and political life, especially once the right to vote was granted to black men through the ratification of the Fifteenth Amendment to the Constitution.

By the end of the 1870s, Reconstruction had failed. Even though each former Confederate state had been readmitted to the Union, African Americans were treated as second-class citizens, without the right to vote and segregated from the white population.

This oppression was legalized by restrictive regulations known as **Jim Crow laws**, which restricted the civil rights of African Americans through limitations on voting rights and a separate-but-equal policy regarding education, employment, and other issues.

Southern states oppressed African-American populations and would not begin to recover economically and repair their fractured social structures for decades to come. Northern states, while less overtly, would continue to restrict the rights of their African-American citizens as well.

27. What is the main idea represented by this political cartoon?

(The caption of this cartoon reads, *The Constitution gives the Negro the right to vote—but what care we for the Constitution.*)

    a. Southern whites did not think voting was important.
    b. Southern whites kept African Americans from voting.
    c. The national government protected African Americans who wanted to vote.
    d. Slaves had trouble voting in the 1840s in the Deep South.

The Birth of Modern America

Following the destruction of the Civil War and the social and political turmoil of Reconstruction, the United States transformed from a rural nation into an urban nation with a massive industrial base connected by railroads. In addition, important inventions and scientific discoveries changed how Americans lived and worked. Large factories employed thousands of workers, cities grew in size, and tens of millions of immigrants from around the world flowed into the nation.

Immigration

Millions of immigrants from foreign shores have made the journey to the Americas since Columbus's first voyage in 1492. The bulk of these immigrants have been of European origin. In what is now the eastern United States, immigrants came from the British Isles, the Netherlands, France, and other nations of northern Europe. But in recent years, immigrants from Latin America have made up a large portion of the immigrant population. Many have settled in adjacent states, such as California, Arizona, and Texas.

Following the settling of the United States by colonists from Great Britain, France, and the Netherlands, other immigrants soon followed, including large groups of Germans, Swedes, and others.

The first great wave of poor immigrants to the United States came from Ireland as a response to the Irish Potato Famine in 1845–1849. Since potatoes were the sole source of food for most poor Irish, many starved in Ireland. Over one million came to the United States.

Unlike other immigrants, the Irish mostly stayed in the cities, where they were discriminated against and exploited. Being the first major group of Roman Catholics to immigrate to the United States, they faced fierce religious discrimination.

In response to their poor treatment, the Irish became involved in politics. Tammany Hall in New York City and the long reign of Mayor James Michael Curley in Boston became synonymous with corruption and patronage. In 1928, Al Smith, the first Roman Catholic of Irish origin to run for U.S. president, was soundly defeated. Thirty-two years later, John F. Kennedy, a descendant of poor Irish immigrants, became president of the United States.

After the end of the Civil War, the United States entered a period of rapid industrial growth. Millions of workers were needed, and the development of steam transport made the voyage across the Atlantic possible for the masses arriving from Europe. Millions of immigrants flooded into America. Many came from southern and eastern Europe and included Italians, Jews, Poles, and other ethnic groups. Chinese immigrants arrived in significant numbers on the West Coast.

The first stop for immigrant-carrying ships at American ports was a processing station where officials decided who could stay in the United States. To enter, immigrants had to be healthy and show that they had money, a skill, or a sponsor to provide for them. Most European immigrants arrived in New York Harbor. Beginning in 1892, they were processed at Ellis Island.

Chinese and other Asian immigrants crossed the Pacific Ocean, arriving in San Francisco Bay. They were processed at Angel Island, which opened in 1910.

Practice

28. In her poem "The New Colossus," which is engraved on the base of the Statue of Liberty, Emma Lazarus wrote: "Give me your tired, your poor, / Your huddled masses yearning to breathe free, / The wretched refuse of your teeming shore. / Send these, the homeless, tempest-tost to me, / I lift my lamp beside the golden door!"

If she were alive today, what immigration policy would Emma Lazarus be most favorable toward?

a. completion of a fence and barrier with motion detectors along the Mexican border

b. increase in the number of work visas for foreign workers with advanced degrees

c. the Dream Act, which provides a path to citizenship to undocumented youth

d. encouragement of potential immigrants to legally apply for permission to enter the United States

Use the following graph to answer questions 29–30.

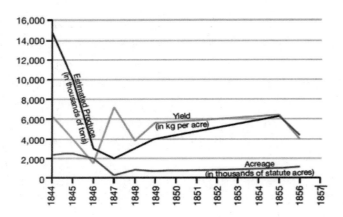

29. Potato production reached a low in Ireland in the year _____.

30. Since the Irish Potato Famine was responsible for mass emigration from Ireland, immigration to the United States was probably highest in the year _____.

This huge wave of new immigrants to the United States transformed American society. Through their labor, immigrants helped fuel industrial growth and expansion in other industries. For example, Mexican Americans in the Southwest brought with them knowledge of effective ranching techniques that they would continue to refine, driving the cattle boom. Chinese and Irish immigrants provided much of the workers who built the growing networks of railroads.

Equally important, immigrants worked in crowded factories and in dangerous coal mines and steel mills. Many labored in the new textile mills. This was work that many Americans were not willing to take. Immigrant women also contributed to the dramatic industrial growth. Many worked in factories. Some became seamstresses or cleaners or performed a variety of piecework jobs.

Immigrants not only helped drive the American economy; they also contributed to and helped shape the evolving American culture. From around the world, immigrants brought their languages, religions, and foods to the United States. These things and the words to describe them soon became part of the American vocabulary. Immigrants also became official citizens and voted to elect politicians.

All of these contributions helped make the United States a world power.

Becoming a World Power

In the late 1800s, the United States began to play a more prominent role in world affairs. Political and industrial leaders encouraged the nation's leaders to make the United States into one of the world's major powers. This led to the United States gaining influence and acquiring territories far beyond its natural borders. Finally, the United States abandoned its isolationism and emerged as a new power.

The period from the mid-1800s through the early 1900s is often called the Age of Imperialism. **Imperialism** is the economic, political, and military domination of a strong nation over weaker nations. During this time, powerful nations tried to project their influence around the world, usually for economic gain. Many Americans also began to consider the benefits of imperialism.

In the 1880s and 1890s, the U.S. dramatically expanded its military and trade operations in East Asia and Latin America. By the early 1900s, it had created an American empire. To maintain this empire, the country created a powerful modern navy. In addition, the United States annexed Hawaii and forced Japan to open its markets to the West.

Victory in the Spanish-American War in 1898 solidified the United States as a world power. It was the shortest war in U.S. history. Within weeks, American forces defeated the Spanish in Cuba while the U.S. Pacific fleet destroyed the Spanish fleet in the Philippines. In defeat, the Spanish gave up Puerto Rico and the Pacific island of Guam to the United States. Spain also sold the Philippines, which it had ruled for more than 350 years, to the United States.

As a result of the Spanish-American War, the United States had an empire and a new stature in world affairs. The war became a crucial event in the history of American foreign policy.

Industrialization and the Gilded Age

Although the Industrial Revolution began in the late 1700s in England, it did not reach its height in the United States until after the Civil War. Unlike some nations, the United States became an industrial power very quickly. Many factors encouraged this rapid industrialization, including abundant supplies of raw materials and natural resources, cheap labor, and a political and economic climate that encouraged the development of new inventions and technology.

The era of industrialization following the Civil War is called the Gilded Age, or the age of the robber barons, named after the ruthless group of industrialists and financiers who made great fortunes controlling monopolies in commodities, transportation, and banking.

Rapid industrialization and innovation created so much new wealth that, even with plundering by robber barons and the influx of the new immigrants, the country's wealth grew and the population nearly doubled.

Visionary American business thinkers harnessed the plentiful resources and the large number of workers to build large, successful corporations, often amassing fortunes. Their factories and operations employed millions of Americans. These large corporations could produce more goods more efficiently and at lower costs for consumers. All these factors spurred the growth of big business.

The Labor Movement

The excesses of the Gilded Age and the poor conditions in which many Americans had to work helped spur the development of the labor movement, which was embraced by many new Americans.

The first truly national labor union, the Knights of Labor, formed in 1869 and reached a peak of 700,000 members in 1886, when the group was blamed for deadly riots at the Haymarket in Chicago. The anti-union backlash that followed the event led to the collapse of the Knights of Labor.

The American Federation of Labor (AFL) formed later that year. While the Knights had been a single national union with membership that included craftsmen and unskilled workers, the AFL was a federation of individual craft unions. In 1905, the Industrial Workers of the World (IWW) was formed and followed a single union model similar to the Knights of Labor model. The IWW tended to be more militant and radical than the AFL. After peaking at 40,000 members in 1923, the IWW declined in numbers and influence.

The Congress of Industrial Organizations (CIO) was formed in 1938, when ten unions left the AFL. The new organization wanted to organize workers by industry rather than by craft. The CIO rejoined the AFL to form the AFL-CIO in 1955.

Instability in the labor movement has continued. The United Auto Workers left the AFL-CIO in 1968 and returned in 1981. Other unions led by the Teamsters left in 2005 to form the Change to Win Coalition.

Practice

Use the following graph to answer questions 31 and 32.

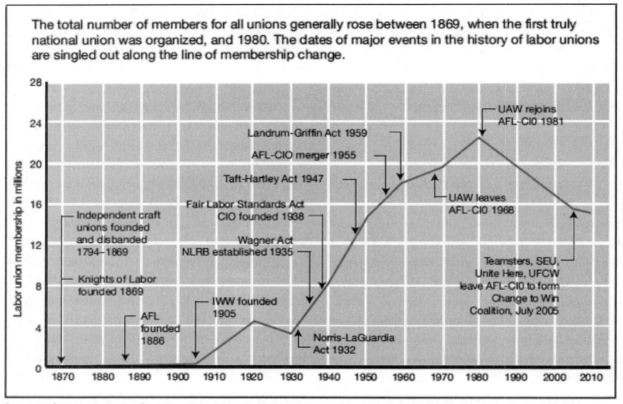

The total number of members for all unions generally rose between 1869, when the first truly national union was organized, and 1980. The dates of major events in the history of labor unions are singled out along the line of membership change.

Source: U.S. Bureau of Labor Statistics, Union Membership, www.bls.gov (accessed April 29, 2010), from *Business*, by William M. Pride, Robert James Hughes, Jack R. Kapoor (Cengage Learning), page 309.

31. According to the graph, which event coincided with the period of greatest union membership?
   a. the founding of the Knights of Labor
   b. the founding of the AFL
   c. the founding of the CIO
   d. the UAW rejoining the AFL-CIO

32. According to the graph, the event that coincided with the period of highest union growth was
   a. the founding of the Knights of Labor
   b. the founding of the AFL
   c. the founding of the CIO
   d. the UAW rejoining the AFL-CIO

Progressivism

Much of the wealth from the nation's new industries went to the owners of very large companies. Most Americans, including its political leaders, believed that the wealthy would reinvest their profits to continue the cycle of economic growth. This would benefit all Americans and keep the American economy running smoothly. But this did not happen as planned, and the wealthy industrialists and financiers continued to grow wealthier with very little trickle-down to the middle and lower classes.

As inequality among Americans grew at the end of the 1800s, many people demanded reforms in government and economic conditions. The excesses of the robber barons helped provoke calls for reform that became known as the **Progressive Era**.

Progressives believed that, in the face of rampant poverty, it was necessary to provide education and adequate housing for the poor as well as fair labor practices and safe workplaces. With the images they created, political cartoonist Thomas Nast and socially conscious photographer Jacob Riis helped stoke public anger over corruption and the terrible living conditions in American cities.

To help spread these new progressive ideas, progressives established political parties, such as the People's Party, that promoted common concepts like "the little man" against "big business." Although these new parties did not score many significant political victories, they did influence the politicians of both parties who eventually held government positions.

Progressives also tried to make government more efficient and more responsive to citizens. Some reformers focused on social welfare problems such as child labor, unsafe working conditions, and alcohol abuse. Many progressives joined the women's rights movement, eventually leading to the ratification of the Nineteenth Amendment in 1920, granting women the right to vote.

Civil Rights

While the modern Civil Rights movement is generally considered to have extended from the 1950s to the 1970s, the struggle for equal rights for African Americans stretched back to the Abolitionist Movement before the Civil War and the passage of the Thirteenth, Fourteenth, and Fifteenth Amendments to the U.S. Constitution after the war.

Separate but Equal

The heart of the Civil Rights movement was the struggle against segregation, which had been upheld by the Supreme Court at the end of the nineteenth century in **Plessy v. Ferguson.**

In 1892, Homer Plessy sat in a whites-only railroad car in Louisiana, challenging the state's 1890 Separate Car Act, and was arrested when he refused to move to the car reserved for African Americans.

Plessy eventually took his case to the U.S. Supreme Court, arguing that separate public accommodations led to unequal treatment in opposition to the Fourteenth Amendment, which guaranteed equal rights and protection under the law for all citizens. In a seven-to-one decision, handed down in 1896, the Supreme Court upheld Louisiana's 1890 Separate Car Act, in effect enshrining separate but equal for decades to come.

Practice

33. As you just learned, in the 1896 case *Plessy* v. *Ferguson*, the Supreme Court found that segregation was legal based on the principle of separate but equal. Plessy, who was one-eighth black, had been arrested when he refused to leave a whites-only railroad car. The Supreme Court upheld his conviction.

In the 1954 case *Brown* v. *Board of Education*, the Supreme Court unanimously ruled that "separate but equal" schools were not achievable, and that they were unconstitutional since they violated the equal protection clause of the Fourteenth Amendment, adopted in 1868.

The most likely reason for this reversal was that

a. nearly 60 years' experience showed that separate cannot be equal.

b. court membership had changed from conservatives to liberals.

c. the 1896 case was about transportation whereas the 1954 case was about education.

d. the equal protection clause of the Fourteenth Amendment was not in effect in 1896.

The Seeds of the Civil Rights Movement

The Civil Rights movement is rooted in the early twentieth century. At the beginning of the twentieth century, Booker T. Washington tried to convince black leaders to support conciliation toward whites.

In 1905, led by W.E.B. Du Bois, the more militant Niagara movement articulated the goals of the

Civil Rights movement and claimed "every single right that belongs to a freeborn American, political, civil and social; and until we get these rights we will never cease to protest and assail the ears of America."

In 1909, Du Bois and other Niagara movement members joined with sympathetic whites to form the National Association for the Advancement of Colored People (NAACP), which for more than a century has been a leader in the Civil Rights movement.

The Twentieth Century

In the first decades of the twentieth century, the United States entered the world arena as a growing economic power. The country's isolationist tendencies gave way to involvement in both World War I and World War II, and this shaped U.S. history in profoundly new ways. Following the second global war, the United States became the most powerful nation in the world, as it emerged relatively unaffected by the carnage and destruction of the war.

World War I

World War I (1914–1918) involved 32 countries, including many European nations, the United States, and other nations around the world. By the war's end, almost 10 million soldiers had been killed and more than 20 million wounded.

Since the mid-1800s, European leaders had been forming military alliances that pitted some nations against others. These alliances encouraged militarism, which is the aggressive build-up of armed forces to intimidate and threaten other nations. These alliances required nations to sign treaties that promised mutual support if any of them was attacked. In June 1914, the assassination of Archduke Franz Ferdinand, the heir-presumptive to the throne of the Austro-Hungarian Empire, sparked conflict and triggered the alliances, thus igniting World War I.

Two coalitions of European nations formed. The Central Powers included Austria-Hungary, Germany, Bulgaria, and Turkey. The Allies included Great Britain, France, Serbia, Russia, Belgium, and Italy.

Technological advancements in weaponry led to the loss of millions of people during World War I. More powerful and accurate artillery guns caused great destruction. Poisonous gas was used for the first time in warfare, and both sides used airplanes, tanks, and submarines with great effect.

Early offensives in 1914 demonstrated that warfare had changed significantly. Powerful long-range artillery forced both sides to build trenches for protection. As if deadly artillery were not enough, both sides used new rapid-firing machine guns that made it very difficult to capture enemy trenches without substantial losses. The results of this kind of warfare were horrific. In major battles, both sides lost hundreds of thousands of soldiers, yet neither side was able to break through the other's lines. The war evolved into a bloody stalemate in Western Europe.

Although many Americans chose sides in the conflict, mostly in support of the Allies, the United States under President Woodrow Wilson remained neutral. The continued targeting and sinking of American vessels on the open seas by German submarines, however, finally brought the United States into the war. In April of 1917, President Woodrow Wilson asked Congress to declare war on Germany.

By the fall of 1917, despite intense and costly fighting, battle lines had changed little over the years. The presence of American troops, however, changed the tide of the war. The United States sent nearly 2 million troops to the Western Front in Europe. This not only significantly increased the Allies' fighting strength, but also boosted the morale of Allied forces. With the addition of American troops on the battlefield, the Allies forced the Germans to finally retreat and then surrender. Fighting in World War I stopped at the eleventh hour of the eleventh day of the eleventh month—on November 11, 1918.

World War I was the most destructive and deadly war the world had seen up to that time.

- 8,528,831 were killed.
- 21,189,154 were wounded.
- An additional 7,750,919 were either prisoners or missing.

President Wilson arrived in Paris for treaty negotiations to put an official end to World War I with the hope of creating a lasting peace. Unlike the other Allied leaders at the negotiations, Wilson argued for the lenient treatment of the defeated nations. Wilson's peace plan, called the Fourteen Points, called for the establishment of a League of Nations. This league, or group, of nations would work to preserve peace by pledging to respect and protect each other's territory and political independence.

The **Treaty of Versailles**, signed on June 28, 1919, ended World War I with the complete defeat of Germany and Austria. The terms of the treaty required that the Austro-Hungarian Empire be dismantled. Germany was humiliated with the loss of territory, huge war reparations to be paid to the victorious nations, and prohibitions against remilitarizing.

Although President Wilson's desire for lenient terms for Germany were ignored and most of the issues in the Fourteen Points plan discarded, the treaty did call for the creation of the League of Nations. The U.S. Constitution dictates that all treaties signed by the United States must be ratified by two-thirds of the U.S. Senate. Senate opposition to the treaty was strong, focusing on the potential loss of sovereignty because of the League of Nations requirements.

The Senate voted twice to ratify the Treaty of Versailles, failing both times. Wilson's plan for a League of Nations and lasting peace took shape without the United States.

Practice

34. The primary reason the United States entered into World War I was
   a. to honor an alliance the United States had with the Allied countries requiring military support.
   b. to stop the rapid advancement of Central Power troops on the Western Front.
   c. the resumption of unrestricted submarine warfare against American vessels.
   d. President Wilson's desire to involve the United States in a foreign conflict.

Use the following song lyrics to answer question 35.

"I Didn't Raise My Boy to Be a Soldier" (1915)
Lyrics by Al Bryan, music by Al Piantadosi
I didn't raise my boy to be a soldier, I brought him up to be my pride and joy. Who dares to place a musket on his shoulder To shoot some other mother's darling boy? Let nations arbitrate their future troubles, It's time to lay the sword and gun away; There'd be no war today if mothers would all say, 'I didn't raise my boy to be a soldier."

"Over There" (1917)
Music and lyrics by George M. Cohan
Johnnie get your gun, get your gun, get your gun. Take it on the run, on the run, on the run. Hear them calling you and me, every son of liberty; Hurry right away, no delay, go today. Make your daddy glad to have had such a lad. Tell your sweetheart not to pine; to be proud her boy's in line.

35. What is the best conclusion based on these two songs?
  a. Americans were proud to have their children join World War I.
  b. Americans had different opinions about World War I.
  c. Most Americans believed World War I was unnecessary.
  d. American soldiers in World War I fought for liberty.

The Great Depression

Throughout much of the 1920s, Americans spent more of their money, leading to a booming economy and high stock market prices. In the late 1920s, the stock market experienced a prolonged period of rising prices; this is called a bull market. Hoping for quick profits, stock buyers speculate, or guess, on future prices. These buyers were betting the market would continue to climb. In October 1929, however, the market collapsed. This sent the financial markets into a panic, which destroyed millions of investors.

Soon, businesses were closing, putting millions of Americans out of work. In addition, banks failed by the hundreds. In order to survive, struggling businesses cut the wages of their workers. This dramatically decreased the amount of money people spent, further damaging the economy. This economic catastrophe was the **Great Depression**, the most severe and longest-lasting economic downturn in the history of the western industrialized world.

The Depression caused large numbers of people to lose their jobs, homes, and entire savings. Some homeless Americans wandered about the country as migrant workers, traveling from region to region in search of short-term employment. Those who did not wander constructed shacks on unused or public lands and formed communities called shantytowns. Since much of the blame for all the economic problems was placed on President Herbert Hoover, shan-

tytown residents began referring to their makeshift communities as Hoovervilles.

Although Hoover did not oppose helping struggling Americans, he did strongly oppose giving direct federal aid to the homeless and jobless. Instead, he relied on providing loans to banks and corporations, and starting public works projects. Hoover thought that any direct aid should come from local governments. By early 1932, however, local governments were running out of money, and were unable to provide the resources necessary to handle the worsening crisis.

To make matters worse, many American farmers faced a new disaster. In 1932, a severe drought hit large portions of the Great Plains. Years of intensive farming had destroyed the region's native grasses and loosened the soil. Lack of rainfall and severe heat dried the used soil into fine particles.

Strong winds blowing across the open plains lifted the dirt into the air and created dust storms, often carrying the dust for hundreds of miles. The region affected by the drought and dust storms became known as the **Dust Bowl**. As the dust storms destroyed their homes and belongings, many farmers abandoned the land and set off for other parts of the country in search of work.

By 1933, with the Great Depression at its worst, between 13 and 15 million Americans were unemployed and nearly half of the country's banks had failed.

The New Deal

In the 1932 presidential campaign, candidate Franklin Delano Roosevelt promised a "new deal" for Americans. Roosevelt won the election and in the first 100 days of his administration he was able to pass 15 major acts of legislation to rescue banks, industries, and the agriculture sector. Many of the acts were also designed to provide jobs for millions of unemployed Americans.

Roosevelt's policies for combating and ending the Great Depression became known as the **New Deal**. Some New Deal programs gave federal aid to small business owners and farmers. Other programs provided job opportunities for artists and musicians through federally funded work programs. New Deal programs also included the following:

- The Public Works Administration (WPA) created work programs to build public projects, such as roads, bridges, and schools.
- The Home Owner's Loan Corporation financed homeowners' mortgages.
- The Social Security Act provided income for senior citizens, disabled, and unemployed citizens as well as a monthly retirement benefit for people over the age of 65.
- The Civilian Conservation Corps (CCC) created forestry jobs for young men.
- The Tennessee Valley Authority (TVA) financed rural electrification and helped develop the economy of a seven-state region.
- The National Labor Relations Board (NLRB) gave workers the right to organize unions and bargain collectively.
- The Federal Deposit Insurance Corporation (FDIC) insured bank deposits to protect Americans' bank accounts, thus increasing public confidence in the banking system.

Though faced with political and legal challenges to his New Deal programs, Roosevelt pushed through a second round of aid legislation in 1935.

The relief and reform measures put into place by Roosevelt helped lessen the worst effects of the Great Depression in the 1930s, but the economy would not fully recover until after 1939, when World War II pushed American industry into high gear.

Practice

Use the following passage and chart to answer question 36.

Economic depression cannot be cured by legislative action or executive pronouncement. Economic wounds must be healed by the action of the cells of the economic body—the producers and consumers themselves. . . . The best contribution of government lies in encouragement of this voluntary cooperation in the community. The government—national, state, and local—can join with the community in such programs and do its part.

—President Herbert Hoover, Annual Message to the Congress on the State of the Union, December 2, 1930

United States Government Finances, 1929–1941 (in Billions of Dollars)

Fiscal Year	Expenditures	Surplus or Deficit	Total Public Debt
1929	$3.127	$0.734	$16.9
1930	3.320	0.738	16.2
1931	3.577	−0.462	16.8
1932	4.659	−2.735	19.5
1933	4.598	−2.602	22.5
1934	6.645	−3.630	27.1
1935	6.497	−2.791	28.7
1936	8.422	−4.425	33.8
1937	7.733	−2.777	36.4
1938	6.765	−1.177	37.2
1939	8.841	−3.862	40.4
1940	9.589	−2.710	43.0
1941	13.980	−4.778	44.0

36. Which is the best conclusion that can be drawn from this information?
   a. Deficit spending contributed to increasing public debt in the 1930s.
   b. The federal government should not be allowed to have deficit spending.
   c. The public debt grew despite annual surpluses in the government's treasury.
   d. The downward economic spiral was resolved only through significant expenditures of the federal government.

The Causes of World War II

In the years after World War I, hostile governments looking to expand their territories took power in Europe and Asia. In addition, dictators gained control of the governments of Italy, Japan, Germany, and the Soviet Union.

Benito Mussolini established one of Europe's first dictatorships when his Italian Fascist Party gained control of the Italian government in 1922. Mussolini promised to return Italy to the glorious times of the Roman Empire and began a large program of bringing political, social, and economic order to Italy.

By 1926, Joseph Stalin had become the new dictator of the communist Soviet Union. He embarked on a massive program to industrialize the country. Although production increased significantly, wages plummeted and family farms were taken over by the government. Stalin's regime did not allow opposition political parties or individuals. Stalin ordered his regime to target political enemies, artists, and intellectuals. He also established concentration camps to which millions were sent to be used as slave laborers.

Harsh reparation requirements placed on Germany in the Treaty of Versailles for causing damage in

World War I crippled the German economy. The hyperinflation resulting from the stock market crash of 1929 destroyed the value of German currency and further sent the country into economic catastrophe.

With the economy devastated and the social order in turmoil, the German people were ready for a radical answer to their problems. They elected Adolf Hitler and his National Socialist Party, or Nazis. The Nazis made sure that the German people never got the opportunity to vote once they were in power.

In Japan, as in Germany, difficult economic times helped undermine the political system. A severe trade imbalance strangled any economic growth. Japanese military leaders and civilian supporters argued that seizing foreign territories was the only way to assure Japan's economic future. Beginning in 1931, with the invasion of Chinese Manchuria, the Japanese military controlled Japan, supported by the civilian government.

The War Begins

During World War II, two powerful alliances, the Allies and the Axis, fought to control much of the developed world. The Allies, led by the United Kingdom and France, were two of the largest democracies. The Allies would later be joined by the communist Soviet Union and the democratic United States.

Fighting the Allies was the Axis alliance, led by the fascist nations of Germany and Italy. Japan was also a member of the Axis powers.

World War II began in September 1939, when Hitler's German army invaded Poland. England and France soon declared war on Germany as part of an alliance agreement. By 1940, France had surrendered, leaving England alone in the fight against the Axis powers in Europe. Germany eventually conquered most of Europe. Meanwhile, the Axis power Japan captured and controlled large territories in East Asia and islands in the Pacific Ocean.

Key events in the first years of the war include:

- The Battle of Britain, 1940: Despite the bombing of London and other major cities in England, the British and their leader Winston Churchill stood firm against the threat of a German invasion.
- Germany invades the Soviet Union: In June 1941, in its largest military operation of the war, German forces attacked the Soviet Union, opening an eastern front and dividing Hitler's armies and resources.
- On December 7, 1941, Japanese naval and air forces attacked the U.S. military installation at Pearl Harbor, Hawaii. The next day, Congress declared war on Japan. Several days later, Germany and Italy declared war on the United States in support of Japan.

As the nation's war mobilization went into high gear, military strategists had to plan for warfare in Europe and Asia. Coordinating military operations and supplying the fighting forces with the necessary materials required the cooperation, participation, and sacrifice of those in the military and of civilians.

Practice

37. This type of stamp was common during World War II, as many items were rationed. Based on the image, what is the best definition of the word *ration*, as used on the stamp?

> **SUGAR ALLOWANCE COUPON**
> 1 Pound — For Home Food Processing — 1 Pound
>
> This coupon authorizes the holder to whom it was issued to receive 1 pound of sugar, which is to be used only to conserve fruit, fruit juices, or other foods as specified in the Regulations for the use of the person or persons listed on the Home Canning Sugar Application (Form No. R-323) or the Special Purpose Application (Form No. R-315) on file at the office of the Board indicated below.
>
> Serial Number of War Ration Book ....
>
> Board No. .... State ....

Accessed through Northwestern University Library
https://images.northwestern.edu/multiresimages/
inu:dil-356cd140-0ef0-4695-90db-052d542a9dc2

a. preferred quota

b. fixed amount

c. passage fare

d. acceleration scale

For the next three years, fighting raged across several continents. Among the key battles and events were the following:

- The Battle of Midway in June 1942 was a turning point in the United States' war in the Pacific. Near the island of Midway, American naval forces sank four Japanese aircraft carriers, which formed a major part of its fleet, and stopped the Japanese advance in the Pacific.
- The Battle of Stalingrad in the Soviet Union was one of the major turning points in World War II. From mid-September 1942 until February 1943, Soviet forces defended the city against massive and constant German attacks, eventually trapping and capturing almost 250,000 German soldiers. The battle stopped Germany's invasion of Russia and put it on the defensive for the remainder of the war on the Russian Front.
- American and British forces invaded and defeated the Axis armies in North Africa in 1943.
- In July 1943, Allied forces invaded the island of Sicily off the southern coast of Italy to begin the liberation of Italy.
- The D-Day landings on the coast of Normandy, France, in June 1944 began the Allied invasion of Europe. Nearly 7,000 ships carrying more than 100,000 soldiers made this the largest seaborne invasion in history.
- The Battle of the Bulge from December 1944 to January 1945 in the Ardennes region of Belgium involved more American soldiers than any other World War II battle. Allied forces in this month-long battle stopped Germany's last major offensive of the war.
- The island of Iwo Jima was the site of one of the bloodiest battles in the Pacific Theater. Around 60,000 American Marines landed on Iwo Jima in February 1945, eventually capturing the heavily defended island after losing more than 6,000 men.

After defeating the Germans in the Battle of the Bulge in early 1945, Allied armies fought their way east into Germany over the next several months while Soviet forces moved west, squeezing the German armies. Germany finally surrendered in May of 1945.

The United States developed the most destructive weapon ever created, the atomic bomb, and dropped one on the Japanese city of Hiroshima and another one on Nagasaki. Although those bombings led to the Japanese surrender, the death and devastation were so extreme that to this day it is debated whether the atomic bombs should ever have been used. While a number of nations currently have nuclear weapons, no atomic bombs have been used since World War II.

World War II was possibly responsible for a greater loss of life than any other event in human history, with total deaths estimated to have been between 60 and 85 million.

The Holocaust

One of the most horrific aspects World War II was the targeting of innocent civilians by the Nazis. The Nazis imprisoned, tortured, starved, and murdered millions of people, including gypsies and homosexuals, but their main target was Jews. The persecution, enslavement, torture, and murder of millions of Jews is known as the **Holocaust**. The attempt to destroy an entire people was given the name *genocide*. After the war, prominent surviving Nazis were put on trial at Nuremberg, Germany, and convicted of crimes against humanity.

Rebuilding Europe

After the war, the United States tried an approach to peace with the defeated Axis powers that was very different from the Treaty of Versailles (the punitive peace treaty imposed on Germany after World War I). Instead of assessing reparations and humiliating Germany, the United States implemented the **Marshall Plan**. The plan provided economic assistance to all of Western Europe, including former Axis countries

Germany, Italy, and Austria. Economic assistance was provided to Japan as well. The aid given to Western Europe helped the entire region recover and start the process of integration that has led to the formation and development of the European Union. And nations that once were adversaries of the United States are now among its closest friends and allies.

Postwar America

Thanks to its military strength and innovative and robust economy, the United States became the richest and most powerful nation on Earth after World War II. Thereafter, it experienced years of steady economic growth. Most Americans enjoyed more prosperity than earlier generations, although not everyone benefited equally.

Returning Soldiers

Millions of returning soldiers, known as GIs, needed education and training to fully participate in the new and growing post–World War II economy. In response to that need, Congress passed the Servicemen's Readjustment Act of 1944, commonly known as the GI Bill. According to the Veterans Administration, the law's key provisions were "education and training, loan guaranty for homes, farms or businesses, and unemployment pay."

"Before the war, college and homeownership were, for the most part, unreachable dreams for the average American. Thanks to the GI Bill, millions who would have flooded the job market instead opted for education."

By the time the original GI Bill ended on July 25, 1956, nearly 8 million World War II veterans had participated in an education or training program.

The new earning power of educated veterans helped increase American consumer spending throughout the nation, leading to a period of postwar abundance. This period also saw an expansion of suburbs, growing families, and more higher-paying white-collar jobs.

This postwar boom also helped bring about the rise of the television as an important social and economic mass-communication medium. Television became so popular that it influenced the movie, radio, and music industries as well. Soon, however, the new media, along with targeted advertising, helped create a generational divide between young people and adults.

Practice

Read the following passage and answer questions 38 and 39.

About the time of World War I, sharp-eyed entrepreneurs began . . . to see ways to profit from the motorist's freedom. . . . Shops could be set up almost anywhere the law allowed, and a wide variety of products and services could be counted on to sell briskly in the roadside marketplace. A certain number of cars passing by would always be in need of gas. Travelers eventually grew hungry, tired, and restless for diversions. Soon gas stations, produce booths, hot dog stands, and tourist camps sprouted up along the nation's roadsides to capitalize on these needs. As competition increased, merchants looked for new ways to snag the new market awheel. Each sign and building had to visually shout: "Slow down, pull in, and buy." Still more businesses moved to the highway— supermarkets, motor courts, restaurants, miniature golf courses, drive-in theaters. By the early 1950s, almost anything could be bought along the roadside.
Source: Chester H. Liebs, excerpt from *Main Street to Miracle Mile*. Little, Brown and Company, 1985.

38. What is the main idea of the passage?
  a. Miniature golf was a very popular sport in the 1950s.
  b. Travelers were looking for sources of entertainment.
  c. Some highway businesses were more successful than others.
  d. Flashy commercial enterprises sprouted along highways, eager to profit from travelers.

39. Given the information in this passage, what appeared to be an important post–World War II trend in the United States?
  a. train travel
  b. car culture
  c. historic preservation
  d. downtown renewal

The Cold War

The end of World War II left the United States and the Soviet Union as the two most powerful nations on Earth. Each nation felt threatened by the other and began a struggle—based on their conflicting ideologies—that involved many regions of the world.

Democracy versus Totalitarianism

The Soviet Union was a totalitarian society run as a one-party state. While the Communist Party was supposedly the highest authority, its secretary, Joseph Stalin, ruled as an absolute dictator. He was responsible for the deaths of millions of Soviet citizens but was never held accountable for his crimes. Economically, in the communist system all property belonged to the state, including the means of production. In practice, this resulted in a top-down command economy where Soviet bureaucrats decided what would and would not be produced.

The United States is a democracy. Two major parties and other smaller and local parties vie for political influence. The United States embraces capitalism, a system in which a country's trade and industry are controlled by private owners operating in a free market.

International Conflict in the Postwar Era

As World War II ended, Western Europe was occupied by the democratic Allied countries while Eastern Europe was occupied by the Soviet Union, which imposed communist governments and economies throughout the region.

Winston Churchill, Britain's prime minister during World War II, referred to the ideological boundary between democratic and communist states as the Iron Curtain. Feeling threatened by the Soviet Union, the United States and its allies formed the North Atlantic Treaty Organization (NATO). In response, the Soviet Union created a military alliance called the Warsaw Pact with the communist nations of Eastern Europe.

Following the war's end, President Harry S. Truman established the **Truman Doctrine** in 1947. The doctrine set U.S. policy concerning engagement with the rest of the world, promising political, economic, and military support to any country that might come under internal or outside threat from authoritarian forces. Under the doctrine, the United States proclaimed a new interventionist approach, which was a turnaround from its previous isolationist foreign policy.

While the United States and the Soviet Union assembled the most powerful arsenals that had ever existed, with hundreds of lethal nuclear missiles pointed at each other, none of these weapons were ever used in direct conflict. As a result, this period was known as the **Cold War**, a war of tension and rivalry but never direct combat.

The two powers were involved in many conflicts across the globe, which often stood as proxies for their own ideological conflict with each other. The first major Cold War conflict was the Korean War.

The Korean War

Using the Truman Doctrine as the basis for postwar American foreign policy, President Truman tried to contain communism by supporting countries that were threatened by Soviet aggression. In 1949, Chinese revolutionaries led by Mao Zedong took control and adopted a communist government. A year later, in 1950, armies from communist North Korea invaded South Korea.

Wishing to keep South Korea free from communism forced the United States to military intervention, resulting in the **Korean War**. For four years, American forces fought alongside armies from the United Nations to prevent the communists from taking control, eventually leading to a stalemate and a cease fire.

The Vietnam War

Although the majority of the fighting occurred in the 1960s and early 1970s, the roots of the Vietnam conflict date back to the 1940s, when the Vietnamese people began an independence movement against the French colonial government.

In the 1950s, U.S. President Eisenhower sent aid and advisers to South Vietnam to prevent communists from North Vietnam from taking control. Presidents Kennedy and Johnson continued the aid throughout the 1960s. By 1968, the United States had more than 500 thousand troops fighting in Vietnam.

Even though the U.S.-led forces had superior weapons and better-trained fighting troops, they could not defeat the communists. After nearly a decade with little progress, many Americans began to question the nation's involvement. The war divided the nation as protests erupted in city streets and on college campuses. In 1973, President Richard Nixon finally pulled American troops from Vietnam, and in 1975 South Vietnam fell to the communists. By the war's end, more than 58 thousand Americans had died or were missing in the conflict.

Practice

In June 1963, President John Kennedy spoke to a crowd of one million people in West Berlin, a city surrounded on all sides by the East German communist state. His most famous statement was "Ich bin ein Berliner," which is German for "I am a Berliner."

Read the excerpt from the speech and answer question 40.

Freedom is indivisible, and when one man is enslaved, all are not free.

When all are free, then we can look forward to that day when this city will be joined as one and this country and this great continent of Europe in a peaceful and hopeful globe. When that day finally comes, as it will, the people of West Berlin can take sober satisfaction in the fact that they were in the front lines for almost two decades.

All free men, wherever they may live, are citizens of Berlin, and, therefore, as a free man, I take pride in the words "Ich bin ein Berliner."

40. What was the significance of Kennedy's statement "Ich bin ein Berliner"?
   a. He revealed to the crowd that he had a German ancestor.
   b. He planned to move to Berlin after his presidency ended.
   c. He wanted to express his affection and admiration for Berlin.
   d. Hw wanted Berliners to know they could trust the United States.

Read the following passage and answer questions 41 and 42.

The Cuban Missile Crisis began in 1962 when U.S. spy planes spotted Soviet missile installations under construction in Cuba. The missiles were capable of carrying nuclear weapons and were within range of major U.S. cities. A 13-day standoff began, during which President Kennedy imposed a naval blockade of Cuba and demanded that the Soviets remove the weapons. Kennedy stated that any missile attack from Cuba would be regarded as an attack from the Soviet Union and would be responded to accordingly. Khrushchev later conceded, agreeing to remove the weapons if, in return, the United States pledged not to invade the island. Details from U.S. and Soviet declassified files and participants in the crisis have surfaced since the incident. Unbeknownst to the U.S. government at the time, 40,000 Soviet soldiers were stationed in Cuba and armed with nuclear weapons. Although Khrushchev's actions helped to avert nuclear war, they made him appear weak to younger Soviet leaders, who ousted him from power. Historians regard the crisis as the world's closest brush with the threat of nuclear war.

41. According to the information given in this passage, it is most likely that Kennedy
   a. viewed this as a regional crisis solely between the United States and Cuba.
   b. trusted Soviet officials who said there weren't any missiles in Cuba.
   c. believed that the conflict was principally between the United States and the Soviet Union.
   d. viewed the situation as serious but felt it could be managed with diplomacy.

42. Which of the following conclusions can you make based on the passage?
   a. Kennedy's first concern during the crisis was the appeal of Communist ideas.
   b. Nuclear war is the only way to win a cold war.
   c. Kennedy knew that Khrushchev would back down.
   d. The U.S. government did not know the full extent of the Soviet threat at the time.

Postwar Movements and the 1960s

The 1960s was one of the most tumultuous decades in American history. The tensions and deep divisions caused by the war in Vietnam were accompanied by the renewed civil rights and women's rights movements. In addition, a youth movement emerged that challenged the American political and social system and conventional American middle-class values.

The 1950s and early 1960s are often thought of as an idyllic time in which an unprecedented number of people joined the middle class and were leading relatively comfortable lives. While there was some evidence supporting this view, millions of Americans were still being left behind, living in extreme poverty. Following the assassination of President Kennedy in 1963, Vice President Lyndon Johnson assumed the presidency. Johnson believed that the federal government should take on the poverty problem, and in 1964 he declared the War on Poverty.

The Great Society

Johnson's War on Poverty worked in conjunction with around 60 other programs that provided assistance to the nation's disadvantaged. All were designed to build a better society, known as the **Great Society**. Among the most significant programs were:

- Head Start to give a boost to poor children in the preschool years
- food stamps to help the poor pay for food
- Medicare health insurance for the elderly
- Medicaid health insurance for the poor

Unfortunately, poverty persists, as does the debate on the role and responsibility of the government to provide a safety net for the country's neediest and most vulnerable people.

Fighting for Rights

Forming a backdrop to President Johnson's Great Society plan was the emergence of a renewed Civil Rights movement.

The success of the Civil Rights movement was incremental, but advances had gathered steam in the middle of the twentieth century:

- In 1947, Jackie Robinson became the first African American to play major league baseball, starting the integration of professional sports.
- In 1948, President Truman ended segregation and integrated the U.S. armed forces.
- In 1954, NAACP lawyer Thurgood Marshall convinced the U.S. Supreme Court in *Brown* v. *Board of Education of Topeka* to end separate-but-equal schools in Topeka, Kansas. This essentially overturned *Plessy* v. *Ferguson* and made segregation illegal throughout the United States.
- In 1955, Rosa Parks challenged the segregation of buses in Montgomery, Alabama, by refusing to give up her seat to a white man. Her action inspired the Montgomery bus boycott, in which blacks refused to ride the buses unless segregation rules were abolished; segregation was abolished a year later.
- In 1957, the city school board and supervisor in Little Rock, Arkansas, had a plan to integrate Little Rock High School. When the governor of the state resisted, President Eisenhower sent in National Guard troops to enforce the desegregation order.

Practice

Use the following excerpt from the U.S. Supreme Court decision Brown *v.* Board of Education *(1954), to answer question 43.*

> Where a State has undertaken to provide an opportunity for an education in its public schools, such an opportunity is a right which must be made available to all on equal terms. . . . Segregation of children in public schools solely on the basis of race deprives children of the minority group of equal educational opportunities, even though the physical facilities and other "tangible" factors may be equal. . . .

43. The legal doctrine struck down by the decision in *Brown* v. *Board of Education* was
   a. the separate-but-equal doctrine
   b. the right to be made available doctrine
   c. the physical and tangible doctrine
   d. the public school or minority group doctrine

In 1963, leaders of the Civil Rights movement organized the March on Washington for Jobs and Freedom to rally for civil rights. On August 28, civil rights leader **Martin Luther King Jr.** delivered his "I Have a Dream" speech to 200,000 to 300,000 people gathered on the National Mall in Washington, D.C., in a massive nonviolent political demonstration to end racism.

EXCERPT FROM MARTIN LUTHER KING'S "I HAVE A DREAM" SPEECH

I say to you today, my friends, that in spite of the difficulties and frustrations of the moment, I still have a dream. It is a dream deeply rooted in the American dream.

I have a dream that one day this nation will rise up and live out the true meaning of its creed: "We hold these truths to be self-evident: that all men are created equal."

I have a dream that one day on the red hills of Georgia the sons of former slaves and the sons of former slave owners will be able to sit down together at a table of brotherhood.

I have a dream that one day even the state of Mississippi, a desert state, sweltering with the heat of injustice and oppression, will be transformed into an oasis of freedom and justice.

I have a dream that my four children will one day live in a nation where they will not be judged by the color of their skin but by the content of their character.

The Civil Rights movement achieved great gains in the 1960s. Ratified in 1964, the Twenty-Fourth Amendment to the Constitution abolished poll taxes in federal elections. These taxes had been used across the South to disenfranchise black voters.

The Civil Rights Act of 1964 prohibited discrimination of all kinds based on race, color, religion, or national origin and addressed segregation in public accommodations, schools, and the workplace.

The Voting Rights Act of 1965 prohibited all states from instituting qualifications, procedures, and regulations for voting that resulted in discrimination against anyone of any race or color.

The Women's Movement

The 1950s are remembered as an era when women retreated to traditional roles, but many women were unhappy in their limited role as housewives. Beginning in the 1960s, women began creating organizations to change society primarily through education by action in state and federal legislatures.

A significant step forward arrived in 1960 with the release of the birth control pill, which helped give women autonomy and allowed them to plan their reproductive lives in ways that might enhance their economic and social well-being.

The Women's Movement gained momentum partly because of the efforts of the President's Commission on the Status of Women, established in the early 1960s by President Kennedy, and headed by Eleanor Roosevelt. The commission issued a report that focused on many of the problems and hurdles women had to overcome in the workplace. Women's rights supporters used the commission's findings to establish networks of activists who then worked to introduce women's issues and solutions as legislation.

One influential member of the movement was Betty Friedan. In 1963, she had written a best-selling book titled *The Feminine Mystique*, which raised awareness and discussion about the role of women in American society. In 1966, she helped found the National Organization for Women (NOW), which became the most prominent group in the Women's Movement.

Additional achievements of the Women's Movement since the 1960s include the following:

- The 1973 *Roe* v. *Wade* Supreme Court decision that legalized abortion, giving women additional control over their choices. This decision has stirred up great controversy and opposition, especially among political conservatives and people of certain religious affiliations.

- In 1967, women earned 58 cents for every dollar a man earned for the same work. By 2012, that number had grown to 77 cents for each dollar—an improvement, but still a long way from equality.
- By the end of the 1970s, for the first time there were more women than men in college. But women are still underrepresented in science, technology, engineering, and mathematics.
- The passage of Title IX legislation in 1972, which created equal opportunities for women in college athletics, including more scholarships.

In the wake of these achievements, Congress passed the **Equal Rights Amendment** (ERA) in 1972. The amendment stated that "Equality of rights under the law shall not be denied or abridged by the United States or by any State on account of sex." At the time of passage, the Constitution required that the amendment had to be ratified by 38 states. Thirty-five states ratified the amendment by 1979, but strong opposition blocked further progress.

Unable to achieve ratification by three-fourths of the states by the deadline set by Congress, the Equal Rights Amendment finally failed in 1982.

The Cultural Revolution

The beginnings of the 1960s youth movement stretched back to the 1950s, when many younger Americans began questioning the actions of their parents' generation as well as the nation's political leaders. The turmoil of the 1960s only heightened these feelings. The arms race with the Soviet Union, the Vietnam War, income inequality, and the Civil Rights movement all contributed to a climate that generated protests and calls for change.

Many young Americans, particularly on college campuses, focused on the injustices they witnessed in the country's political and social system. Some galvanized into a movement that became known as the New Left. The most influential group of the New Left was Students for a Democratic Society (SDS). SDS chapters focused on ending the Vietnam War and on addressing issues such as racism, poverty, and campus regulations.

Instead of fixing or transforming American society, some young Americans rejected it altogether. They created what became known as the counterculture and were often called *hippies*. Hippies advocated peace, love, and freedom. They experimented with new styles of dress and ways in which to wear their hair, especially long hair, beards, and mustaches on young men. Counterculture musicians also experimented with their music, blending folk styles, rock-n-roll rhythms, and other genres that greatly changed the sound of rock music. Hippies also promoted freer attitudes toward sexual relationships and the recreational use of drugs.

Their values were so different from traditional American values that many experts described the situation as a generation gap, which made it difficult for the generations to effectively communicate or understand each other.

Practice

44. What happened to the ERA?
   a. It was passed by a majority of states and became a constitutional amendment.
   b. It was no longer needed because women had made significant strides forward.
   c. It did not receive the votes needed in Congress to become a constitutional amendment.
   d. It did not receive the support needed by states to become a constitutional amendment.

45. In the 1960s, young people known as *hippies* began the _____ movement.
   a. beat
   b. women's
   c. counterculture
   d. equal rights

The Cold War Ends

After several decades in which progressive and liberal ideas dominated American politics and the social agenda, conservatism made a comeback in the 1970s. In 1980, voters elected conservative Republican Ronald Reagan as president.

Reagan cut taxes, deregulated several industries, and appointed conservative justices to the federal courts.

In foreign policy, Reagan believed that the United States needed to weaken communism by challenging it as much as possible without provoking war. Reagan encapsulated this concept with the phrase "peace through strength." The Reagan administration developed policies aimed at toppling communist nations, ranging from building new nuclear missile systems to funding covert operations against Soviet troops and allies around the globe. Under Reagan, the United States committed itself to the largest peacetime military buildup in its history.

Reagan supported this massive military buildup, in part, because he did not believe that the Soviet Union could afford to spend as much on defense as the United States could. By the mid-1980s, the Soviet Union's economy was in deep trouble. The nation faced regular shortages of food. In addition, its factories and workers were not as competitive as those in the west. As Reagan had hoped, a huge portion of the Soviet economy was focused on funding its military. Soviet leader Mikhail Gorbachev realized that his nation could not match the military buildup initiated by the Reagan administration.

In August 1991, three years after the end of Reagan's two terms as president, hard-liners in the Soviet Union attempted to stage a coup in an attempt to revive the tradional communist rule. Millions of Russians rallied in the streets of Moscow in support of Gorbachev, forcing the coup to fall apart. Not long afterward, the Communist Party lost power, and the Soviet Union separated into 15 independent republics. The Cold War was over.

The 1990s and the New Century

A computer and technology boom swept the United States in the 1990s. The development of new technology, including personal computers, mobile phones, and the Internet, has revolutionized the way people live, work, and communicate. The massive developments and investments in technology spurred economic growth in the 1990s, making it one of the longest sustained periods of growth in American history.

Also in the 1990s, the number of immigrants coming to the United States significantly increased. Large numbers of non-European immigrants changed the ethnic makeup of the United States. By 2000, immigrants made up more than 10 percent of the U.S. population. The largest groups of these new immigrants came from Latin America and Asia.

The Interconnected World

During the 1990s, the technological, political, economic, financial, and cultural exchanges between peoples and nations grew substantially, making the world a more interconnected and interdependent place. In the business world, this involved huge increases in trade between nations and and the rise of large corporations that operated in many countries throughout the world. These were the first multinational corporations. The process through which the world has become increasingly interconnected is called **globalization**.

Technological advances, including mobile phones and the Internet, have contributed to globalization by connecting people all over the world. The World Wide Web has the power to connect billions of people through their digital devices. This provides new opportunities for people to do business, exchange information, or even build new forms of communities.

Globalization also spreads through the signing of free trade agreements, such as the North American

Free Trade Agreement (NAFTA), which the governments of the United States, Canada, and Mexico signed in 1992. This agreement removed barriers that had restricted the movement of both people and economic goods and services. NAFTA greatly expanded the amount and value of trade between the countries, but it also exposed the risk of job losses, as many companies closed U.S. operations and moved to locations where labor costs were lower.

In 1993, the European Union was created to promote economic and political cooperation among a number of European countries. The following year, 120 nations formed the World Trade Organization (WTO) to oversee international trade agreements and help resolve trade disagreements.

The increasing interconnectedness of the world economy and international finance has also heightened the risk of global economic catastrophe. Because national economies and the world financial markets have become so interconnected, economic or financial failures in one country can lead to crises in other countries, spreading throughout the world rather than remaining isolated in one country or region. This is what happened in the Great Recession of 2008–2009, during which the financial crisis in the U.S. subprime mortgage market led to a global economic meltdown.

American Foreign Policy since September 11

On September 11, 2001, members of the Islamic terrorist organization al-Qaeda hijacked four passenger jets and flew two of them into the World Trade Center in New York City and one into the Pentagon in Washington, D.C. The fourth plane crashed in a field near Shanksville, Pennsylvania, after passengers retaliated and attacked the hijackers. The attacks resulted in the deaths of close to 3,000 people, nearly all of them civilians, and the devastation of a large area of lower Manhattan, the site of the World Trade Center.

The rise of al-Qaeda was a result of the Soviet Union's invasion of Afghanistan in 1979. Muslims from around the world traveled to Afghanistan to help fight and drive out the Soviets. A wealthy Saudi Arabian named Osama bin Laden founded al-Qaeda to recruit fighters and to fund the Afghan resistance.

Like many Muslims in the Middle East, bin Laden opposed the Western presence in the region. The oil industry brought the Western powers to the Middle East, bringing money to the oil-rich nations. Western ideas were also traded in the Middle East, and many Muslims feared that their traditional values were being weakened. In addition, American support for Israel over the years has angered many in the Middle East. The long-running struggle between the Muslim Palestinians and the Jewish Israelis has only heightened the animosity many Islamic fundamentalists feel for the United States.

To advance their causes, bin Laden and other Islamic fundamentalists have used and continue to use terrorism to try to undermine and overthrow pro-Western governments in the Middle East and create a pure Islamic society.

In the aftermath of the 9/11 attacks, the administration of President George W. Bush launched the War on Terror. This war, as Bush's Secretary of Defense Donald Rumsfeld noted, would be a war like none other the nation had faced. Its strategies included the following:

- open and covert military operations
- new security legislation
- efforts to block the financing of terrorism
- increased domestic policing and intelligence gathering
- engaging other countries to support the War on Terror

Proponents of the War on Terror point to the fact that, since the attacks of September 11, no large-scale attack has occurred on U.S. soil.

Criticism against this strategy is multifold, including these arguments:

- The War on Terror is based on an ideology of fear and repression that creates enemies and promotes violence rather than mitigating acts of terror and strengthening security.
- The worldwide campaign has too often become an excuse for governments to repress opposition groups and disregard international law and civil liberties.
- Governments should address terrorism through international cooperation, using international law and respecting civil liberties and human rights.
- Governments should address the root causes of terrorism, notably political alienation resulting from prejudice, state sponsored violence, and poverty.

Since the War on Terror began in 2001, U.S. and coalition forces have invaded and overthrown the governments of Afghanistan and Iraq. In early May 2011, President Barack Obama gave the go-ahead on a U.S. special forces mission that killed Osama bin Laden in a compound in Abbottabad, Pakistan.

Although the invasions of Afghanistan and Iraq removed oppressive and brutal regimes, establishing stable, effective governments has proven difficult, as both Iraq and Afghanistan remain politically uncertain.

Practice

Use the following excerpts, taken from the inaugural addresses of President Barack Obama, the nation's first African-American president, to answer questions 46 and 47. Note that President Obama references many issues, including the economy and war in Iraq.

Excerpt from President Barack Obama's Inaugural Address, 2009

That we are in the midst of crisis is now well understood. Our nation is at war against a far-reaching network of violence and hatred. Our economy is badly weakened, a consequence of greed and irresponsibility on the part of some but also our collective failure to make hard choices and prepare the nation for a new age.

Homes have been lost, jobs shed, businesses shuttered. Our health care is too costly, our schools fail too many, and each day brings further evidence that the ways we use energy strengthen our adversaries and threaten our planet . . .

Excerpt from President Barack Obama's Inaugural Address, 2013

This generation of Americans has been tested by crises that steeled our resolve and proved our resilience. A decade of war is now ending. An economic recovery has begun. America's possibilities are limitless, for we possess all the qualities that this world without boundaries demands: youth and drive; diversity and openness; an endless capacity for risk and a gift for reinvention. My fellow Americans, we are made for this moment, and we will seize it—so long as we seize it together . . .

46. In these two inaugural addresses, some statements express optimism, while others do not. Which of these statements expresses the greatest optimism?
   a. That we are in the midst of crisis is now well understood.
   b. Our nation is at war against a far-reaching network of violence and hatred.
   c. This generation of Americans has been tested by crises that steeled our resolve and proved our resilience.
   d. America's possibilities are limitless, for we possess all the qualities that this world without boundaries demands: youth and drive; diversity and openness; an endless capacity for risk and a gift for reinvention.

47. In 2009, Obama stated: "A decade of war is now ending." Select the part of the world where this war had been fought.
   a. Africa (sub-Sahara)
   b. East Asia and the Pacific
   c. Middle East
   d. South and Central Asia

United States History Summary

The foundational documents that shaped U.S. history, such as the Declaration of Independence, the Constitution, and the Emancipation Proclamation, contain ideas that determined the country's progress as a society and its response to the rest of the world. The adoption of the Bill of Rights, the waging of the Civil War, the Civil Rights Movement, the struggle for women's suffrage, and the progressive era were all carried out in the quest for freedom and justice.

During the twentieth century, the United States turned outward as its economic and military power increased and as the world became more interconnected. Today, the United States still leads the world in economic and military power and continues to uphold the founding ideals of the right to life, liberty, and the pursuit of happiness for all.

Practice Answers and Explanations

1. The king. In the Magna Carta, *we* refers to the king, also known as the royal *we*. The Magna Carta cites barons and freemen, and common people are not referred to at all.

2. Answers will vary. Possible reply: The colonists agreed to form a government that would make laws. They also agreed to obey the laws and listen to officials appointed by the government.

3. b. The Declaration of Independence laid out the justification for a revolution against the rule of Great Britain. In declaring independence, the authors and signers of the Declaration were revolting against the current government. At the signing of the Declaration, the future of the colonies was at stake. Members of the Continental Congress would not have been thinking about the colonies becoming the most powerful nation on Earth (choice **a**). As with choice **a**, members of the Continental Congress would not have been thinking about spreading democracy (choice **c**) to the rest of the world. The Declaration was primarily a political document and statement, not an economic or technological one presented to seed the nation for the Industrial Revolution (choice **d**).

4. c. The Continental Congress appointed a Committee of Five members to write the document that would become the Declaration of Independence. Jefferson, in consultation with the other members, wrote the first draft and the subsequent revisions. Thomas Paine (choice **a**) was the author of the influential pamphlet *Common Sense* and was not involved in the writing of the Declaration. John Adams (choice **b**) was a member of the Committee of Five, but did not draft the versions. Like Adams, Benjamin Franklin (choice **d**) was a member of the Committee of Five, but did not draft the versions.

5. a. Unalienable rights are explained in the excerpt. Based on the explanation, they are absolute rights to which people are inherently entitled. The excerpt explains that historical rights (choice **b**) have long been abused by various forms of government. Resolute (choice **c**) means *unwavering*. Unalienable rights are those that people are born with simply because they are human. Governmental rights (choice **d**) would mean the rights are granted by a government, which is just the opposite of how the excerpt defines *unalienable*.

6. b. The excerpt states: "mankind are more disposed to suffer, while evils are sufferable, than to right themselves by abolishing the forms to which they are accustomed," so people are likely to be accustomed to an unfair government that has been governing for a long time, and they are less likely to move forward to "throw off" this type of government.

7. d. The Constitution was established to fix the weaknesses of the Articles of Confederation, primarily by giving more power to the central government. State boundaries (choice **a**) were not discussed in the Constitution. Both the Constitution and the Articles of Confederation were representative governments (choice **b**). Both the Constitution and the Articles of Confederation had the authority to raise an army during times of war (choice **c**).

8. a. The Preamble lists six reasons why a new governing document is needed. The Preamble lists the reasons for the Constitution; it does present an outline (choice **b**). The Preamble does not describe the new system (choice **c**) of government; it explains why it is needed. The Constitution was written after the colonies had already broken from England (choice **d**).

9. b. The framers solved this problem with the Connecticut, or Great, Compromise, by creating a two-chambered legislature. The House would be based on population and the Senate on equal representation. The problem with western territories (choice **a**) had already been solved by the Articles of Confederation. A greater geographic problem was between the northern and southern states. The framers dealt with an "uncrowned king" (choice **c**) by carefully limiting the powers of the president with a strong system of checks and balances. Experience under the Articles of Confederation had shown the framers that they needed a stronger federal government, not a weaker government (choice **d**).

10. c. A major concern for the Anti-Federalists was that a strong federal government could be used to restrict or deny individual rights and liberties. The Bill of Rights proposed by the Federalists addressed this concern. Delegates at the Constitutional Convention had already agreed to create a bicameral, or two-chambered, Congress (choice **a**). The Supreme Court (choice **b**) was an element of the Constitution, as outlined in Article III. The Preamble (choice **d**) was already a part of the Constitution that had been agreed to at the Constitutional Convention.

11. c. Although somewhat loosely governed, the French built a colony and lucrative fur trading network by partnering with Native Americans in present-day Canada and the Great Lakes regions. The English (choice **a**) initially settled primarily along the Atlantic Coast, where agriculture was the primary economic activity. The Dutch (choice **b**) explored and established a settlement on Manhattan Island, but were eventually forced out by the British. The Spanish (choice **d**) had settlements in the southern regions of North America, where fur trading was not a primary economic activity.

12. c. Evidence suggests that millions of Native Americans died from diseases carried by European settlers, drastically reducing populations. The introduction of new foods (choice **a**) did not necessarily have a negative effect. In many ways, new foods, plants, and livestock were beneficial to the diets and health of many Native Americans. The horse (choice **b**) greatly increased the range that many Native Americans could travel, as well as expanding their hunting abilities. Gunpowder and muskets (choice **d**) did affect tribal relations, but not always negatively. The greatest negative effect came from diseases.

13. c. The author states that American Indians "were virtually destroyed by the subsequent immigration that created the United States." Choice c is a good paraphrase of that excerpt from the passage. The passage clearly states that treaties negotiated with Native Americans were broken (choice **a**). The indigenous peoples of North America were not homogeneous (choice **b**), but rather incredibly diverse. The author of the passage does not mention if the Native Americans were unsophisticated (choice **d**).

14. a. The New England Colonies occupied land that was rocky and had poor soil. Consequently, industries that were connected to the Atlantic Ocean, such as fishing, whaling, and shipbuilding, became vital economic engines. The Southern Colonies, not New England, were located in the warmer climates (choice **b**). The Middle Colonies, not New England, attracted many diverse peoples from Europe (choice **c**). The New England Colonies did not have large plantations (choice **d**).

15. d. The rule of law would dictate that every accused person is entitled to a competent defense and a fair trial. As the ruling authority over the colonies, the British would not have been considered underdogs (choice **a**). Individual rights (choice **b**) includes a broad range of civil and legal rights. Rule of law is a much more specific and pertinent choice. The right to bear arms (choice **c**) is an American right granted by the Second Amendment to the U.S. Constitution. The Boston Massacre occurred nearly 20 years before the Constitution was ratified and amended.

16. d. Although the peace treaty was not signed until September 1783, Yorktown marked the last major battle of the war. The Battle of Saratoga (choice **a**) was not the first battle of the war and the Americans won the battle, not the British. The war began with the battles of Lexington and Concord in 1775. The British Army was the best equipped and trained army in the world at the time, and enjoyed superiority over the Americans (choice **b**). France began supporting the American cause (choice **c**) following the Continental Army's victory at Saratoga.

17. d. After Britain implemented the Intolerable Acts, many colonists thought that the British were trying to seize control of the colonial governments. Colonists formed the Continental Congress, which escalated tensions, leading to the start of the war. Almost all town hall meetings (choice **a**) were banned by the Intolerable Acts. The Proclamation of 1763 prohibited colonists from settling west of the Appalachian Mountains (choice **b**). Boston Harbor was closed (choice **c**) to all economic activity, not just American shipping.

18. a. While U.S. military focus was on Canada, British forces easily marched on Washington and captured the city. The British set fire to the White House and the Capitol. American forces made several attempts to occupy Canada (choice **b**) but were unsuccessful on each attempt. The British failed in their attack on Baltimore (choice **c**). The United States purchased the Louisiana Territory (choice **d**) from the French in 1803, nine years before the War of 1812.

19. c. Manifest Destiny, a term coined by newspaper editor John Louis O'Sullivan in 1845, was the idea that God had given the entire North American continent to Americans and wanted them to settle and control western lands. Although most Americans felt great pride in the country and held great optimism for it, few would have imagined it becoming the most powerful nation (choice **a**). Settling European conflicts (choice **b**) was an idea that almost all American leaders rejected. Although many Americans may have believed that United States was the greatest country (choice **d**), this belief is not the definition of Manifest Destiny.

20. b. The Monroe Doctrine was the principle of U.S. policy expressed by President James Monroe in 1823, stating that any intervention by external powers in the politics of the Americas is a potentially hostile act against the United States. The Treaty of Paris (choice **a**) was the document that ended the Revolutionary War. The Louisiana Purchase (choice **c**) did not outline a principle of American foreign policy; it gained vast amounts of new lands for the United States. The Treaty of Ghent (choice **d**) ended the War of 1812; it did not establish a long-term American policy.

21. b. The women in the photograph hold posters, one of which asks, "Mr. PRESIDENT HOW LONG MUST WOMEN WAIT FOR LIBERTY." Their protest is directed at President Wilson and not at other women (choice **a**), abolitionists (choice **c**), or suffragettes (choice **d**).

22. b. By portraying the women picketing outside the tall gates of the White House, the photographer is making a visual statement that concurs with choice **b**.

23. a. Traditionally, complex products were built one at a time by skilled artisans who made each part and assembled the device from start to finish by hand. As a result, a part that would work in one gun or clock might not work in any other. The use of interchangeable parts made the production of a wide range of manufactured goods much more efficient because identical components could be used in place of one another. Free enterprise (choice **b**) is an economic philosophy that greatly encouraged the growth of the Industrial Revolution. Home-based workshops (choice **c**) were among the traditional manufacturing processes that were replaced by the use of new procedures. Water-driven machines (choice **d**) did change manufacturing processes, but they did not have the impact on complex products that interchangeable parts did.

24. d. According to the table, there were more free African Americans in the South than in the North. In the South, free African Americans made up only a small portion of the total African American population; according to the table, more than 90 percent of southern African Americans were slaves. This means that there were well over 1 million African Americans in the South between 1820 and 1860. Therefore, the table supports the conclusion that there were many more African Americans in the South than in the North between 1820 and 1860.

25. c. Clay's compromise stated that the northern district of Massachusetts would enter the Union as the free state of Maine to balance admission of Missouri as a slave state, thus adding an equal number of Southern and Northern senators. Parts of the Louisiana Territory (choice **a**) were located south of the slave/free line drawn up in the Missouri Compromise. New states that were south of the line would be admitted as slave states. Massachusetts (choice **b**) was already a free state. To balance the admittance of the slave state of Missouri, the northern part of Massachusetts would become a separate free state. The Missouri Compromise also established a line across the continent from the southwestern corner of Missouri to the nation's western boundary. Territories north of that line would enter as free states (choice **d**).

26. d. Noting the year of the Gettysburg Address, 1863, is important in determining the answer to this question. The question explains that Lincoln is referencing 1776, so:

$$4 \times 20 = 80$$
$$80 + 7 = 87$$

1863 (the year of the Gettysburg Address) $- 87 = 1776$. Choices **a**, **b**, and **c** are mathematically incorrect.

27. b. The cartoon depicts a courageous and unarmed African-American male attempting to vote. An angry-looking group of scraggly whites, including two wearing hoods to hide their identity, confronts him. The group is preventing the man from reaching the polls. Southern whites, like most Americans, thought voting was very important (choice **a**). Following the collapse of Reconstruction in the late 1870s, the federal government was unable to protect the voting rights of African Americans (choice **c**). Enslaved people in the 1840s did not yet have the right to vote (choice **d**).

28. c. Emma Lazarus would be most favorable toward the Dream Act if she were alive today. In her poem, she expresses support for immigration of the least fortunate and the idea of the United States as a country that welcomes needy individuals hoping for a better life. Completion of a fence and barrier with motion detectors along the Mexican border (choice **a**) is opposite to the greeting of poor immigrants that Lazarus supports in her poem. She would be less concerned with immigrants complying with bureaucratic details in order to gain entry to the United States (choices **b** and **d**).

29. 1846.

30. 1847.

31. d. Union membership was close to its all-time peak of approximately 23 million when the UAW rejoined the AFL-CIO in 1981.

32. c. At the time of the founding of the CIO, the slope of the membership line was steeper than it was at the other times.

33. a. The reason for the reversal between the 1896 and 1954 cases is that nearly 60 years of experience showed that *separate but equal* was a fallacy. By 1954, the evidence was overwhelming that segregation was very damaging for black people. Although the court membership had more liberals in 1954 than in 1896 (choice **b**), the decision was unanimous, so that could not have been the most important reason. While the 1954 case was about education (choice **c**), it was also influential in ending segregation in transportation and public accommodations. The equal protection clause (choice **d**) had been in effect since 1868.

34. c. In 1916, Germany agreed to stop submarine attacks on American ships. In 1917, however, they resumed attacking all ships on sight, including six American vessels in February and March. This pushed Wilson and Congress to enter the war. The alliances (choice **a**) that triggered World War I were between European nations and did not involve the United States. By 1917, when the United States entered the war, fighting had reached a stalemate, with neither side making significant advancements (choice **b**). From the outbreak of fighting in 1914, Wilson was determined to keep the country out of the war and declared the United States to be neutral (choice **d**).

35. b. The two songs take opposite views as to the value of enlisting and fighting in World War I, reflecting how the American public was conflicted about the war. The lyrics of "I Didn't Raise My Boy to Be a Soldier" reflect that not all Americans were proud to have their sons fight in the war (choice **a**). Neither song lyrics reflect the belief that the war was unnecessary (choice **c**). Neither song provides a reason as to why American soldiers should fight in the war (choice **d**).

36. a. The government had a deficit from 1931 to 1941, which contributed to its debt. During the Depression and to this day, economists continue to argue about the efficacy of deficit spending (choice **b**). The chart shows that the public debt grew in conjunction with increasing annual deficits, not surpluses (choice **c**). The chart does not reflect a resolution of the downward economic spiral (choice **d**).

37. b. The ration is the fixed amount people were entitled to obtain. A preferred quota (choice **a**) implies that the holder of the coupon has a choice about how much to receive, which the coupon clearly states is 1 pound of sugar. Passage fare (choice **c**) and acceleration scale (choice **d**) do not make sense in this context.

38. d. Each of the incorrect choices (choices **a**, **b**, and **c**) identifies a detail from the passage. The main idea summarizes the entire passage; a detail does not.

39. b. Roadside commercial enterprises flourished with highway construction and car travel.

40. d. President Kennedy used metaphorical language to let Berliners know they could trust the United States. By identifying with Berliners, he was saying that he and the United States would protect West Berlin. Kennedy and Berliners did have a special rapport, but it was the unspoken security guarantee that was most important.

41. c. Kennedy proclaimed that any nuclear missile attack from Cuba would be regarded as an attack by the Soviet Union; thus, it is reasonable to conclude that he saw the Cuban Missile Crisis as a conflict between the United States and the Soviet Union. Kennedy's demands were made to the Soviet Union, thus he saw the conflict mainly between the U.S. and the Soviet Union, not Cuba (choice **a**). The passage clearly states that U.S. spy planes spotted Soviet missiles in Cuba (choice **b**). Kennedy hoped the crisis could be solved with diplomacy; however, he had to threaten military retaliation as well as diplomacy to influence the Soviet Union (choice **d**).

42. d. According to the passage, the United States did not know how many Soviet troops were present in Cuba, and so the United States did not know the full extent of the Soviet threat at the time. Kennedy's first concern was the safety and security of the United States, not Communist ideals (choice **a**). Kennedy tried diplomacy, naval blockades, and military retaliation to avoid using nuclear weapons (choice **b**). The information in the passage does not support the idea that Kennedy knew what actions Khrushchev would take (choice **c**).

43. a. The excerpt states that segregation solely on the basis of race deprives children of equal educational opportunities. Segregated facilities are separate facilities, and the excerpt makes it clear that even though physical facilities may be equal, students are still deprived of equal opportunities when separation through segregation exists. The other possible answers (choices **b**, **c**, and **d**) are either nonexistent or do not make sense in this context.

44. d. A proposal to amend the Constitution needs to be ratified by three-quarters of the states. There are 50 states, so this means 38 states would need to ratify the amendment. The ERA did not meet the three-fourths requirement, so it finally failed.

45. c. Hippies were young Americans who embraced and promoted values that ran counter to mainstream American values, hence the name *counterculture*. The beat movement (choice **a**) emerged in the 1950s and was made up of people who openly criticized American society. Although some hippies supported the women's movement (choice **b**), they did not create it. The Equal Rights Movement (choice **d**), an offshoot of the women's movement, was started by prominent women's rights groups, not hippies.

46. d. After events during President Obama's first term in office, he expressed great optimism in this excerpt from the second address. Phrases such as "possibilities are limitless" and "endless capacity" provide guides to recognize Obama's optimism.

47. c. The introduction to the excerpts explains that President Obama referenced the war in Iraq, which is located in the Middle East. None of the other options is located in the Middle East.

ECONOMICS

Acommon definition of economics is "the study of the way society uses limited resources to meet its material needs through the production, distribution, and consumption of goods and services." Economic concerns and processes have been crucial components of societies and governments since they were first established thousands of years ago. The first attempt at a formal examination of economics as an academic study, however, was made in 1776 by Scottish philosopher Adam Smith in his *Inquiry into the Nature and Causes of the Wealth of Nations*.

The Relationship between Political and Economic Freedoms

Many people have argued that an intimate link exists between political and economic freedoms. Ideas about that relationship have been explored throughout American economic and political history.

Milton Friedman and Economic Freedom

In his 1962 book *Capitalism and Freedom*, economist Milton Friedman argued that economic freedom and political freedom are linked, claiming, "It is no accident that modern capitalism and democracy arose at the same time in the same nations . . . Civil liberties, political freedom, and the existence of free markets are all necessary as a whole for each to exist."

Fundamental Economic Concepts

A knowledge of key concepts in economics is critical to understanding how societies operate. The operation of capitalism—the economic system in place in the United States and throughout much of the world—revolves around several basic ideas.

Markets and Competition

A **market** is a venue where buyers and sellers exchange goods and services for money. A market can be physical, virtual, or a combination of the two. For example, the New York Stock Exchange is a physical place located on Wall Street in New York City, but many investors participate in this market electronically from their computers, never actually visiting the stock exchange.

The U.S. economic system is **capitalistic**. Another name for capitalism is **free enterprise**. Free enterprise is based on a principle known as the **free market system**. A **free market** is a market that, theoretically, has little or no government intervention, such as taxes, subsidies, or regulation. In reality, in free-market economies such as in the United States, the government intervenes in the market to a lesser or greater extent to ensure its smooth operation.

Americans highly value the freedom to make personal economic decisions. For example, every American can decide what type of job or career he or she would like to have. In addition, as consumers, American citizens can freely choose the goods and services they wish to purchase. People who start businesses also have the freedom to decide in which industries they will do business and which products they will make and sell. It is important to note the other side of making personal economic decisions, and that is that each person must take responsibility for their decisions and the consequences that result.

Competition is the situation in which two or more sellers create the same types of goods and services to sell. In economics, competition is often thought of as "the struggle between buyers and sellers to get the best products at the lowest prices." Competition between sellers helps to keep the cost of making things low while at the same time making sure that the quality of the goods produced stays high. In other words, competition rewards those who can most efficiently make products. A direct result of competition is that it can force the least efficient producers out of business because they will not be able to sell as many products as the efficient producers. In the end, competition forces producers to be more efficient and create higher-quality products, while passing on their savings to customers, who then become more satisfied.

It is important to note that in a free market system, the competitive struggle over prices, production, and distribution of goods is determined by the market rather than by the government. A free market government will only get involved when the best interest of the public is threatened.

A **monopoly** exists when a single company or group dominates all or nearly all of the market for a given type of product or service. Competition and monopoly are often seen as opposites. While for the most part the U.S. financial system encourages competition, there are a few instances where monopolies are allowed and even encouraged. For example, public utilities, such as supplying water to homes, stores, and factories, are often set up as monopolies.

Practice

1. In a free market, or free enterprise, system, competition is allowed to flourish with a minimum of _____.
   a. investment
   b. choices
   c. government interference
   d. risk

Use the following passage to answer questions 2 and 3.

In economics, a monopoly exists when a seller or producer is the only one that supplies a particular product or service. The problem with a monopoly is that it can control the price of the goods or services it sells within the entire market. Congress has passed several laws to prevent monopolies and to maintain healthy competition within the market. The best-known of these laws are the Sherman Antitrust Act and the Clayton Antitrust Act.

2. Which of the following is a fact based on the passage?
   a. Big business is bad for the economy.
   b. Monopolies are no longer a problem in the U.S. because of the Sherman and Clayton Acts.
   c. Congress must regulate businesses or they will exploit consumers.
   d. Congress has laws to prevent or manage monopolies.

3. By 1878, the Standard Oil Company, owned by John D. Rockefeller, had bought out most of its business rivals and controlled 90 percent of the petroleum refineries in the United States. Which of the following was a likely effect of Standard Oil's business practices?
   a. The company set limits on its prices.
   b. The company increased oil prices.
   c. Competition in the oil market flourished.
   d. Standard Oil increased its efforts to attract needed customers.

Economic Production

The types and amount of goods and services a nation can produce depends on its resources. **Resources** are the things used to make goods or provide services. **Economic production** is the capacity to produce goods. Inputs of economic production include labor and capital. **Labor** is the work of people that provides goods and services. **Capital** is money and assets for the production of goods and services. Examples of assets include tools, such as an electric drill; infrastructure, such as a road or the Internet; and buildings, such as a factory.

A nation with many resources is able to satisfy most of its citizens' wants and needs. But when resources are scarce, or limited, economic decisions become much harder to make for the government, for businesses, and for consumers. **Scarcity** affects decisions that determine what and how much to produce, how to produce those goods and services, and how those goods and services will be distributed.

As discussed earlier, a capitalist economy is a system based on the private ownership of capital. When people engage in a business, they usually expect to make a **profit**. Profit, which is usually measured in terms of money, is what a business has left after all operating expenses have been met.

A key element of a capitalist economy is its ability to develop new businesses that produce new products and services. **Entrepreneurship** is the capacity and willingness to develop, organize, and manage a business venture while taking on the possible risks.

An entrepreneur takes on risk for the potential to make profit. This desire to risk investments in the hope of creating more wealth is called the **profit motive**. The profit motive has long been a huge factor in the growth of the free enterprise system. Entrepreneurship combined with land, labor, natural resources, capital, expertise, and ideas can produce profit. For example, Bill Gates started Microsoft with little more than his understanding of computer programming and his capacity to develop a computer operating system. He built his company into one of the most successful and influential companies in the world.

While entrepreneurs start companies and come up with innovations, investors provide a company with money that can be spent to grow and run the business. The money that an investor gives to help finance a company in return for partial ownership is called an investment. Sometimes an entrepreneur provides investment to start his or her own company. Investments can consist of time as well as money.

Practice

The following is an excerpt from a campaign speech by Elizabeth Warren when she ran for a U.S. Senate seat from Massachusetts. Use the excerpt to answer question 4.

There is nobody in this country who got rich on his own. Nobody. You built a factory out there? Good for you. But I want to be clear: you moved your goods to market on the roads the rest of us paid for; you hired workers the rest of us paid to educate; you were safe in your factory because of police forces and fire forces that the rest of us paid for. You didn't have to worry that marauding bands would come and seize everything at your factory, and hire someone to protect against this, because of the work the rest of us did.

Now look, you built a factory and it turned into something terrific, or a great idea? God bless. Keep a big hunk of it. But part of the underlying social contract is you take a hunk of that and pay forward for the next kid who comes along.

4. Based on the views expressed in this excerpt, Elizabeth Warren would most likely support which of the following policies?
   a. a tax cut for small businesses so that they have a better chance to succeed and hire more workers
   b. higher taxes on corporate profits so that successful companies help support infrastructure
   c. cutting the federal deficit so that future generations are not saddled by the debts we incurred
   d. privatization of much of our infrastructure, including major roads, water supply, police, and firefighters

Alternative Views

As discussed earlier, free market, or capitalist, systems like in the United States require a great amount of individual and economic freedoms. Some systems, however, do not allow for much freedom. As nations evolve and adapt, the relationship between political and economic freedom has been, and will be, tested. In **Russia**, following the breakdown of the Soviet Union in 1991, an experiment in increasing personal freedom did not lead to economic freedom, and the country has even seen an erosion of individual rights, as a corrupt and coercive economic system developed.

In **China**, the growth of the economy has been proceeding in concert with an improvement in economic freedom. But even though China seems to be on track to become the world's largest economy, it is unclear whether political freedoms are on the rise. It is an open question whether in coming years economic prosperity will lead to political freedom or the lack of political freedom will undermine the thriving economy.

Many economists and development experts have linked the level of inequality in a society with negative economic, as well as social, results. For instance, in *Why Nations Fail* (Crown, 2012), Daron Acemoglu and James Robinson argue that a country's economic health and success rise the more individuals across the spectrum share in a country's wealth. If the wealthy elite of a nation successfully control a disproportionate amount of its resources and production, they conclude, that nation is in danger of falling into a downward spiral of authoritarianism and corruption.

Maximizing Economic Growth

Economies grow when a nation's total output of goods and services increases over time. Economic growth is beneficial because it raises people's **standard of living**. Economists measure various economic factors to determine whether the economy is healthy. Some economists argue that economic growth and raising the standards of living of a country's citizens might be the main function of the economy.

As mentioned earlier, resources used to produce goods and services are often scarce, so it is crucial that they be used efficiently. **Productivity**, the efficient use of resources, is a measure of output in relation to the inputs of raw materials, labor, and capital. Productivity increases when more output is produced using the same amount of input in the same amount of time. Productivity also increases when the same amount of output can be produced with less input.

Usually, companies that are more productive, producing quality products for less cost than their competition, will survive best in a free market.

People and companies have discovered that it is often more profitable and efficient to focus on what each does best to increase production. **Specialization** means that each person or company in the production effort creates what each is best at creating. For example, expert welders would probably buy their safety shoes rather than make their own. They specialize in welding and use earnings from their work to pay for their other needs. Most people depend upon others to produce the goods and services they consume. Specialization is important in that it improves productivity.

Another way that productivity is increased is through **division of labor**. Division of labor means breaking down a job into small tasks performed by different workers; it relies on the differences in skills and abilities of workers or on specific methods of production. When producers take advantage of the division of labor, they are more likely to develop better production techniques and thus improve productivity.

Economic Interdependence

On a much larger economic scale, American society has a high degree of division of labor through which people depend on each other to produce most of the goods and services required to sustain life. This economic interdependence exists even in remote areas. People depend on each other for protection, for keeping roads open, and for information, such as weather reports.

The discussions in this section highlight how consumers and producers are interconnected through a continuous **circular flow** of buying and selling through a wide range of markets. An important element of the circular flow model is that one person's spending is another person's revenue. The income a person earns through labor and then spends to purchase products ends up as income for those who produce or sell those products. These people then spend this revenue to purchase other products, which then becomes income for other producers, and so the cycle continues.

Practice

Use the following passage to answer question 5.

A standard of living is essentially the minimum of the necessities or luxuries of life to which a person or a group is accustomed. The average standard of living in a country may be measured by first determining the country's gross national product, or GNP (the value of the goods and services produced in the national economy in a given year), and then by calculating per capita GNP (the GNP divided by the number of people in the country). Per capita GNP tells how much each person would receive if all the goods and services produced in the country during the year were divided equally.

An individual's standard of living, of course, may improve or decline depending on circumstances. Retirement from employment, for instance, often leads to a decline in the standard of living as retirees attempt to live on a percentage of their former income. The average standard of living in a country may be subject to change due to political upheaval, forces of nature, or global economics.

5. Which of these circumstances would almost certainly improve a person's standard of living?
   a. divorcing a spouse
   b. having a child
   c. receiving a college diploma
   d. filing tax forms on time

Key Economic Events

The foundation of a healthy economy is trust, and throughout its history, the United States developed institutions such as the **Federal Reserve Board** to help ensure trust by safeguarding financial and economic stability.

Reliable Currency

A crucial component of a stable economy is a reliable currency. This belief was promoted by Alexander Hamilton, the first secretary of the treasury, who successfully argued that the new government of the United States should pay back all the debts that the Continental Congress had incurred during the American Revolutionary War. As secretary of the treasury, Hamilton was responsible for managing the country's large debts and developing plans to promote economic stability. Hamilton was a Federalist who thought that the nation needed a strong, centralized government to preserve the young union.

He also wanted to build an economy that was based on industry and commerce. Only then, he argued, would the country be able to support a large federal government and a powerful military.

Unlike most political leaders at the time, Hamilton viewed the national debt as an asset and not a liability. Rather than pay down those debts with money the government held in reserves, Hamilton wanted to borrow money by selling government bonds. After a specific amount of time, the bonds would be repaid with interest to the holders. Hamilton's plan was put into action and eventually the debt was repaid, speculators who bought the government bonds prospered, and the financial reliability of the United States was established and trusted by Americans and investors around the world.

The Foundations of the Banking System

Hamilton also argued for a Bank of the United States, which would be able to make loans and have its bills received for payment by the federal government. He believed that such a bank would be helpful for the development of manufacturing in the United States. The First Bank of the United States was established and lasted for 40 years.

In the country's early history, opposition to the federal government's involvement in banking was strong. In 1836, President Andrew Jackson let the Charter of the Second Bank of the United States expire, leaving the nation without a central bank until the Federal Reserve System was created in 1913. Through 1836, state legislatures had the right to charter banks, and they did so.

Despite the Constitution stating that only the federal government had the right to coin money, in 1837 in *Briscoe* v. *Bank of Kentucky* the Supreme Court ruled that state banks and the notes they issued were also constitutional. More than 700 individual banks had the right to issue paper money. Starting in 1837, the United States passed laws and allowed a free banking system, which did not include any form of government restriction on banking activities, except for the enforcement of legal contracts and provisions to prevent fraud.

In practice, this system was unstable. As economic growth began to expand during economic upturns, banks would issue more banknotes, but **inflation** would result as credit was extended too widely. These business cycles would repeat themselves, leaving the country's economic health subject to wild fluctuations.

The free banking era came to a close with the passage of the National Banking Acts of 1863 and 1864. These laws created a system of national banks and a uniform national currency that helped finance the Civil War.

The banking system still had a problem. Money supply issues caused financial panics in 1873, 1884, 1893, and 1907. Each of these panics was followed by a depression and then by renewed prosperity. However, the 1907 panic was so severe that the richest man in the world, J.P. Morgan, loaned money to key banks to keep the entire financial system from collapsing.

The Federal Reserve System

In reaction to the crisis of 1907, the Federal Reserve Act of 1913 created the earliest version of the current Federal Reserve System.

To put it simply, the Federal Reserve is the central banking system of the United States. The Federal Reserve, or *the Fed*, manages the total amount of money available for lending and borrowing in the private banking system and partially controls interest rates. When individuals or businesses need money, they usually borrow from banks. When banks need money, they borrow from the Fed. Essentially, the Fed is a bank for banks.

The Structure of the Federal Reserve

The United States is divided into 12 Federal Reserve districts. Each district has a main Federal Reserve Bank and many branch banks. The Fed system is made up of several thousand banks located throughout the United States. They are considered members of the Federal Reserve System. Because these member banks buy stock in the Fed system and earn dividends from it, they are also considered partial owners of the Fed.

The biggest banks in the country were forced to buy stock in the Fed when it was established in 1913. Laws were implemented to limit the power of these banks from influencing the Fed. Authority to choose the leaders of the Fed—the Board of Governors—was given to the U.S. president. The Senate either confirms or rejects the president's nominees. The head of the Board of Governors is the Chairman/Chairwoman, and is picked by the president for a four-year term.

The Board of Governors is in charge of all the Federal Reserve's actions. A primary responsibility is to establish overall policies and goals for the Fed. Once determined, all the Fed's member banks follow these policies. A key component of the makeup of the Fed is that board members and the chairperson are considered outside the political sphere of influence of the president and Congress. Not being tied to the political process helps the Fed make the best economic decisions possible without partisan or interest-group pressures.

The Federal Open Market Committee (FOMC) is the Fed's monetary policymaking body. Its primary job is to formulate policies that promote economic growth while keeping prices stable. Simply put, the FOMC manages the nation's money supply.

The Role of the Federal Reserve

The Federal Reserve's mandate is "to promote sustainable growth, high levels of employment, stability of prices to help preserve the purchasing power of the dollar and moderate long-term interest rates."

The Fed conducts **monetary policy** to achieve these goals. Monetary policy refers to actions that either increase or decrease the supply of money. Monetary policy also affects the cost of borrowing money, which is credit, and is based on the health and needs of the economy. The Fed has the power to increase or decrease the supply of money that is circulated.

The Fed relies on several methods to control the money supply. First, it can lower or raise the interest rate it charges its member banks for loans. This is called the discount rate. If the economy is showing signs of slowing, the Fed can lower the discount rate to stimulate the economy. Because money is cheaper to borrow, banks are motivated to borrow more, which they then lend to their customers.

If the Fed wants to slow the economy, it can raise the discount rate. Higher interest rates means that money is more expensive to borrow, which discourages borrowing. This reduces the money supply, causing interest rates to rise. High discount rates result in banks borrowing less money from the Fed, and so they will have less money available to lend to customers.

As mentioned above, two primary responsibilities of the Federal Reserve are to maintain high levels of employment and to preserve the purchasing power of the dollar. Manipulating interest rates affects these goals significantly. When the Fed lowers interest rates, it makes the economy grow faster and creates jobs.

If the economy grows too much, it triggers inflation. **Inflation** is the rising price of goods and services over time, whereas **deflation** is a drop in the general level of prices of goods and services. When prices rise, it takes more money to buy fewer goods and services; thus, inflation reflects a lowering in the purchasing power per unit of money. At this point, the Federal Reserve would want to use monetary policy that slows, or contracts, the economy. The quickest way to do this would be to raise interest rates. As mentioned above, high interest rates make borrowing more expensive. This slows growth, reduces the number of purchases people make, and makes it less likely that businesses will raise prices.

The Federal Reserve can also manipulate the money supply by raising or lowering the reserve requirement for its member banks. The reserve requirement is the amount of money banks must keep as a reserve, or safeguard, against their deposits. When the Fed raises this rate, banks have to deposit more money in the Federal Reserve, leaving them with less to lend to their customers. When the Fed lowers the rate, banks are left with more money to lend to their customers.

The Fed can also control the money supply through open market operations. This involves the buying or selling of United States government bonds and Treasury bills. When the Fed buys bonds from investors, it gives the investors more money. This increases the money supply and lowers interest rates; it also ripples through the economy by encouraging borrowing and consumer demand and an increase in business output. As a result, the economy grows. If the Fed thinks interest rates are too low, it can sell bonds. This decreases the amount of money in circulation and interest rates rise.

The Fed's Role as Regulator

The Federal Reserve's two main regulatory responsibilities are overseeing regulations in the banking industry and monitoring issues with consumer credit.

As the nation's central banking system, the Fed monitors the activities of the nation's large commercial banks. The Fed must also scrutinize the interactions between foreign banking interests and American banks, especially international banks that have operations in the United States.

Monitoring and regulating the consumer borrowing industry is the Fed's other responsibility. The Federal Reserve establishes the laws that dictate what information lenders must provide to borrowers.

The Government's Bank

All money collected by the U.S. government is deposited in the Federal Reserve. Whenever the government purchases something, it uses money from its account with the Fed. In this way, the Fed is the U.S. government's bank. It holds the government's money just as a local bank holds the money of its customers. The Fed also manages all United States currency. Although paper money and coins are produced by government agencies, the Fed is in charge of how that money is circulated.

In addition, the Federal Reserve sells U.S. government bonds and Treasury bills. The government uses these to borrow money.

Practice

"Every nation on the Earth that embraces market economics and the free enterprise system is pulling millions of its people out of poverty. The free enterprise system creates prosperity, not denies it."
—Marco Rubio, U.S. Senator from Florida, August 24, 2011

6. Based on the quote, which inference could most clearly and reasonably be drawn regarding Rubio's opinion with regard to the free enterprise system?
   a. Poverty causes the existence of the free enterprise system.
   b. Without prosperity, poverty and the free enterprise system would be stronger.
   c. Poverty in nations is caused by prosperity in the free enterprise system.
   d. Without the free enterprise system, many more people would be experiencing poverty.

7. Monetary policy is the control of the supply of money and interest rates by the monetary authority of a country. Which of the following controls monetary policy in the United States?
   a. the president
   b. the Congress
   c. the Supreme Court
   d. the Federal Reserve

8. The interest rate that the Federal Reserve charges on loans to its member banks is

   _____.
   a. the money supply
   b. the inflationary rate
   c. the discount rate
   d. the bond rate

9. Which of the following policies might the Federal Reserve implement to slow rapid economic growth and to decrease the risk of inflation?
   a. Buy back government securities from bondholders.
   b. Sell government bonds and Treasury bills to investors.
   c. Lower income tax rates on all citizens.
   d. Lower the discount interest rates it charges banks to borrow money.

Modern Fiscal Policy

Fiscal policy—how government raises revenue and budgets its expenditures—became more important in shaping the economy in the first half of the twentieth century, especially as the Great Depression devastated livelihoods and destroyed wealth. Today, governments have significant influence over their economies by manipulating or implementing fiscal policies. Through the use of fiscal policies, a government can sometimes manage the pace of economic activity. For example, if the economy is sluggish and the government wants to encourage growth, it might cut taxes. Lowering tax burdens allows citizens to keep more money. They can spend this extra money to buy more goods and services. When consumers buy more goods and services, demand increases throughout the economy, and when this happens, businesses must hire more workers to produce more goods and services. This lowers unemployment. The government can also increase its spending, thereby increasing demand, which might encourage businesses to hire more workers and increase production.

Fiscal policies implemented by the U.S. government in the twentieth and twenty-first centuries have included significant actions that resulted in both success and failure. The Sixteenth Amendment to the Constitution, ratified in 1913—the same year the Federal Reserve System was established—made it possible for Congress to authorize a graduated income tax.

The Federal Reserve System and enhanced government fiscal powers were not strong enough to enable the country to avoid the stock market crash of 1929, which was preceded by extensive uncontrolled speculation in real estate and stock markets in the earlier part of the decade.

Following the crash of 1929, the economy headed into a long downward spiral known as the Great Depression. Businesses closed, people withdrew their savings in runs on banks, and millions of people lost their jobs. Many economists suggest that the economy did not fully recover from the Depression

until spending on defense increased substantially during the war mobilization effort and the years during World War II.

The election of Franklin Delano Roosevelt in 1932 was the beginning of a new era of government involvement in the national economy and the personal welfare of millions of Americans. Roosevelt proposed and Congress approved a series of federal programs called the New Deal to help the country combat and recover from the effects of the Depression. The New Deal included the creation of the following:

- The Tennessee Valley Authority (TVA) was established in 1933 to build dams to control floods, conserve forests and other sensitive lands, and supply electricity to communities in rural areas in the Tennessee River region and surrounding areas.
- The National Industrial Recovery Act (NIRA) enabled the president to regulate industry and suspend antitrust laws.
- The Glass-Steagall Banking Act instituted safe banking policies by separating commercial banking from investment banking. Commercial banks handle the routine, everyday banking transactions. Glass-Steagall prohibited commercial banks from risking depositors' money by using it to speculate on the stock market.
- The Works Progress Administration (WPA) provided jobs for the unemployed. The WPA was the largest public works program of the New Deal, involving $11 billion and more than 8 million workers who constructed highways, roads, bridges, airports, and public buildings and parks.
- The National Labor Relations Act, also known as the Wagner Act, created the National Labor Relations Board (NLRB). This piece of legislation guaranteed the right of workers to organize labor unions and to bargain collectively.
- The Social Security Act of 1935 guaranteed pensions to millions of older Americans, as well as

assistance to dependent children and the disabled. The key component of the Act was a monthly retirement benefit that people could collect when they stopped working at age 65. The money came from a federal tax that was deducted from employees' paychecks. The Social Security Act also established unemployment insurance for workers who lost their jobs.

Practice

10. Which of the following is an accurate statement about how the government manages fiscal policy?

   a. It requires the president and Congress to work together.

   b. It requires the input of the Supreme Court.

   c. It is voted on by citizens of the country.

   d. It is left entirely to the Congress.

11. John Maynard Keynes was an economist whose prescriptions for managing a national economy included increasing public spending and public employment during economic downturns when the private sector has cut back on its spending. President Franklin Roosevelt's New Deal included many programs that followed the advice of Keynes. One part of the New Deal that would not fall under the above Keynesian recommendation was

   a. the Tennessee Valley Authority, which built hydroelectric dams along the Tennessee River.

   b. the Works Progress Administration, which provided jobs to the unemployed.

   c. the Social Security System, which provided pensions to millions of the elderly and the disabled.

   d. the Glass-Steagall Banking Act, which separated commercial banking from investment banking.

Types of Energy

Wind and water power allowed parts of northern Europe to become the first countries in world history not dependent on animals and people for the bulk of their energy needs. After 1600, thousands of windmills were built, with the greatest concentration in Holland. About 500,000 water mills and 200,000 windmills in Europe helped create economies totally based on renewable energy.

At the beginning of the industrial age, steam engines powered mainly by coal, the first widely used fossil fuel, became the most important source of power. In the nineteenth and twentieth centuries, electric motors and internal combustion engines powered by oil and gas fossil fuels became key components of the energy needs of the United States and other industrialized economies.

Since the first commercial oil well was drilled in 1859, and through most of the twentieth century, the United States was the world's leading oil producer. But by the 1970s, the United States and other industrialized nations were importing a substantial amount of oil from the Middle East.

The 1970s Energy Crisis

Energy is an important part of any nation's economy. Fossil fuels, including oil, coal, and gas, have powered much of the economic development of the modern era. In the 1970s, the price of oil, one of the main energy sources, skyrocketed. This had serious effects on the economic health of the country and stimulated debates about energy policy in the United States and around the world.

The Energy Crisis in the 1970s was an international event. It arose from the manipulation of oil prices by the Organization of Petroleum Exporting Countries (OPEC), a group of Middle Eastern countries that control much of the world's oil production.

In 1973 and 1974, led by Saudi Arabia, OPEC restricted the supply of oil in response to the Yom Kippur War between Israel and Arab nations, resulting in oil prices more than tripling.

In 1979, there was a second energy crisis set off by the Iranian Revolution, which resulted in decreases in the amount of oil being produced. Because the United States had price controls on oil, supplies of oil dropped, resulting in shortages.

Since the 1970s, the United States and many other countries have been encouraging the development of alternative forms of energy to offset reliance on fossil fuels. Governments and the private sector have also been encouraging the development of new methods of drilling for oil and mining for other resources. Beginning around 2008, U.S. oil production has significantly increased from 5 million barrels per day to an average of 8.7 million in 2014. This increase is mostly due to technological innovations, such as horizontal drilling, hydraulic fracturing, and seismic imaging. These innovations have made the United States the world's leader in total oil production.

Practice

The following table shows world crude oil prices from 1965 to 2004. For each year, two prices are given, the actual price of oil that year and the price adjusted for inflation in U.S. dollars in 2004. Use this table to answer questions 12 and 13.

WORLD CRUDE OIL PRICES (U.S. DOLLARS PER BARREL)					
YEAR	ACTUAL PRICE	2004 DOLLARS	YEAR	ACTUAL PRICE	2004 DOLLARS
1965	1.80	8.64	1985	27.53	42.74
1966	1.80	8.41	1986	14.38	21.84
1967	1.80	8.15	1987	18.42	27.24
1968	1.80	7.82	1988	14.96	21.39
1969	1.80	7.45	1989	18.20	25.08
1970	1.80	7.80	1990	23.81	31.59
1971	2.24	8.39	1991	20.05	25.70
1972	2.48	8.90	1992	19.37	24.27
1973	3.29	11.18	1993	17.07	20.91
1974	11.58	36.09	1994	15.98	19.16
1975	11.53	32.84	1995	17.18	20.19
1976	12.38	33.34	1996	20.81	24.00
1977	13.30	33.67	1997	19.30	21.89
1978	13.60	32.17	1998	13.11	14.71
1979	30.03	65.60	1999	18.25	20.18
1980	35.69	71.48	2000	28.26	30.59
1981	34.28	62.76	2001	22.95	24.26
1982	31.76	54.81	2002	24.10	25.06
1983	28.77	47.76	2003	28.50	29.10
1984	28.06	44.89	2004	36.20	36.20

Source: U.S. Energy Information Administration, U.S. Departments of Commerce and Labor. Nominal prices are not adjusted for the effects of inflation. www.econlib.org/library/Enc/OPEC.html.

12. Adjusted for inflation, the cost of oil was the highest in the year _____.

13. Adjusted for inflation, the cost of oil was the lowest in the year _____.

Microeconomics and Macroeconomics

The study of how economies work is commonly divided into microeconomics and macroeconomics. Both deal with important concepts, such as supply and demand and the price and cost of production. But each branch of study comes at these concepts from a different perspective.

Microeconomics is the part of economics that explores the decisions made by individual customers, workers, households, and businesses. **Macroeconomics** examines either the economy as a whole or its major components, such as key business sectors and government.

Small Details and the Larger Picture

Microeconomics deals with how factors such as price feed into the decisions of buyers and sellers in a marketplace. It looks at the smaller picture and focuses on

- basic theories of supply and demand
- how businesses decide how much of something to produce
- how businesses decide what to charge for a commodity

Macroeconomics considers the national economy as a whole, looking at the factors that influence aggregate supply and demand. Since macroeconomics is associated with national economies, it deals among other variables with

- unemployment rates
- gross domestic product (GDP)
- overall price levels, including inflation

To understand the difference between microeconomics and macroeconomics, consider the price of a smartphone. Microeconomics looks at the demand for a smartphone at different price points and with different amounts of supply. Macroeconomics looks at the current state of prices in general as measured by the **consumer price index**, which is based on data collected nationwide.

Practice

14. What does microeconomics deal with?
   a. the production of whole industries
   b. the distribution of goods worldwide
   c. the economic decisions of individuals
   d. the allocation of resources by governments

Use the chart below to answer question 15.

YEAR	CPI (Annual Average)
1966	32.4
1971	40.5
1976	56.9
1981	90.9
1986	109.6
1991	136.2
1996	156.9
2001	177.1
2006	201.6
2011	218.0

The consumer price index (CPI) is an indicator of the general level of prices. It measures the average change of prices over time. The CPI consists of a set market basket of typical goods and services such as energy, food, housing, clothes, transportation, medical care, and entertainment. When the CPI goes down, consumers have to pay less for the same amount of goods and services. The CPI for all urban consumers covers about 80 percent of the total population.

15. Based on the data in the chart, what is the most likely prediction for 2017?
  a. The U.S. trade deficit will worsen.
  b. Inflation will continue.
  c. Unemployment will rise.
  d. Americans will be able to afford more goods.

Supply and Demand

The primary force and one of the basic principles of economics is that of **supply and demand**. Economists state that prices are determined by the relationship between supply and demand. **Supply** is the quantity of a good or service that a producer is willing to sell at a certain price at a given place and time. The law of supply says that if the price of a product is high, producers will be willing to sell more of it to increase the amount of money they will make. If the price is low, they will want to sell less of it. **Demand** is the degree to which people want a product and are willing and able to pay for it. The law of demand states that if the price of a product is high, consumers will demand less of it. If the price is low, they will demand more of it. These factors working together make up the principle of supply and demand.

Price is the amount charged for a good or service at a given place and time. In a free market economy, the price of a product is determined at the point where the quantity that consumers want to buy is equal to the quantity that producers want to sell. This is called the **market price**, or **equilibrium**. Equilibrium is reached when the supply of a product or service equals the demand for it. When the price of a product is more than the equilibrium point, demand

decreases and there is an oversupply of the product on the market.

It is important to note that the laws of supply and demand are accurate only in an economic system based on unregulated markets or those that have not been manipulated in uncharacteristic ways. For example, national crises can force governments to manipulate the supply of certain products. In addition, governments that operate under command economies exert too much control over supply and demand in the markets. In these situations, the laws of supply and demand break down.

Practice

The following graph shows the relationship between supply and demand. Equilibrium is the point where the two lines cross and represents a balance of supply and demand. Use the graph to answer questions 16–18.

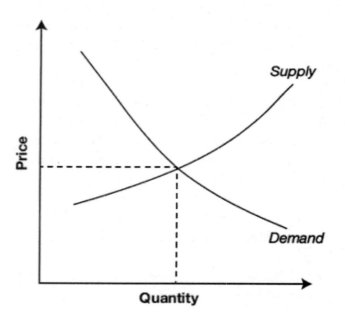

16. After the introduction of the new model, the price and quantity of the current model truck would likely _____.

17. When a new model truck is introduced, demand for the current model would likely

_____.

18. Based on the principles of supply and demand, which factors might cause a retailer to lower the price of an item?
   a. small supply and high demand
   b. large supply and high demand
   c. small supply alone
   d. large supply and low demand

Key Components in Economic Policy

Inflation is a rise in the general level of prices of goods and services in an economy over a period of time, whereas **deflation** is a drop in the general level of prices of goods and services. While excessive inflation is commonly seen as a threat to the economy by eroding the purchasing power of individuals, deflation can be a problem as well. If prices are generally perceived as falling, an incentive exists to delay purchases until a later time when they will cost less; this depresses economic activity.

The **gross domestic product (GDP)** is the monetary value of all finished goods and services produced within a country's borders in a specific time period, usually a year. The size of a nation's GDP as well as changes to the GDP from year to year are strong macroeconomic indicators of an economy's overall health.

Gross national product (GNP) is the monetary value of all finished goods and services produced within and outside a nation's borders in a given period. Economists generally consider the GDP to be a more accurate indicator of a nation's economic health. In 1991, the U.S. government switched from reporting its GNP to reporting its gross domestic product (GDP).

Unemployment means that people are looking for work and cannot find a job. The best-known measure of unemployment is the unemployment rate, which is a macroeconomic measure of economic health.

Economists measure the employment rate by first determining how many people are in the civilian labor force. The civilian labor force includes all civilians who are 16 years old or older who are either currently working or are looking for work. The **unemployment rate** is the percentage of people in the civilian labor force who are not working but have actively looked for jobs within a certain amount of time. The unemployment rate tends to rise sharply during recessions and then comes down slowly afterward.

Unemployment affects the people who do not have jobs, primarily economically because it makes it very difficult for them to buy the things they need to survive and to pay off their debts. Unemployment, however, negatively impacts the economy as a whole. Unemployed citizens usually have to reduce their discretionary spending, including on such basic needs as healthcare. Another way people try to get by is by using credit, which further adds to their debt. All these cutbacks in total spending slow the economy and create a drag on growth.

Surpluses, Deficits, and Debt

Governmental budgeting can be a difficult and complex undertaking. To create a government budget, leaders must study a great deal of information and then make predictions, or forecasts, to determine how much money should be allocated to specific government operations. A major issue is that forecasts are not always accurate. For example, if a government collects fewer taxes than it expected, the budget it created will not be enough to handle all that it wanted to accomplish. In addition, unexpected events that must be dealt with will force the government to spend money that it had not planned on and therefore did not put into the budget. This leaves less money to pay for the operations that were originally in the budget.

When a government spends less money than it collects, it runs a **surplus**. A government runs a **deficit** when it spends more than it collects. A government has a **balanced budget** when the amount of money it collects equals the amount of money it spends. The U.S. government is not required to have a balanced budget, however. Most states and smaller levels of government are required by law to operate on balanced budgets. If they cannot do this, then they usually have to make cuts or shut down.

The federal government has to borrow money when it runs a deficit in order to pay for all its operations. It can continue to operate by borrowing money or by selling bonds. As described earlier in the chapter, this is what Alexander Hamilton accomplished in the early years of the United States. People who buy U.S. savings bonds are basically providing the federal government with a loan. Many state and local governments also sell bonds to pay for their operations.

Debates about the nation's debt and deficits have always been heated. But these concepts are often confused. The U.S. federal **national debt** includes all the money over the years that the government has borrowed but has not paid back. The **national deficit** is the difference between how much the government collects and how much it spends in a single year, based on the annual budget. If the government continues to run deficits, its total debt will continue to increase as well. Budget surpluses, however, can be used to reduce the total debt. It is important to note that governments can reduce their deficits but still add to the total national debt. This is because deficit reductions are not large enough to offset the increases in the amount of money needed to run all government programs, which also includes interest payments on borrowed money.

As discussed previously, when the economy slows, people often lose their jobs and cut back on spending. This reduces the amount the government can collect in taxes and other revenues. Periods of economic weakness, however, are exactly the times when governments need to provide *more* assistance to citizens in need. These periods create budget problems because the only way government can help people is by borrowing money. This, of course, leads to higher deficits and more overall debt.

The national debt also has a significant effect on the government's annual budget. Because the government must make payments on the interest on the national debt each year, it must set aside money for that purpose. This reduces the amount of money that can be budgeted for other things. To make up the shortfall in revenues, the government often turns to the American taxpayers. As the amount of the payments on the accumulating debt increases, more taxes are needed to pay them. This ripples through the economy because when citizens have to pay more taxes to the government, they have less money to spend. As mentioned earlier, this usually hurts the economy as a whole.

Practice

Use the following graphs to answer questions 19–21.

Unemployment Rates in Selected Countries, 1995

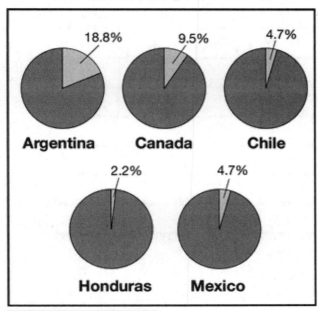

18.8% Argentina
9.5% Canada
4.7% Chile
2.2% Honduras
4.7% Mexico

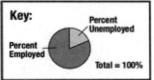

Key:
Percent Unemployed
Percent Employed
Total = 100%

19. What was Canada's approximate rate of unemployment in 1995?
a. 40%
b. 25%
c. 10%
d. 3%

20. Which two countries had about the same unemployment rate?
a. Chile and Mexico
b. Canada and Argentina
c. Chile and Argentina
d. Argentina and Mexico

21. High unemployment is generally associated with a low growth rate and a low level of inflation. Based on the graphs, which country would you expect to have the lowest level of inflation?
a. Argentina
b. Chile
c. Honduras
d. Mexico

Use the following graph and text to answer question 22.

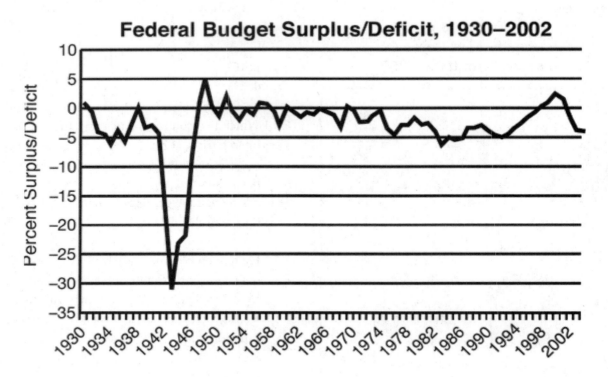

Federal Budget Surplus/Deficit, 1930–2002

Each year the federal government collects revenues in the form of taxes and other fees. It also spends money on such necessary functions as national defense, education, and healthcare. When the government collects more than it spends, it operates at a surplus. According to the graph, the government operated at a surplus for every year in which the line is above 0%. When the government spends more than it collects, it operates at a deficit. According to the graph, the government operated at a deficit for every year in which the line is below 0%.

22. In what year between 1930 and 2002 did the federal government operate with the greatest budget deficit?
a. 1930
b. 1945
c. 1951
d. 1994

Keynesian Economics and Supply-Side Economics

Two opposing views of monetary and fiscal policy are Keynesian and supply-side economics. **Keynesian economic theory**, or demand-side theory, is named after its founder, British economist John Maynard Keynes. He described his theory in 1936 in his *General Theory of Employment, Interest and Money*. First proposed during the Great Depression, Keynesian theory was the dominant economic theory until the stagflation period of the 1970s, in which the U.S. economy suffered from high inflation coupled with poor job and economic growth.

One of the key principles of Keynes's theory was his assertion that total demand in an economy is the most important driving force. As Keynes described it, total, or aggregate, demand is the sum of all spending on goods and services by all participants in the economy. Keynesian economists argue that governments should adopt aggressive spending policies during economic downturns. Because the private sector usually reduces spending in these times, it is up to the government to try to increase or maintain demand in the economy. According to the theory, this would keep businesses running that might otherwise lay off workers, which would then create more drag on the economy.

Supply-side economics was proposed in the 1970s as a conservative alternative to Keynesian economics. Supply-side economics suggests that the supply of money, labor, and goods or services creates demand. It is the opposite of Keynesian theory, which states that aggregate demand is the primary driving force.

Supply-side proponents argue that by lowering tax rates, businesses and investors could have more money to make new investments. This would lead to the formation of many new businesses, as well as motivating established businesses to expand, creating new jobs and more goods and services throughout the economy. Consumers could then take advantage of the tax cuts by spending more of their money.

Debates between supply-side proponents and Keynesians were sparked by the **Great Recession** that began in 2008. Keynesians called for government stimulus spending to jump-start the economy, even if it resulted in high federal budget deficits. Supply-siders argued for tax cuts and sharp cuts in government spending. In the end, a combination of the two was implemented to alleviate the effects of the recession.

Practice

23. A _____ economist would be more likely to support a very high sugar tariff.
    a. supply-side
    b. Keynesian

International Institutions

At the national level, the key banking institution in the U.S. is the Federal Reserve System. It is the central bank of the United States supporting its mandates for maximum employment, stable prices, and moderate long-term interest rates.

At the international level, two major institutions are the **International Monetary Fund (IMF)** and the **World Bank**. In addition to promoting economic growth, these institutions also act to protect and stabilize the world economy.

The IMF, also known as the Fund, was created at a United Nations conference in Bretton Woods, New Hampshire, in July 1944 during World War II. The goal for the IMF hammered out at the conference was to create the processes and an international economic institution that could help countries work together to rebuild once the war ended.

The IMF's mission statement declares that its main objectives are to "ensure the stability of the international monetary system—the system of exchange rates and international payments that enables countries (and their citizens) to transact with each other."

Like the IMF, the World Bank was established at the Bretton Woods conference in 1944. Its initial goal was to help in the rebuilding of the Western economies destroyed by World War II. The World Bank provided financial support for many countries to rebuild their national infrastructures and commercial sectors. In the years since, the World Bank's mission has changed. Currently, the organization's chief goal is the "present-day mandate of worldwide poverty alleviation." World Bank member countries must also be members of the IMF.

Trade

From the earliest societies to the present, **foreign trade** has been a key component of almost all economic systems. Foreign trade, also called international trade, involves the exchange of goods and services across international borders and among people and institutions of different countries. Very few, if any, countries contain all the resources to be self-sufficient. Therefore, to acquire the resources necessary to meet their citizens' wants and needs, nations must trade with other countries.

Foreign trade is usually described through the terms **imports** and **exports**. Goods and services brought into a country from another country are called **imports**. Goods that are traded out from one country to another are **exports**. Government leaders and economists always try to export more goods than they import, a situation economists call a **favorable balance of trade**. Countries who have a favorable balance of trade are producing and selling more goods and services than they are buying. In simple terms, it is like making a profit. The more money a nation earns from this advantage the better off its businesses and citizens are. Businesses can grow, employees can earn higher wages, and most will experience a higher standard of living.

Because international trade can have profound effects on national economies, governments around the world are constantly struggling to protect their trade interests. Many governments establish trade barriers to restrict or manipulate the exchange of goods and services between themselves and others. One type of barrier is a tariff. A **tariff** is a tax imposed on imported goods and services. In addition to raising revenue, tariffs on imported products give an advantage to competitors producing domestically. Other barriers include quotas, currency controls, administrative red tape, and export controls. Politicians and economists throughout the world have long argued about the benefits and costs of trade policies. Most will agree, however, that in the long run free trade among nations raises worldwide living standards. Most will also admit that some people and groups will suffer because of foreign trade and international competition. Those who support trade barriers often point to the need to protect domestic workers from foreign workers who earn lower wages, and to the need to protect young, potentially lucrative industries.

In today's interconnected global economy, there are many regional trading communities, or blocs, that work to increase free trade among countries. These include the European Union (EU) and the North American Free Trade Agreement (NAFTA). There are arguments for and against free trade and trade barriers. The issue ultimately boils down to whether it is free trade or protectionism practices that benefit economies the most, and which is more likely to raise the living standards of the most people, and improve the quality of life for as many people as possible.

Practice

Use the following graphic to answer question 24.

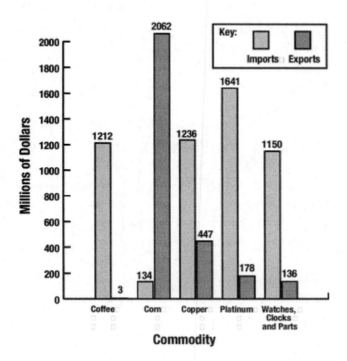

24. According to the graphic, which of the following items, if found in a store in the United States, would most likely be entirely American made?
a. copper tubing
b. a platinum wedding band
c. a package of frozen corn
d. a can of coffee

Use the following chart to answer question 25.

UNITED STATES FOREIGN TRADE PARTNERS			
COUNTRY	TOTAL TRADE	EXPORTS TO UNITED STATES (in millions)	IMPORTS FROM UNITED STATES (in millions)
Canada	407,995	178,786	229,209
Mexico	246,837	110,926	135,911
Japan	211,831	65,254	146,577
China	116,316	16,253	100,063
Germany	87,981	29,244	58,737
United Kingdom	85,038	41,579	43,459
Korea (South)	68,202	27,902	40,300

Source: U.S. Census Bureau.

25. Which of the following conclusions can you draw from the information in the chart?
a. The United States trades the most with the countries geographically closest to it.
b. Geographic location does not influence international trade.
c. There is a relationship between the size of a country and its economic status.
d. There is a relationship between the population density of a country and its economic status.

Consumer Economics

All of us are consumers. Nearly all activities we engage in have an economic component. Going out to dinner, buying a home, and attending college all involve decisions that have economic aspects and outcomes.

Savings and Banks

For an individual or a family, savings is the difference between the amount of money spent in a time period and the amount of money earned. Savings can either be set aside for future use or be invested.

Most people save their money in a **bank**, a financial institution that accepts deposits and makes loans. A bank's customers include individuals, nonprofit organizations, and businesses. Banks offer their customers savings and checking accounts, certificates of deposit, credit cards, automobile and student loans, mortgages, and lines of credit.

Different kinds of banks provide different kinds of services for their customers. **Commercial banks** are those that offer general or full banking services to businesses as well as individuals. Because commercial banks throughout the United States provide services for the majority of small businesses in the country as well as for tens of millions of Americans, they are probably the most important segment of the American financial system.

Savings and loan associations, or **S&Ls**, are a type of financial institution that traditionally lent money to people who were in the process of buying homes. Like commercial banks, S&Ls also take deposits from their customers, which the customers can then access by creating a savings account with the S&L. S&Ls in operation today provide many of the same services as commercial banks.

Some businesses, government institutions, and labor unions establish financial institutions only for their members. These are called **credit unions**. Unlike commercial banks and S&Ls, credit unions are not-for-profit organizations. Their nonprofit status makes credit unions exempt from taxes, while also lowering their overall operating costs. These factors generally allow credit unions to offer better rates on savings and loans than S&Ls or commercial banks.

Credit

Sometimes people purchase a good or service and enter into an agreement to pay for it later, usually with interest. That agreement is a request for **credit**. Credit provides a method for consumers to make purchases that they may otherwise have put off because they simply did not have enough money.

Consumers use various types of credit. Common types of consumer credit include:

- credit cards
- personal loans
- home mortgages
- installment plans
- home equity loans
- charge accounts

The use of **credit cards** exploded in the 1960s and 1970s, becoming one of the most popular and most used types of credit. **Credit cards** are used to purchase many goods and services at all types of businesses throughout the world. Consumers using credit cards should be aware of potential costs associated with them. These include annual fees that some credit card companies charge for the use of their cards; late charges, or a late payment fee, that is added to the card holder's total account if the minimum monthly payment is not made within a determined number of days; and interest rate charges, which are required for customers who do not pay the whole balance on their monthly bills.

Banks and other financial lending institutions provide **personal loans** to their customers. Personal loans are based on trust and confidence. Lenders must be confident that the borrower has the ability to repay the loan on a regular payment schedule over a set amount of time.

The largest credit commitment that most people enter into is a **mortgage** for a home. The home buyer pays a down payment to the seller while the bank or other lender pays the balance. The home buyer agrees to pay the bank back, with interest, in payments that can be spread out over as many as 30 years. Unlike most personal loans that are based on trust and confidence, home mortgage loans require collateral, or a way for the lender to protect the investment if it goes bad. In most cases, the collateral for the mortgage loan is the home itself. Most mortgages require a down payment followed by equal monthly payments until the mortgage is paid off. Each payment covers two aspects of the mortgage. One part of the payment is used to pay down the principal of the loan. The principal is the total amount that was borrowed. The other part of the payment covers the **interest** charges. Interest is what lenders charge customers for the privilege and convenience of borrowing money that they otherwise would not have had.

Student loans now comprise the second largest form of consumer debt after home mortgages. The federal government helps students finance their education because it is considered an investment in the productive capacity of the nation. However, the rising debt burden faced by students is considered by some to threaten the economic health of future workers and of the country itself.

When consumers buy goods or services on credit, they may be victimized by theft or fraud. Consumer credit laws protect buyers and limit their liability in situations such as identity theft, especially if the fraud or abuse is reported quickly. Other consumer credit laws are written to protect companies.

In many ways, the American economy relies on consumer credit to grow and expand. Consumer credit creates more demand for goods and services and pumps more money into the economy, leading to a healthier and more robust economy. Although there can be negative consequences of relying on credit, the positive side is that people make more purchases, especially on expensive items, when they have access to credit. And in the long run, increased spending benefits the entire economy.

Practice

26. If a person wants to avoid paying interest charges on a credit card, he or she must

_____

a. pay the minimum monthly amount.
b. pay half the monthly balance.
c. make no charges at the end of the month.
d. pay off the full balance each month.

Use the following passage to answer questions 27 and 28.

Before lending money to potential customers, most businesses will contact a credit bureau. Credit bureaus collect information about the credit habits of consumers, which can then influence whether they will lend money to prospective customers. The United States has several laws that aim to protect American consumers. The U.S. Fair Credit Reporting Act guarantees the right of all consumers to contact a credit bureau to make sure their credit files are accurate. Consumers denied credit because of wrong information on their credit reports have a right to review and challenge any information that might be wrong or inaccurate. It is the responsibility of the credit bureau to investigate and correct or remove any inaccurate information. The credit bureau may also be required to contact any business, bank, or individual who received the inaccurate credit reports within the past six months.

27. Which of the following is a basic principle supporting the passage of the Fair Credit Reporting Act?
   a. The government wanted to reduce the usage of consumer credit.
   b. Banks and other financial institutions are often dishonest.
   c. Individual credit ratings can have a huge impact in people's lives.
   d. Individuals need complete privacy when applying for loans.

28. Based on information in the passage, which of the following best describes the key purpose of the Fair Credit Reporting Act?
   a. The act was passed to protect the rights of consumers.
   b. The act is intended to make the loan process more difficult.
   c. The act was implemented to increase the amount of consumer credit.
   d. The act was created to grow the credit bureau industry.

Economics Summary

Economic and political freedoms are closely linked in capitalist systems, which are based on free markets and the ability of consumers and producers to engage in economic activity of their own choosing without much government regulation. In practice, however, governments regulate economic activity to ensure safe financial practices and healthy levels of competition.

Markets and competition, supply and demand, and division of labor are among the cornerstones of the U.S. capitalist system. Just about everyone participates in this system, as suppliers of capital, labor, or investment and as consumers and producers of goods and services.

Given the high level of freedom allowed, entrepreneurship is a hallmark of the U.S. economy. This spirit of economic freedom fuels the growth of new products and services, and government involvement, limited as it is, aims to protect the consumer and business from excesses and abuses of this very freedom.

Practice Answers and Explanations

1. c. In a free market system, the market and not the government ultimately determines whether a business succeeds or fails. Because individuals and organizations are free to invest (choice **a**) their resources as they choose, the amount of investment is determined by the needs of the market, with no minimum or maximum amount established. Healthy competition in a free market system seeks to maximize choices (choice **b**), not minimize them. The free market system allows individuals to pursue their ventures in any legal manner they choose, even if that involves great financial risk (choice **d**).

2. d. The passage clearly states that Congress has passed laws to prevent monopolies. Since this statement can be verified, it is indeed a fact. The statement that big business is bad for the economy (choice **a**) is implied in the passage; it is, however, an opinion, and not a fact. The passage does not state that monopolies are no longer a problem in the United States. Because Congress has passed laws, it is assumed that the possibility of a monopoly emerging is still a threat (choice **b**). The passage implies that businesses have the potential to exploit consumers (choice **c**) but does not make the claim that all businesses will do so.

3. b. By eliminating its competitors, Standard Oil controlled most of the production of oil and could artificially drive up prices.

4. b. Elizabeth Warren would most likely support higher taxes on corporate profits so that successful companies help support infrastructure. She makes it clear that the existing infrastructure helped these companies succeed, and that everyone must contribute and pay for that infrastructure and the climate that helps drive successful businesses. That means paying a fair share of taxes, not less in taxes (choice **a**). Implicit in Warren's statement is the idea that with every citizen contributing, the economy can continue to grow without focusing on cutting spending (choice **c**) and restricting the factors that allow businesses to grow. Warren's remarks emphasize the concept that all citizens, along with public agencies or departments, work together to foster economic growth, not just private entities (choice **d**).

5. c. Data show that a college degree generally raises a person's earning power because jobs or occupations that require a degree usually pay more. The passage says that an individual's standard of living may improve or decline depending on personal circumstances, such as retirement or having a child (choice **b**). However, divorcing a spouse is no guarantee of improvement; in fact, many divorced people (choice **a**) experience a decline in living standards. Filing tax forms (choice **d**) has no bearing on a person's standard of living.

6. d. Rubio states that the free enterprise system is pulling millions of people out of poverty, so it is reasonable to infer that he believes that without the free enterprise system, many more people would be experiencing poverty, as they would not be pulled out of poverty. Choices **a**, **b**, and **c** all run counter to what Rubio states in the quote.

7. d. The Federal Reserve controls monetary policy in the United States. The president (choice **a**) has appointment powers to the Federal Reserve, but does not control the supply of money. In order to limit the amount of political pressure on critical economic matters such as the supply of money, Congress (choice **b**) was not given authority over the supply of money. The Supreme Court (choice **c**) plays no role in determining the money supply.

8. c. The discount rate is the rate the Fed charges to member banks for loans. The money supply (choice **a**) is the total amount of money in circulation in the economy, not something that the Fed charges member banks. The inflationary rate (choice **b**) would be the rate of inflation in the economy, not a borrowing cost. The bond rate (choice **d**) is the amount of interest paid by the Fed to a buyer of a government bond over a certain amount of time.

9. b. When the Federal Reserve sells government bonds and Treasury bills, it decreases the money supply by removing cash from the economy and raises interest rates. All the other policies (choices **a**, **c**, and **d**) are enacted to stimulate the economy.

10. a. Fiscal policy involves regulating taxes and spending, so it is crucial that the president and Congress cooperate because taxes and spending are part of the normal budget process that involves both the legislative and executive branches. The Supreme Court (choice **b**) is not involved in crafting legislation concerning taxing and spending. Citizens (choice **c**) mainly influence fiscal policy through voting or other outside channel activities; they do not write tax and spending bills. All issues related to taxing and spending must be approved not only by Congress (choice **d**) but also by the president.

11. d. The Glass-Steagall Banking Act, which separated commercial banking from investment banking, addressed an inherent conflict of interest in the banking system but did not directly increase investment during economic downturns. All the other options (choices **a**, **b**, and **c**) involved increasing public spending.

12. 1980. Adjusted for inflation, the cost of oil was the highest in the year 1980, when it was $71.48 a barrel in year 2004 dollars.

13. 1969. Adjusted for inflation, the cost of oil was the lowest in the year 1969, when it was $7.45 a barrel in year 2004 dollars.

14. c. In economics, the prefix *micro-* refers to the smallest entity—individuals. The keywords in all the other choices (**a**, **b**, and **d**) signal large groups.

15. b. CPI is a measure of inflation, and it has been rising consistently for the past 50 years. The chart does not deal with the U.S. trade deficit (choice **a**). The chart does not deal with unemployment (choice **c**). The chart shows that Americans will have to pay more for the goods they purchase and therefore will not be able to afford more goods (choice **d**).

16. Decrease. When demand drops, the price drops. With fewer sales, the quantity of unsold cars would likely increase until a new equilibrium is established.

17. Decrease. When a new model truck is introduced, demand for the current, outdated model would likely drop off.

18. d. If a retailer has a large quantity of a product and customers are reluctant to purchase it (low demand), a retailer will lower the price in order to sell the product. When demand for a product is high (choices **a** and **b**), a retailer can increase the price. A small supply of a product (choice **c**) does not necessarily mean that demand for the product is high. Therefore, a retailer will not move the price unless customers are actually buying the product.

19. c. In the circle graph for Canada, the shaded portion is about 10% of the whole. Therefore, unemployment was about 10%.

20. a. In the circle graphs for Chile and Mexico, the shaded portions are about the same; each is about 5%.

21. a. If high unemployment is associated with low inflation, then the country with the highest unemployment rate is likely to have the lowest level of inflation. Of the countries shown, Argentina has the highest unemployment rate.

22. b. The graph shows that the federal government operated approximately at a 30% deficit in 1945. This is by far the largest deficit shown on the graph, much greater than choices **a**, **c**, and **d**.

23. a. Tariffs give an advantage to domestic supply, so they would more likely be supported by a supply-side economist.

24. c. The graphic shows that the United States imports large quantities of coffee, copper, platinum, and watches and clocks. It also shows that the United States exports only very small amounts of these same commodities. These two facts suggest that the United States does not produce large amounts of these particular items. The United States exports a great deal of corn, however, and imports very little; therefore, it is reasonable to conclude that the United States produces most of the corn available on its domestic market. And it follows that if you bought a package of frozen corn in a store in the United States, that corn would likely be American made. All of the other choices (**a**, **b**, and **d**) are incorrect based on the information in the graphic.

25. a. The countries that the United States trades the most with—Canada and Mexico—are also its geographic neighbors. The chart clearly shows that geographic location (choice **b**) does influence trade. The chart does not present information about the size of the countries (choice **c**). Information about population density and economic status (choice **d**) is not included on the chart.

26. d. The only way to avoid interest charges is to keep a zero balance by paying the full balance each month. All of the other options (**a**, **b**, and **c**) do not keep a zero balance and would therefore accrue interest charges.

27. c. Because almost everyone will eventually rely on credit at some point, an accurate credit rating is crucial in securing necessary loans. Choice **a** cannot be substantiated from the information in the passage. The Act does not claim that lending institutions engage in dishonest practices (choice **b**). Although privacy (choice **d**) is often important in credit reports and business transactions, the Act's main purpose is to provide accurate information for use by lenders and consumers.

28. a. The passage clearly describes what consumers can do to make sure that their credit reports are accurate. This helps protect consumers. The Act focused on the accuracy of information needed to secure a loan, not on making the process harder (choice **b**). Choice **c** cannot be supported by information in the passage. The Act outlines specific responsibilities and restrictions on credit bureaus, which is counterproductive if the goal was to boost the industry (choice **d**).

7 ▶ GEOGRAPHY AND THE WORLD

Understanding the world around you—its history, its environmental processes, and its cultures—is critical to living as an informed citizen.

The Beginnings of Human Societies

The longest era in human history is called the **Paleolithic Era**, or the **Old Stone Age**. This period ranged from the beginning of human existence until around 10,000 years ago. Paleolithic peoples invented tools and languages that allowed them to live in all regions of the world. The principal characteristic of humans during this era is that they foraged for their food by hunting wild animals or gathering edible plants.

Much of the Paleolithic Age occurred during the earth's Ice Age, when glaciers flowed and retreated multiple times. Experts think that the last of the major glacier eras ended about 10,000 years ago.

Around 12,000 years ago, humans in warmer climates learned to grow plants to eat. This advancement brought about the **Neolithic Revolution**, or the **agricultural revolution**.

Many experts theorize that warming climates brought about the agricultural revolution. Rising temperatures would have made the growing seasons longer and produce more fertile soil. However, not all experts agree.

Agriculture most noticeably emerged in fertile river valleys. Another key development was the domestication, or taming, of animals. Humans were soon keeping goats, camels, sheep, and other animals to help supply life's necessities.

Archaeological evidence suggests that Neolithic humans throughout the world all developed forms of agriculture independently. Developing initially in the fertile river valleys, agriculture spread to other regions.

This shift from hunting and gathering to food producing is one of the great breakthroughs in human history. People began living in larger, more organized permanent communities, creating the foundation of a much more complex way of life—civilization.

Early Civilizations

As agriculture advanced and food surpluses could be accumulated, larger population centers could be supported. By 3500 BCE, this led to the development of the early civilizations we are familiar with today.

A civilization is usually defined as "a complex culture in which large numbers of people share common elements. Among the most important elements of civilizations are large cities, organized government, religion, social structure, writing, and art."

The Sumerians and Mesopotamia

First among these early civilizations were the Sumerians, who settled in the valley between the Tigris and Euphrates rivers in present-day Iraq. This area is also known as Mesopotamia. By 3000 BCE, the Sumerians had built a number of cities that were supported by fields used for the cultivation of crops.

This civilization developed characteristics common to those that followed it, including a large population center, art and monumental architecture, a system of government, division of labor and social classes, and written language. Key Sumerian contributions include the development of the wheel, the plow, and the sail used for sea travel. In addition, the Sumerians made great advances in science and technology. Sumerian scientists studied astronomy and chemistry and even made early investigations into human diseases.

By 2000 BCE, nomadic warriors known as Amorites had invaded and taken control of Mesopotamia. These peoples created the first human empires. The largest and most influential empire during this period established its capital in the city of Babylon. King Hammurabi, who ruled from around 1792–1750 BCE, was the most influential of the leaders. He developed the first recorded set of laws. Hammurabi recognized that a single, uniform code would help to unify the diverse groups within his empire. Two centuries after Hammurabi's reign, the Babylonian Empire fell to newer nomadic warriors.

With the invention of written language, humanity moved from prehistory to history. In the eastern hemisphere, ancient civilizations developed in a number of river valleys, including

- the Nile in Egypt, where civilization remained stable for centuries
- the Huang Ho or Yellow River in China, where another civilization also lasted for centuries
- the Indus in India, where the civilization vanished around 1500 BCE until archaeologists rediscovered it

In the western hemisphere, civilization developed independently a few thousand years later. None of these ancient civilizations developed an alphabet for written language such as we use today.

The first written language, Phoenician, was developed in the area that is present-day Lebanon. The oldest surviving alphabetic written language still in use today is Hebrew, developed in what is now called Israel, which is south of Lebanon. For the most part, pictographic written languages, such as Egyptian hieroglyphics, which could contain thousands of different symbols, have disappeared. Chinese and Japanese are the only two surviving pictographic written languages.

Practice

Use the following chart to answer questions 1–3.

The Neolithic Era saw significant climatic changes that allowed for the beginning of farming in many parts of the world.

The Rise of Farming in the Neolithic Era

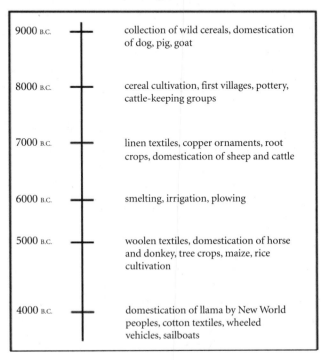

9000 B.C.	collection of wild cereals, domestication of dog, pig, goat
8000 B.C.	cereal cultivation, first villages, pottery, cattle-keeping groups
7000 B.C.	linen textiles, copper ornaments, root crops, domestication of sheep and cattle
6000 B.C.	smelting, irrigation, plowing
5000 B.C.	woolen textiles, domestication of horse and donkey, tree crops, maize, rice cultivation
4000 B.C.	domestication of llama by New World peoples, cotton textiles, wheeled vehicles, sailboats

1. How did people's lives change when they began cultivating cereal crops?
   a. They stopped being afraid of wild animals.
   b. They started painting on the walls of caves.
   c. They started using fire to cook their food.
   d. They started settling down in villages.

2. Based on the chart, which statement is an opinion rather than a fact?
   a. The wheel was invented long after people settled down in villages.
   b. Dugout canoes preceded sailboats by thousands of years.
   c. Olive trees and fruit trees were first cultivated around 5000 BCE.
   d. Irrigation was the Neolithic era's most important innovation.

3. Most ancient civilizations began in
   _____.
   a. mountains
   b. river valleys
   c. deserts
   d. plateaus

Ancient Egypt

The Ancient Egyptian culture emerged along the banks of the Nile River in northern Africa. Egyptians had been living in farming villages for centuries, perhaps as far back as 5000 BCE. The longest river in the world, the Nile, was essential to the development of ancient Egypt. Every year, the river flooded the valley, enriching the soil with silt and minerals. The Egyptians could grow a variety of crops in this fertile black soil. Eventually, Egyptian traders developed lucrative trading networks with the people of Mesopotamia and societies in central Africa.

By 3000 BCE, the kingdoms of Lower and Upper Egypt were united, creating the first Egyptian dynasty. The history of Ancient Egypt was to consist of 32 dynasties, spanning roughly 2,600 years.

Like the people of Mesopotamia, the early Egyptians were polytheistic, which means that they believed in many gods. Whereas in Mesopotamia, the kings were considered to be the representatives of the gods, the Egyptian kings, called pharaohs, were considered actually to *be* gods, who continued to rule even after they died.

Since pharaohs were expected to reign forever, the tombs for their afterlife were very important. During the Old Kingdom, pharaohs were buried in structures called pyramids, which is why the Old Kingdom is often called the great age of pyramid building. The largest tomb, called the Great Pyramid, was completed around 2556 BCE. The base of this massive pyramid covers an area of 13 acres.

Like the Mesopotamians, the Egyptians developed their own system of writing, called hieroglyphics. This system of writing was a key to the growth of Egyptian civilization. Also, in order to protect their crops and maximize yields, it was crucial for the Egyptians to be able to predict the flooding of the Nile River. This led to the development of a calendar. Egyptian scientists were eventually able to calculate the number of days between one rising of a star and the next as 365 days, which today we call a solar year.

Egyptian mathematicians also invented a system of written numbers. Using this system, they could count, add, and subtract. To survey and measure property boundaries, Egyptian engineers developed an early form of geometry. In addition, Egyptian medicine was much more advanced than in many other civilizations. Egyptian physicians learned how to check heart rates, fix broken bones, and even perform surgery.

The Indus Valley

The region that includes present-day India, Pakistan, and Bangladesh is known as the Indian subcontinent. The region is isolated from the rest of the Asian continent by the tallest mountain ranges in the world.

Two large rivers, the Indus and the Ganges, cut through the subcontinent, creating a large area of rich, fertile land. As in other areas of the world, societies formed near the rivers and developed agriculture. Archaeological evidence suggests that the inhabitants of the region were farming and tending animals as far back as about 7000 BCE. Villages supported by farming developed on the banks of the Indus River by about 3200 BCE.

Around 2500 BCE, a civilization emerged in the valley of the Indus River. Scholars have not yet deciphered the Indus system of writing, and so what is known and understood of this civilization comes mostly from archaeological digs at more than 100 settlements. At its height, this Indus Valley civilization was larger than both Mesopotamia and Egypt.

Prominent Indus Valley archaeological sites include that of the former settlement of Harappa, and so experts often refer to it as the Harappan civilization. A strong agricultural economy made it possible for the Harappan civilization to build a complex society that included trade with cultures as far away as Mesopotamia. Like the other early civilizations, the Harappan culture developed a written language, but experts have yet to discover bilingual texts that might decipher the Harappan language.

The Harappan people constructed complex and very organized cities. Instead of randomly building structures and roads as other early civilizations did, Harappan engineers built their cities using a rigid grid system. Structures in these cities were built using oven-baked bricks of uniform size. In addition, archaeological evidence shows that these early Harappan cities even had plumbing and sewage systems.

Ancient China

China's first cities were built around 4,000 years ago, nearly a thousand years after the civilizations of Mesopotamia, Egypt, and the Indus Valley. As in other early civilizations, Chinese peoples settled near fertile river areas. In China, these were the areas along the Huang He River, or Yellow River.

Historians mark off Chinese history by a succession of **dynasties**. Historically, Chinese dynasties emerge and decline and are then replaced by a new dynasty, in a pattern known as the dynastic cycle. In about 1700 BCE, along the banks of the Huang He River in northern China, the first powerful and long-lasting civilization emerged, the Shang Dynasty. This dynasty lasted from around 1700 BCE to 1027 BCE.

Shang leaders were the first Chinese rulers to develop written records. The people living under the Shang Dynasty were very diverse and often spoke different languages and followed different customs and traditions. Shang rulers, however, relied on their written language to bring order to the empire and to unite these different peoples.

From earliest times, Chinese culture has placed the well-being of the community above the interests of individuals. Above all, people were driven by their duties to their families and their king or emperor.

Around 1027 BCE, the Shang dynasty collapsed and was replaced by the Zhou dynasty. The Zhou controlled a vast expanse of territory, relying on **feudalism** to rule the empire. Feudalism is a loosely organized political system in which nobles or local lords are allowed to rule over lands that are actually owned by a king or emperor. The lords owe military service and loyalty to the emperor.

The Zhou built roads and canals to supply their empire, to develop trade routes, and to increase food supplies. The Zhou also used coined money for business and legal transactions. Among the technological advancements in the Zhou Dynasty was the use of iron. The Zhou developed blast furnaces that enabled them to make cast iron.

Practice

4. Which conclusion can most fairly be drawn from this map?

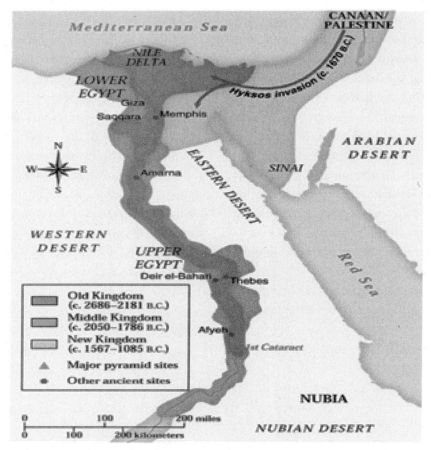

Credit: *The Making of the West*, Vol. 1: to 1740, by Lynn Hunt et al., Copyright © 2001 by Bedford/St. Martin's. Reproduced by permission of Bedford/St. Martin's.

a. Egyptian civilization predated Chinese civilization.
b. More than two-thirds of Egypt's population lived along the Mediterranean Sea.
c. Palestine served as a potential route for Asian invasion into Africa.
d. The Nile Delta was one of the last areas settled by the Egyptians.

Use the following passage to answer questions 5 and 6.

From 2000 BCE until the twentieth century, a succession of dynasties ruled China. The word *China* comes from the Ch'in Dynasty (221–206 BCE), which first unified the country by conquering warring land-owning feudal lords. King Cheng named himself Shih Huang-ti, or first emperor, and consolidated his empire by abolishing feudal rule, creating a centralized monarchy, establishing a system of laws and a common written language, and building roads and canals to the capital. Scholars speculate that construction of the Great Wall or *chang cheng*, meaning *long wall*, began during the Ch'in Dynasty in order to protect China's northern border from invaders. Shih Huang-ti ruled with absolute power, imposing strict laws and heavy taxes and doling out harsh punishments. He also is reputed to have burned books on topics that he did not consider useful. Shih Huang-ti died in 210 BCE. His son succeeded him but soon peasants and former nobles revolted and overthrew the dynasty. The Han Dynasty replaced it, ruling China until CE 220.

5. Which of the following is NOT a contribution of the Ch'in Dynasty?
   a. unification of territory
   b. feudal aristocracy
   c. road construction
   d. standardized written script

6. Which of the following conclusions can you make based on the passage?
   a. The Ch'in Dynasty enjoyed a stable and long-lasting rule.
   b. By abolishing feudalism, Ch'in Shih Huang-ti promoted democracy in China.
   c. The Ch'in Dynasty was popular among peasants and displaced nobles.
   d. The Ch'in Dynasty had long-lasting influence.

Rising Populations, Technology, and Warfare

At the beginning of the Neolithic period, roughly from 10,000 BCE to 2000 BCE, there might have been as few as five million people on Earth. By the time of the Roman Empire (which began in 27 BCE), that number had probably increased to about 200 million people.

While warfare became one destructive way to deal with rising populations in limited territory, a more constructive approach was the development of tools that allowed the creation of more wealth and increased the capacity of the planet to support more people. The development of metals such as bronze and iron resulted in more durable and effective farming tools that could increase crop yields. On the other hand, these new technologies were also used to make more lethal weapons to kill more adversaries.

While today we know about the rise and fall of many ancient civilizations, we are still not sure why warfare developed as a way of settling disputes. A number of factors were most likely involved, including the pressure of expanding populations, the greed and ambition of the most powerful, and the temptation of great wealth generated in the large cities.

The Rise of the Classical Civilizations

Two major civilizations rose to power in Southwest Asia before the emergence of the Ancient Greek city-states. In about 850 BCE, **Assyria** established a large empire throughout the region. The Assyrians defeated the peoples of Syria, Palestine, and Babylonia. Eventually they would control the lands not only of Mesopotamia, but also of territory in Egypt as well.

The last of the major Mesopotamian empires was the **Persian Empire**, centered in what is now Iran. Although it built a powerful military force, Persia's success in expanding and holding its empire was due to the tolerance of conquered peoples and to wise political diplomacy. Cyrus the Great established the Persian Empire after defeating his enemies between 550 and 539 BCE. His empire would eventually span more than 2,000 miles, from the Indus River in the east to present-day Turkey and the Mediterranean Sea in the west.

Cyrus laid the foundation for the Persian governing system by emphasizing tolerance and kindness in his dealings with the people he conquered. Unlike other conquerors in the past, Cyrus did not try to replace local customs, religions, and traditions with Persian ones.

Darius, another influential Persian leader, seized the throne in about 522 BCE. The empire had been thrown into chaos after the death of Cyrus. Darius managed to restore peace and order by reorganizing the Persian government system. His key achievement was dividing the empire into provinces in which people of different cultures could live peacefully under Persian control. Darius allowed these people to maintain their cultural identities and even practice some elements of local self-government. By doing this, Darius and his administration helped preserve these cultures for the future.

Ancient Greece

The failure of the Persians to defeat the Greek city-states, followed by the Greek conquest of the Persian Empire in 334 BCE, led to a major cultural change throughout the Middle East. But the most important legacies of the Greeks were cultural, not military.

The ancient Greeks built city-states on the lands surrounding the Aegean Sea. Each Greek city-state was like an independent country with its own government and laws. Many political systems today reflect the forms of government developed by the ancient Greeks. These include **monarchies, aristocracies**, and **oligarchies**.

By 500 BCE, a new form of government called **democracy** emerged. In Athens, the most influential Greek city-state, citizens participated directly in political decisionmaking. In a democracy, it is ultimately the people who rule.

Democratic Athens was at its height between 480 and 430 BCE. This is often referred to as the

Golden Age of Athens, during which Greek culture flourished. Much of the golden age occurred during the reign of Pericles, an influential politician and military leader. In fact, Pericles was so influential during his 32-year reign from 461 to 429 BCE that the era is called the **Age of Pericles**. With support from Pericles, Greek artists, writers, and poets created works that have become classics in literature and art.

Greek architecture also made great advancements during this time. Among the achievements was the Parthenon, a large temple built to honor Athena, the Greek goddess of wisdom and the guardian of Athens.

In addition, Greek playwrights introduced the principles of modern drama, including early examples of the genres of tragedies and comedies. The Greeks also made key discoveries in the sciences and mathematics. Hippocrates played a key role in medical discoveries, including the writing of a code of ethics for doctors.

Perhaps the Greeks' greatest contribution was in the field of philosophy. Socrates, Plato, and Aristotle were three influential Greek philosophers who lived in the city-state of Athens. These Greek thinkers pioneered the idea that the universe operates in an orderly way, governed by unchanging, or absolute, laws. They also argued that people can learn about and understand these laws by using reason and logic.

The philosophical foundation built by these Greek thinkers has supported philosophers and scientists up to the present.

Constant wars weakened the Greek city-states. In 338 BCE, Philip of Macedonia conquered Greece. Philip's son, Alexander the Great, would eventually conquer most of the lands between Greece in the west, Egypt in the south, and India in the east. Because Alexander's empire was so large, its peoples came from many different cultures, including Egyptian, Indian, and Persian. The merging of these diverse peoples with Greek culture led to the emergence of a new culture, known as **Hellenistic** culture.

Ancient Rome

Between prehistoric times and 500 BCE, various groups including Latins, Greeks, and Etruscans lived in and near the region around the present-day city of Rome. But it was the Latins who built the first significant settlement. Eventually, the Etruscans came to rule over Rome, but in the early 500s BCE, the Romans overthrew the Etruscan king and established a new form of government and called it a **republic**. A republic is a form of government in which power rests with citizens who elect representatives to run their government. The Roman republic would last for more than 500 years as the strongest empire in the Mediterranean region and one of the most influential cultures in history.

By the first century BCE, the Roman Republic in many ways reflected aspects of many different forms of government, including monarchy, aristocracy, and democracy.

Rome expanded its territories through conquest and trade. By 70 BCE, Rome's Mediterranean territories stretched from Anatolia (modern-day Turkey) in the east to Spain in the west. Its location on the Mediterranean Sea gave it access to the rich lands in the region.

Roman leaders maintained peace and governed the empire by establishing a unified set of laws. Like the Persians, they created a skilled force of civil servants to run and manage government affairs. Rome's well-disciplined army also provided security and maintained peace and stability throughout its territories.

Even with stunning military conquests and great wealth flowing into Rome, political and social strife were slowly corroding its stability. The great amount of wealth that came from conquest and lucrative trade networks was shared only by Rome's wealthy class, with very little trickling down to the vast majority of citizens. Growing inequality between the wealthy and the lower classes created great social upheaval. In addition, Roman generals who com-manded the Empire's many far-flung armies often developed great power and earned strong loyalty from the soldiers they commanded. One such general was Julius Caesar. In 46 BCE, Caesar marched his armies on Rome and defeated his political rivals. Caesar became dictator and governed as an absolute ruler until his assassination in 44 BCE.

Rome plunged into civil war after Caesar's death. In 31 BCE, Octavian emerged as the most powerful leader. Julius Caesar's grandnephew Octavian was given the title of Augustus, which means *exalted one*. During Augustus's reign, the 500-year-old Roman Republic ended and the Roman Empire emerged.

Rome was at its peak of power from 27 BCE to 180 CE. For 207 years, the empire experienced peace, order, and prosperity throughout much of its territories. This period of peace and prosperity is known as the *Pax Romana*, or Roman peace.

During the *Pax Romana*, the Roman Empire controlled more than 3 million square miles of territory, about the size of the continental United States. The empire's population numbered between 60 and 80 million people.

By the third century CE, Rome faced many problems, from both inside and outside the empire. Frequent conflicts with hostile people outside the empire disrupted Roman trade and severely weakened its economy. Infighting and the loss of loyalty within the Roman military weakened the armies that had once kept peace and stability.

In 330, the emperor Constantine moved the capital of the empire from Rome to the Greek city of Byzantium, in present-day Turkey. This divided the empire into Western and Eastern empires. In 476, invading Germanic tribes overthrew the Western Roman Empire. The Eastern Empire eventually evolved into the Byzantine Empire, and would flourish for another thousand years until it too was overthrown, by the Muslim Ottoman Turks in 1453.

The many achievements and contributions of Ancient Rome include the following:

- the development of aqueducts
- the invention of cement
- the refinement of the arch for architectural purposes
- the development of representative democracy the establishment of military medical corps

Practice

7. Cyrus, the founder and first king of the Persian Empire, carried out a foreign policy based on
  a. tolerance of other cultures.
  b. the teachings of the Zoroastrian religion.
  c. military aggression and strict authoritarian leadership.
  d. torture and submission to Persian culture and traditions.

8. Which of the following best explains why Greek architectural styles were found throughout the Middle East and the Mediterranean?
  a. The Romans adopted Hellenic culture and then spread it to all parts of the empire.
  b. Greek trading empires and the conquests of Alexander the Great spread Hellenic culture across these areas.
  c. The Persian conquest of the Greek city-states allowed for Greek culture to spread into its empire.
  d. The decline of Southwest Asian empires made Greek culture the most influential.

The Major Religions

The five largest religions in the world today—Christianity, Judaism, Islam, Hinduism, and Buddhism—all emerged in some of the world's earliest civilizations. Through the centuries, religious followers have shaped and transformed these religions into many variations.

Buddhism

Buddhism began during the sixth century BCE in India, based on and inspired by the teachings of Siddhartha Gautama, who is known as the Buddha, *the enlightened one*. Buddhism focuses on the goal of spiritual enlightenment and an understanding of the Buddha's Four Noble Truths: existence is suffering; suffering has a cause; there is an end to suffering that is called *nirvana*; and there is an eightfold path to the end of suffering.

Hinduism

Hinduism originated in India in the second and first millennia BCE. It comprises a diverse set of beliefs and practices with no single founder or religious authority. Hindus may worship one or many deities. The most common gods are Vishnu, Shiva, and a mother goddess, Devi. The goal of Hindu religious life is to learn to act so as to finally achieve liberation (*moksha*) of one's soul, escaping the rebirth cycle.

Judaism

The eastern shore of the Mediterranean Sea, in present-day Palestine, was the ancient home of the Hebrews, later called the Jews. Judaism, the religion of the Jews, emerged as the first of the Abrahamic religions (Judaism, Christianity, Islam). Judaism has greatly impacted Western culture through its history, legends, and moral laws. Unlike other early religions, Judaism taught that there was only one god rather than many gods. The belief in one god is called monotheism. The history of the Hebrews is contained in the first five books of the Hebrew Bible, the Torah, which are considered to be the most sacred writings in their tradition.

Christianity

Christianity grew out from Judaism and emerged in the same location. Central to Christianity is the belief that Jesus of Nazareth is the promised messiah—the son of God—of the Hebrew Scriptures. Christianity's sacred text is the Bible. Rome, the center of Western civilization at the time, eventually became the home of the Church. Primarily through the influence of the Roman Empire, Christianity spread throughout Europe and eventually the rest of the world.

Islam

Islam emerged as the last of the three Abrahamic religions. It originated in what today is Saudi Arabia with the teachings of Muhammad in the seventh century and was eventually spread by Arab traders, armies, and settlers. Followers of the teachings of Islam are called Muslims. Muslims believe that Muhammad is the final of all religious prophets and that the Quran, which is the Islamic scripture, was revealed to him by God, or Allah.

Practice

9. Judaism and Christianity were born in the
   _____.
   a. Eastern Mediterranean
   b. Arabian Peninsula
   c. Sahel of North Africa
   d. Central Asian steppe

10. Arab expansion brought _____ to North Africa, Southwest Asia, and Central Asia.
    a. Islam
    b. Buddhism
    c. Judaism
    d. Hinduism

The Environment and Societal Development

For much of human history, societal development did not appear to have major consequences on the environment. The earth is so huge and its resources are so vast that human impact seemed negligible. However, even in prehistory, humans did in fact have significant impact on the environment. For example, humans probably played a role in the extinction of large Ice Age mammals, such as the mammoth, the mastodon, and the saber-toothed cat.

Environmental Issues and Sustainability

Ongoing societal impacts have placed increasing pressure on the environment. These impacts include population growth, economic activities, and consumption patterns. Humanity has reached a point where environmental degradation threatens sustainable development as well as human health and well-being.

Humans use **natural resources**, naturally occurring from the earth, for food, fuel, and other necessities. **Sustainable resources** are those that can be used or harvested without exhausting their supply. According to the Merriam-Webster dictionary, sustainable means *of, relating to, or being a method of harvesting or using a resource so that the resource is not depleted or permanently damaged.*

Some natural resources can be used over and over because there is an unlimited supply. These are **renewable resources**. Wind, sunlight or energy, and water (in most cases) are examples of renewable resources.

There are many resources, such as minerals and fossil fuels, that people cannot renew or continue to use. These resources are called **nonrenewable resources.**

Because nonrenewable resources cannot be replaced, they must be conserved. Experts and others who advocate conservation—conserving resources—have two major goals. First, resources must be managed wisely so that current needs are met. Second, resources that are necessary to sustain societies must be carefully looked after to make sure the needs of future generations are met.

One of the major debates about conservation and natural resources today deals with the issue of nonrenewable resources such as fossil fuels. **Fossil fuels** are resources such as oil and coal. Conservationists argue that people should lessen their dependence on these forms of energy and look to replace them with renewable energy sources, such as wind and solar power. In many countries today, this transition is already happening. Some countries are producing hydroelectric power, which is energy generated from falling or moving water. Another example is using solar energy, which is generated by the sun's heat.

Of great concern to many environmental scientists at the moment is the mass consumption of fossil fuels. Most environmental scientists think that human activities have significantly affected the environment. A major environmental challenge around the world is pollution, which is the release of unclean elements into the air, water, and land.

While the developed worlds of Europe and North America have contributed the most to environmental degradation, rapidly industrializing countries such as China, India, and Brazil are starting to take a larger role.

Environmental issues include air pollution, deforestation and desertification, and climate change.

Air Pollution

The major contributor to air pollution is the burning of fossil fuels by industries and vehicles, primarily internal combustion engines. When these fuels ignite and burn, they release poisonous gases into the air. Another type of harmful air pollution is acid rain. Many industrial factories or plants release acidic chemicals into the air during the manufacturing processes.

These chemicals combine with precipitation to form acid rain, which can destroy forests, poison water, and even slowly erode the surfaces of buildings.

Deforestation and Desertification

Increasing human populations can also have a profound effect on natural environments. More people living on the planet means that more food is needed to feed them. In many areas of the world, people have been forced to remove natural forests to make room for additional fields of vital crops. This process is called **deforestation**. It has been occurring in the Amazon rain forest, which helps supply a large portion of oxygen for the earth and a large share of the ingredients used in many of the world's medicines.

Similar to deforestation is the condition of **desertification**, which occurs when once-fertile topsoil dries out and turns into soil similar to that found in deserts. A key cause of desertification is the removal of large numbers of trees and other plants that hold in place and maintain the quality of the topsoil.

Climate Change

A majority of climate scientists argue that high levels of harmful pollutants in the atmosphere are causing earth's temperatures to rise gradually. This trend is called **global warming**. The National Aeronautics and Space Administration (NASA) defines global warming as "the increase in earth's average surface temperature due to rising levels of **greenhouse gases**." A greenhouse gas is any gaseous compound in the atmosphere that is capable of absorbing infrared radiation. When this happens, heat is trapped in the atmosphere, leading to higher temperatures.

Many scientists who support the global warming theory predict disastrous consequences if the problem is not reversed. Unchecked rising temperatures have already started the melting of glaciers and ice caps. This has started to raise the level of the world's oceans, putting coastal cities and smaller islands at risk.

Global warming is just one aspect of a larger theory called climate change. **Climate change** is the long-term change in the earth's climate, or of a region on earth. NASA states that climate change includes global warming and everything else that increasing greenhouse gas amounts will affect.

Many experts argue that rising temperatures may not be the most severe effect of changing climate. For example, some scientists theorize that changes to precipitation patterns and rising sea levels could pose more severe risks to humans around the world than the higher temperatures alone.

Practice

11. Which of the following recommendations would most support sustainable development?
    a. Allow workers to telecommute and work from home.
    b. Use fracking mining techniques to extract oil from shale.
    c. Increase the usage of water from underground aquifers in dry regions.
    d. Increase industrial development in young or struggling economies.

Use the following passage to answer questions 12 and 13.

Even though acid rain looks, feels, and even tastes like clean rainwater, it contains high levels of pollutants. Scientists believe car exhaust and smoke from factories and power plants are the main causes of acid rain, but natural sources like gases from forest fires and volcanoes may also contribute to the problem. Pollutants mix in the atmosphere to form fine particles that can be carried long distances by wind. Eventually they return to the ground in the form of rain, snow, fog, or other precipitation. Acid rain damages trees and causes the acidification of lakes and streams, contaminating drinking water and damaging aquatic life. It erodes buildings, paint, and monuments. It can also affect human health. Although acid rain does not directly harm people, high levels of the fine particles in acid rain are linked to an increased risk for asthma and bronchitis. Since the 1950s, the increase of acid rain has become a problem in the northeastern United States, Canada, and western Europe. Some believe it is the single greatest industrial threat to the environment, although most feel that the emission of greenhouse gases is a far larger problem.

12. Which of the following natural resources is least likely to be affected by acid rain?
    a. animal life
    b. plant life
    c. coal reserves
    d. water

13. According to some analysts, a temperate climate is most conducive to human productivity. Which of the following would be the best evidence to support this claim?
    a. Many areas of the temperate region are rich in natural resources.
    b. Tropical regions are most attractive to tourists and vacationers.
    c. The world's five largest economies are all located in the temperate region.
    d. The most severe damage from the two world wars was in the temperate region.

Population Growth and Urban Development

Human population has been exploding since the beginning of the Industrial Age, when it was less than one billion. Population has increased massively since then, but growth has begun to slow.

- The current world population is around 7.4 billion.
- The world population will reach 9.9 billion in 2050 and 10 billion by 2054.
- Population growth peaked at 2.2% in 1963, and by 2012 had declined below 1.1%.
- Some nations, such as Japan and Russia, are already experiencing an aging of the total population as birth rates remain below replacement rates.
- Projections show that Africa's population will reach 2.5 billion by 2050, while the number of people in North and South America will increase by only 223 million to 1.2 billion. Asia's population will jump from 900 million to 5.3 billion, while Europe's population will fall from 740 million to 728 million.

The populations of various regions of the world change at different rates. In most places, death rates have significantly dropped because of better healthcare, more reliable food supplies, and overall better living conditions. Some places have not only seen declining death rates but also falling birth rates. This is especially the case for some Western industrialized nations. These countries have **zero population growth**. This occurs when the birth rate and the death rate are equal.

Many countries in Asia, Africa, and Latin America, however, continue to have high birth rates. High birth rates in these regions are often due to cultural beliefs about marriage, family, and the high value societies and families place on having children. For example, in many agricultural areas of the world, families may choose to have many children to help with the many jobs required to farm land.

Large increases in populations create many issues for societies and countries. For example, as mentioned earlier, larger populations require larger amounts of food. Almost all regions of the world have managed to increase food production, with the exception of Africa. This has mainly been due to frequent wars and uncontrollable weather conditions that hinder crop production.

Early civilizations were marked by the development of urban centers. However, since the beginning of the Industrial Revolution, urban settlement has dramatically increased, first in the developed world and now in regions of the developing world as well.

To support growing cities and populations, rural areas have had to adapt. While a much smaller percentage of the population lives in rural areas, these areas must still produce sufficient food for a growing population while maintaining an environment that protects biodiversity and mitigates the impact of climate change.

Practice

14. According to the information given in the table, what do you think will be the most pressing issue in Russia in 2025?

#	Top Ten Most Populous Countries	World Population (millions)			
		1980	1990	2008	2025*
1	China	981	1,141	1,333	1,458
2	India	687	849	1,140	1,398
3	United States	228	250	304	352
4	Indonesia	151	178	228	273
5	Brazil	122	150	192	223
6	Pakistan	81	108	166	226
7	Bangladesh	81	116	160	198
8	Nigeria	76	94	151	208
9	Russia	n/a	148	142	137
10	Japan	117	124	128	126

*2025 projections based on 2008 figures.

Source: Based on data from the International Energy Agency.

a. food supply
b. housing
c. aging population
d. unemployment

15. Not including migration, negative population growth simply means _____.
a. the birth rate exceeds the death rate
b. the death rate exceeds the birth rate
c. the birth rate is not recorded
d. the birth rate and the death rate are equal

16. Which of the following predictions is best supported by the world population growth data in the graph?

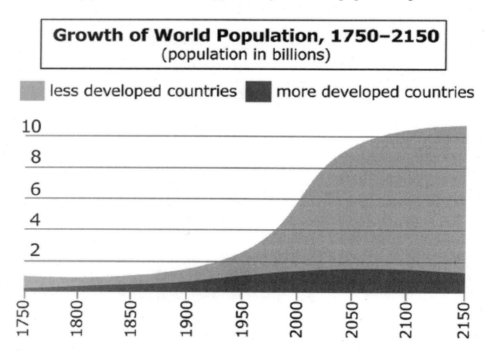

Growth of World Population, 1750–2150
(population in billions)

less developed countries more developed countries

a. The world population growth rate will be declining starting by 2050.
b. The less-developed countries will continue to grow rapidly for the next 150 years.
c. The developed countries will experience a population collapse in the next century.
d. Within the next century, world population will level off and begin to decline.

17. Fill in the blank with the correct term.
Birth rates are high in the _____ world.
a. developed
b. industrial
c. Western
d. developing

Peoples and Nations

Along with culture, place, region, and nation are critical concepts in geography and help us analyze variations across physical and political boundaries. Recognizing these variations in human society allows for increased understanding between peoples around the globe. The ways physical and cultural life is organized form some of the key concepts in geographic study.

Places and Regions

In geography, it is important to understand the difference between a place and a region. A **place** is a particular location that has some meaning to an individual or group of individuals. That meaning can have a physical and/or a human dimension. Every place on earth has its own unique characteristics, which are usually established by the surrounding environment and those who live there.

A fundamental goal of geographers is to try to understand and explain how places are similar to and different from one another. One of the most effective ways of doing this is to group places into regions. A **region** is an area that is distinct for either physical or social reasons. Regions are bounded by homogeneous characteristics.

Regions may be defined in terms of similar or common physical characteristics, such as climate, plant life, or river systems. Regions may also be defined in terms of the unique or common characteristics, such as language, religion, and cultural traditions, of the people who live within them.

Types of regions include the following:

- continental
- geographical
- historical
- paleogeographic (or historical geographic)
- natural resource
- religious
- political
- administrative
- regions controlled by military force

Culture

Geographers also study culture. **Culture** is the way of life of a group of people who share similar beliefs and customs. When studying a culture, geographers will examine fundamental characteristics, such as the languages people speak and the religions they follow.

Language is one of the principal foundations upon which all cultures are built. Language is also vital in allowing cultures to evolve, providing a way for people to interact with one another, share information, and pass on cultural values and traditions. It is not uncommon, however, to have language differences within a culture. Language differences may include distinct ways to pronounce specific words or variations in the definitions of words.

Like language, **religion** is another key element of culture. Religious beliefs are often some of the most personal and influential beliefs people have, affecting their daily lives as well as determining moral values and interpreting life experiences. Religious beliefs, however, have often been—and continue to be—contributors to many conflicts around the world.

Culture is one factor that helps to define regions, nations, and states. According to Article 1 of the **Declaration on Cultural Diversity** issued by the **United Nations Educational, Scientific, and Cultural Orga-**

nization **(UNESCO)**, "Culture should be regarded as the set of distinctive spiritual, material, intellectual, and emotional features of society or a social group, and . . . it encompasses, in addition to art and literature, lifestyles, ways of living together, value systems, traditions and beliefs."

The Declaration goes on to say

Culture takes diverse forms across time and space. This diversity is embodied in the uniqueness and plurality of the identities of the groups and societies making up humankind. As a source of exchange, innovation and creativity, cultural diversity is as necessary for humankind as biodiversity is for nature. In this sense, it is the common heritage of humanity and should be recognized and affirmed for the benefit of present and future generations.

As discussed in Chapter 4: Civics and Government, the type of government a society establishes is often based on cultural traditions, values, and other characteristics. Although governments around the world exhibit differences, they also share specific characteristics. For example, all governments provide security and public services as well as guide communities toward goals by making public policies that support the economic well-being of their citizens.

Nations and States

A **nation** is a group of people who are bound together through history, culture, language, religion, customs, and values. Geographers study political science to help them see how people in different places are governed. Geographers also investigate how political boundaries were established and how they have changed over time.

A **state** is a portion of land with a sovereign government and laws. (The term *state* can refer to the subnational areas in the United States and other countries, but it also applies to completely separate countries as well.) The difference between nation and state can be considered the difference between ethnicity and citizenship, though the terms are often used interchangeably.

Governments around the world vary greatly. Since each has unique characteristics that reflect that nation's past and its traditions and customs, governments are structured in a variety of ways to help them run effectively.

Large countries around the world today usually have several levels of government. For example, the United States has a central, or federal, government, but also state, county, township, and city, town, or village governments.

Practice

18. Russell lives in Chicago and Javier lives in Los Angeles. Both boys speak English but have different names for soda. Russell calls it *pop* and Javier calls it *coke*. How might you explain this difference?

   a. different cultures

   b. different dialects

   c. different languages

   d. different educations

Use the following maps and passage to answer questions 19 and 20.

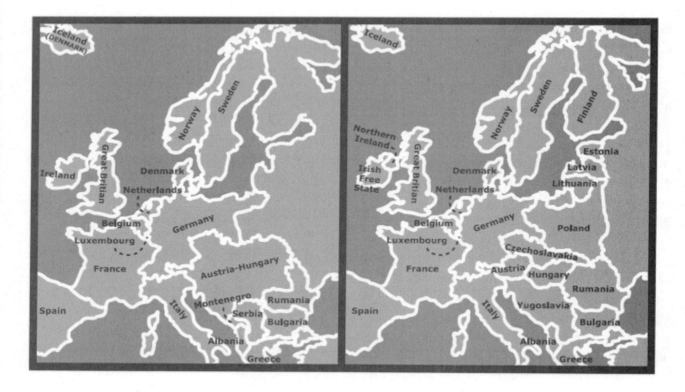

The maps show the political borders of European nations before the start of World War I (the map on the left) and after the war concluded (the map on the right). At the end of World War I, Germany was required to sign the Treaty of Versailles, which demanded that Germany accept responsibility for causing the war. The treaty also required Germany pay the victor nations over 6 million pounds in reparations and to cede some of its land, including its valuable coal mines on the German-French border. In addition, Germany had to give up all of its colonies, which had provided it with a steady source of income. Finally, strict limitations were placed on the size and weaponry of the German military, and the country was forbidden from entering into an alliance with neighboring Austria.

19. Which country increased in size at the conclusion of World War I?
   a. Austria-Hungary
   b. Norway
   c. Rumania (Romania)
   d. Ireland

20. Which of the following is a *fact* about the Treaty of Versailles?
   a. The Treaty of Versailles harmed the German economy.
   b. Germany deserved the harsh terms of the treaty because Germany started the war.
   c. If the Treaty of Versailles had been fairer to Germany, the Nazis would never have gained power.
   d. The United States was the country that benefited the most from the Treaty of Versailles.

Human Migration and Cultural Diffusion

The United Nations defines **migration** as "the crossing of the boundary of a political or administrative unit for a certain minimum period of time." People who migrate are called **migrants**. Large numbers of people throughout the world today are migrating, either as a result of national disasters, warfare, or regional conflicts or for more complex social, political, or economic reasons. People are not only migrating from one country to another, but also within countries. Many people in the United States and other developed countries are moving from city to city or from rural areas to urban areas, usually in pursuit of better economic opportunities or in the search for more fulfilling lives.

Human migration has been a constant throughout history. People migrate for a wide range of reasons, including the need for food and livelihood, greater economic opportunity, and freedom from oppression. Few regions of the world today are not the products of wide-ranging human migration and cultural exchanges that result from migration.

The process of spreading new knowledge and skills from one culture to another is called cultural diffusion. **Cultural diffusion** or **exchange** occurs between groups of people as they spread their products or ideas to one another, often through migration or trade. It is nearly impossible for a culture to isolate itself to the extent that it has no contact with outside peoples. Consequently, cultures change and evolve over the course of time. New political concepts, ways of living, and technical or scientific innovations and inventions can all lead to cultural evolution. These may come from within or without a culture.

Cultural changes pushed by outside influences have historically come about because of trade, human migration, and even war.

From the very first human societies, cultural diffusion has always played a role in how cultures grow and evolve. For example, early people who had once been nomads became farmers living in permanent villages. Once they learned to grow crops, they no longer had to move from place to place.

Innovations brought about by the Industrial Revolution in the 1700s and 1800s greatly increased the scope of cultural diffusion. The early technological innovations had profound social and economic consequences. The prospect of finding steady employment in urban factories motivated many rural people to move to cities. This changed the way millions of people lived, while also instigating cultural changes.

Cultural diffusion has increased greatly in the past few decades as globalizing forces, including the Internet, have taken hold in all regions of the world. Internet technology, which emerged out of the Information Revolution in the 1990s, allows people thousands of miles apart to interact and share information in an instant. Computer technology and innovations in communications have linked the world's cultures more closely than ever before.

Assimilation occurs when a minority group or an individual adopts the customs and ideas of the dominant culture. Assimilation is an issue of considerable debate as populations have become more mobile and immigration across national borders has escalated during the current era of globalization.

Practice

21. Which of the following is the most common migration trend for many developing countries at the end of the twentieth and into the twenty-first century?
   a. interior to exterior migration
   b. urban to rural migration
   c. industrialized to farming migration
   d. rural to urban migration

22. How would a list of today's top 10 cities compare to this list from 1790?

Population of Top Ten U.S. Cities in 1790

Rank	City
1	Philadelphia, PA
2	New York, NY
3	Boston, MA
4	Charleston, SC
5	Baltimore, MD
6	Salem, MA
7	Newport, RI
8	Providence, RI
9	Marblehead, MA
10	Portsmouth, NH

   a. All of the cities listed would be the same.
   b. Some of the cities would be the same, but the list would include cities in the South and West.
   c. Some of the cities would be the same, but there would be more cities in New England.
   d. None of the cities would be the same.

Out of Africa and Early Migrations

Between 250,000 and 100,000 years ago, many scientists contend, a new group of hominids—the group that includes humans and their closest relatives—emerged. This new group was named *Homo sapiens*. Modern humans are *Homo sapiens*. Based on current evidence, many experts suggest that modern humans evolved from archaic humans primarily in East Africa.

Although scientists still have much to discover, a leading theory is that the first humans emerged in Africa and then migrated to other areas of the world. This is often called the *Out of Africa* theory. Eventually, two more groups of *Homo sapiens* arose, Neanderthals and the earliest modern humans. Early modern humans eventually spread all over the world, while Neanderthals lived mostly in Europe and western Asia. However, for reasons not yet understood, the Neanderthals disappeared between 50,000 and 30,000 years ago. This left humans as the only hominids on earth.

From these origins in Africa, humans have spread to every continent on Earth.

Human migration has continued throughout history. One example was the migration of the Germanic peoples into Europe, which helped bring an end to the Roman Empire. Another was the migration of Turks from Central Asia to what is now Turkey.

The following map illustrates human migration routes out of Africa and Asia.

Practice

23. Based on the map, humans first entered Western Europe from what direction?

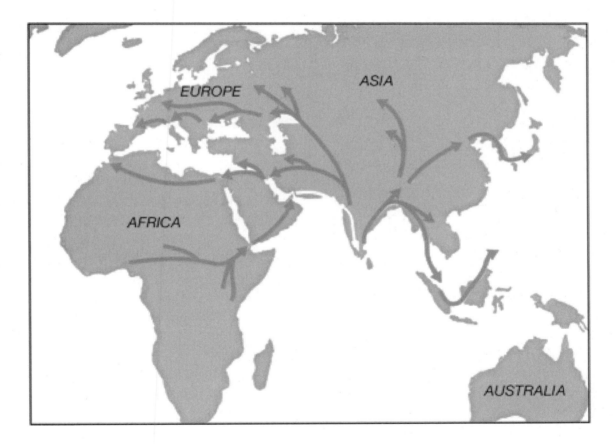

    a. North
    b. South
    c. East
    d. West

Migration in the Modern Era

Human migration continues today, aided by modern technology. Immigrants from all over the world have been moving to the Americas, especially to the United States. People from Africa and the Middle East have been immigrating to Europe. The benefits and costs of immigration are a topic of debate around the world.

Migrations can also occur within a country. For example, in nineteenth-century America, many pioneers migrated from the east to the west. In the twentieth century, Southern rural African Americans moved to Northern cities. This movement of people has come to be known as the Great Migration. In 1910, 89 percent of African Americans lived in the South. By 1970, this figure was down to 53 percent. The Great Migration represents the largest internal movement of any group in American history.

The Great Migration greatly altered the racial makeup of such cities as Chicago, Detroit, and Cleveland, as well as having a huge social and economic impact. Politically, the large influx of African-American voters created a new voting bloc that eventually grew to have significant electoral influence.

Along with African-American migration at this time, Mexican Americans also moved north in search of new opportunities in factory jobs in Chicago, St. Louis, Omaha, and other cities. In addition, political turmoil in Mexico impelled many Mexicans to leave their country and move to the United States.

Beginning in the 1940s, following World War II, millions of Americans moved to states in the South and West. By the mid-1960s, California surpassed New York as the state with the largest population. The migration to Sunbelt cities such as Houston and Los Angeles continued for the rest of the twentieth century. These migrations of Americans to suburbs and to cities in the Sunbelt have had a momentous impact on American society, and have altered the nation's political and economic landscape.

Migration is an ongoing feature of human history. It began when our ancient ancestors migrated from Africa and peopled the continents. It continues today as the increasing interconnectedness across the world allows people to seek new opportunities and better lives in other countries.

Practice

24. The _____ is the term used to describe the area in the U.S. South and West that became more important economically than the Northeast.
   a. Sunbelt
   b. rural South
   c. air-conditioned South
   d. suburbs

25. Which of the following is an accurate description of the Great Migration that occurred during the twentieth century?
   a. African Americans eventually gained more power in southern states.
   b. States in the West and the Southwest—the Sunbelt—lost political power.
   c. The migration affected the balance of regional political power in the United States.
   d. Mexican Americans abandoned the United States and returned to Mexico.

Geography and the World Summary

The earliest human civilizations emerged more than 5,000 years ago, after people learned to grow crops and tame wild animals to create reliable sources of food. Several large and powerful empires developed along fertile river valleys, including the Sumerians, the Egyptians, and the people of China and the Indus Valley.

Increasing world population, technological innovations, and warfare all contributed to a complex cycle in which empires such as the Greek and Roman emerged, prospered, and were eventually replaced by new empires.

Civilizations today face many of the same challenges those early civilizations faced, as well as some new ones. The impact humans have on the environment, natural resources, and the overall health of the planet has emerged as one of the most important issues humans have ever had to deal with.

Practice Answers and Explanations

1. d. According to the time line, the cultivation of cereal crops occurred around 8000 BCE. At that time, the most significant development was the appearance of villages in which people settled.

2. d. This choice is the only opinion among the five choices. The words *most important* give a clue that the statement is a value judgment, not a fact.

3. b. Most ancient civilizations began in river valleys.

4. c. The Hyksos were among the first of several invaders to attack Africa through Palestine. Information about Chinese civilization (choice **a**) is not presented on the map. Likewise, statements about Egyptian population (choice **b**) cannot be supported by this map. The Nile Delta had been settled during the Old Kingdom, and was not one of the last areas settled (choice **d**).

5. b. Shih Huang-ti abolished the aristocracy of feudalism, instead appointing officials to carry out his rules in all of China's provinces. Shih Huang-ti unified territories (choice **a**) by building roads (choice **c**) and canals. He also established a system of laws and a common written language (choice **d**).

6. d. The Ch'in Dynasty introduced a centralized government ruled by monarchy, a form of government that lasted in China until 1911, when revolutionaries overthrew the last dynasty. The Ch'in Dynasty did not last long (choice **a**) because the Han Dynasty overthrew it after Shih Huang-ti died. Shih Huang-ti ruled with absolute power, imposing strict laws and heavy taxes and doling out harsh punishments. He did not promote democracy (choice **b**). Although he rid the empire of feudalism, his harsh rule would not have made him popular with peasants nor with the displaced nobles (choice **c**).

7. a. Perhaps Cyrus's most enduring legacy was his method of governing. His kindness toward conquered peoples revealed an insightful and tolerant understanding of how to govern an empire. Cyrus did not try to impose his religious beliefs (choice **b**) on the peoples he conquered. Cyrus believed in honoring local customs and religions. Although he was a military genius who won many victories in expanding the Persian Empire, he did not allow his soldiers to loot or burn the lands that he conquered. Cyrus understood that in order to keep his empire stable, he had to learn from the conquered peoples and adopt their best aspects to the new empire (choice **c**). Cyrus was very accommodating of conquered peoples. He pacified local populations by supporting their local customs and even sacrificing to the local deities (choice **d**).

8. b. The Greeks developed strong trade networks across these regions to provide food and luxury goods to the city-states. Furthermore, Alexander the Great's army included thousands of Greek soldiers and advisors who spread Hellenic culture through their conquests. The Romans (choice **a**) did adopt aspects of Hellenic culture but transformed it into their own. The Persians (choice **c**) did not conquer the Greeks. Greek culture spread because of the conquests of Alexander the Great, not because of the decline of preclassical civilizations (choice **d**).

9. a. Judaism and Christianity were born in the Eastern Mediterranean. Islam, not Judaism and Christianity, was born in the Arabian Peninsula (choice **b**). Neither of these religions emerged from Africa (choice **c**) or the Central Asian steppe (choice **d**).

10. a. Arab expansion brought Islam to North Africa, Southwest Asia, and Central Asia. Buddhism (choice **b**) emerged out of India. Judaism (choice **c**) is the religion of the Hebrews and Jews. Like Buddhism, Hinduism (choice **d**) emerged out of India.

11. a. Encouraging workers to telecommute, or work at home, would most support sustainable development, since energy from fossil fuels is saved when workers do not have to use cars or other transportation to get to work. Using recently developed fracking technology to get oil from oil shale (choice **b**) would result in more CO_2 in the atmosphere, worsening global warming, plus it is not sustainable. Pumping more water from underground aquifers in dry areas of the world (choice **c**) is not sustainable because the underground water will be depleted. Industrial development (choice **d**) uses a great deal of resources and may not be sustainable.

12. c. All of the natural resources in choices **a**, **b**, and **d** are negatively affected by acid rain except coal reserves. The passage identifies coal burning as a source of acid rain. It does not say that coal reserves are harmed by acid rain.

13. c. According to some analysts, the fact that the world's five largest economies are all located in the temperate region offers strong evidence that a temperate climate is most conducive to human productivity. Although some temperate regions are rich in natural resources (choice **a**), it cannot be assumed that all are. Areas attractive to tourists and vacationers (choice **b**) may or may not be conducive to human productivity. Not all regions damaged by the two world wars (choice **d**) were in temperate regions, for example the Soviet Union.

14. c. With a steadily declining population involving fewer new births, Russia's population will be older; that will most likely be the most pressing of the listed issues. Russia will have fewer people than it has today, which means it will need less food (choice **a**). Since housing (choice **b**) requires maintenance, it will need some attention, but not as much as dealing with the needs of the aging population. Unemployment (choice **d**) will not likely be the most pressing issue.

15. b. Not including migration, negative population growth simply means the death rate exceeds the birth rate. A birth rate higher than the death rate (choice **a**) will lead to a positive population growth. Negative population growth means the death rate exceeds the birth rate, not that it is not recorded (choice **c**). A birth rate that is equal to the death rate (choice **d**) is known as zero population growth.

16. a. That the world population growth rate will be declining by 2050 is the prediction best supported by the graph. While the total population continues to increase, the slope of the line, or rate of growth, is decreasing. The graph shows that the growth rate in less-developed countries (choice **b**) will slow after 2050. The graph shows that the growth rate in developed countries will hold fairly steady, not collapse (choice **c**). The graph shows no decline in the world population (choice **d**).

17. d. Birth rates are high in the developing world. The text clearly states that developed nations (choice **a**) have experienced declining birth rates. The term *industrialized* (choice **b**) means the same as *developed*. These nations have experienced declining birth rates. The majority of Western world nations (choice **c**) are developed, and therefor have experienced declining birth rates.

18. b. People from the same country and culture who speak the same language may have different words for certain items or variations in pronunciation or meanings of words because of a difference in dialects. Because both Russell and Javier live in the United States, they are both from the same culture (choice **a**), not from different cultures. The question clearly states that both Russell and Javier speak English (choice **c**), so this could not account for the difference. A popular beverage such as a soda would be known to almost every American, so a difference in education (choice **d**) would not account for this difference.

19. c. Of the countries listed, according to the maps only Rumania increased in size. Austria-Hungary (choice **a**) was broken up by the Treaty of Versailles. Norway (choice **b**) remained the same size after the war. Ireland (choice **d**) was divided into the Irish Free State and Northern Ireland, hence it became smaller.

20. a. According to the passage, the Treaty of Versailles imposed huge fines on Germany and stripped the country of valuable property. These provisions harmed the German economy by depriving it of cash and income, which it needed to rebuild the country after an extremely costly war. Choices **b**, **c**, and **d** each state an opinion, not a fact.

21. d. The developing world is rapidly becoming industrialized, so consequently many rural citizens have been displaced and are moving to cities in search of industrial jobs. The migration trend is based primarily on economic factors, not necessarily on geographic factors like interior or exterior (choice **a**). Urban to rural (choice **b**) is the opposite of the correct answer. The majority of people migrating are moving from traditionally agricultural areas to industrialized areas (choice **c**).

22. b. In 1790, the United States extended only as far as the Mississippi River, and the largest cities hugged the Atlantic Coast. Today's population has moved west and south. The United States has expanded dramatically since 1790, and many large cities have been established throughout the country, making the list highly likely to be vastly different (choice **a**). As the country expanded, people moved away from the Atlantic coast, so having more cities in New England (choice **c**) is not viable. Many of the cities on the list from 1790 remain some of the largest in the country (choice **d**).

23. c. According to the map, humans first entered Western Europe from the east. There are no immigration routes from any other direction entering Western Europe.

24. a. The Sunbelt is the region in the United States that stretches across the southern and southwestern portions of the country from Florida to California. Beginning during World War II, the Sunbelt experienced a dramatic increase in population and industrial and economic growth that made it the leading economic engine in the country. *Rural South* (choice **b**) is a term used to describe the traditional agriculture-based economy of the region, which never was more important economically than the Northeast. The term *air-conditioned South* (choice **c**) is not a commonly used expression. Suburbs (choice **d**) are located throughout the country, not just in the South or the West.

25. c. By moving to northern cities and regions, African Americans could vote as members of a powerful voting bloc, giving them influence over the policies of Northern politicians while also increasing the populations and thus political representation. The Great Migration involved large numbers of African Americans leaving the South for the North. It did not involve them gaining power in the South (choice **a**). The large movement of people to the Sunbelt states (choice **b**) occurred after World War II and was not called the Great Migration. During the rise of the Sunbelt, states in the region gained power, not lost it. The Great Migration is used to describe the movement of African Americans, not Mexican Americans (choice **d**).

8 ▶ GED® SOCIAL STUDIES PRACTICE TEST

This practice test is modeled on the format, content, and timing of the official GED® Social Studies test and, like the official exam, presents a series of questions that focus on the fundamentals of social studies reasoning.

You'll be asked to answer questions based on brief texts, maps, graphics, and tables. Refer to the information provided as often as necessary when answering the questions.

- Work carefully, but do not spend too much time on any one question. Be sure to answer every question.
- Set a timer for 70 minutes, and try to take this test uninterrupted, under quiet conditions.

35 total questions
70 minutes to complete

Please use the following chart to answer questions 1–3.

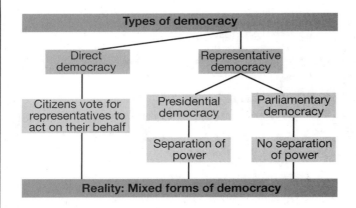

1. Which of the following is generally unique to presidential democracy?
   a. Citizens participate in voting.
   b. The executive power is separate from the legislature.
   c. The executive power is a part of the legislature.
   d. The head of state is not directly elected by the people.

2. Which specific type of democracy is the United States?
   a. direct democracy
   b. representative democracy
   c. parliamentary democracy
   d. presidential democracy

3. Using the chart, what can you infer about representative democracy?
   a. Each individual's choices are not represented when lawmakers make decisions.
   b. Every citizen's vote on laws is represented when lawmakers make decisions.
   c. The president or prime minister writes the laws.
   d. It is the same as direct democracy.

Please use the following chart to answer questions 4 and 5.

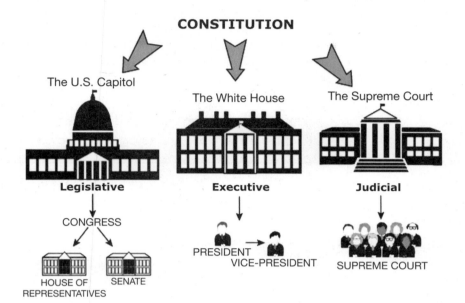

4. What are the branches of government?
   a. the House of Representatives and the Senate
   b. the House of Representatives, the Senate, and the Supreme Court
   c. the president and the vice president
   d. the legislative, the executive, and the judicial

5. The _____ branch interprets and applies the law.

The following excerpt was spoken by Sojourner Truth. Please use it to answer questions 6 and 7.

That man over there says that women need to be helped into carriages, and lifted over ditches, and to have the best place everywhere. Nobody ever helps me into carriages, or over mud-puddles, or gives me any best place! And ain't I a woman? Look at me! Look at my arm! I have ploughed and planted, and gathered into barns, and no man could head me! And ain't I a woman? I could work as much and eat as much as a man—when I could get it—and bear the lash as well! And ain't I a woman? I have borne thirteen children, and seen most all sold off to slavery, and when I cried out with my mother's grief, none but Jesus heard me! And ain't I a woman?

6. Sojourner Truth is making the case for
   a. women's rights.
   b. the abolition of slavery.
   c. the opportunity to work.
   d. special treatment for women.

7. The most important source of Sojourner Truth's credibility was
   a. her physical toughness.
   b. her personal beauty and charm.
   c. her moral strength.
   d. her eloquent use of language.

Please use the following passage to answer questions 8 and 9.

When the Spanish Conquistadors came to the Americas in the sixteenth century and destroyed Native American civilizations, one of the greatest civilizations, the Classical Maya, had already disappeared. The archeological evidence shows that a relatively peaceful civilization became more violent with the conquest of Tikal, the greatest Mayan city, in 378 by the mysterious warrior Fire Is Born. Even though Tikal was rebuilt and remained one of the dominant Mayan city-states for hundreds of years, it and the other Mayan cities fell into disrepair and were eventually abandoned.

Researchers have worked for years to identify the causes for this collapse. According to the *National Geographic* article "The Maya: Glory and Ruin," by Guy Gugliotta,

Scholars have looked at various afflictions across the Mayan world, including overpopulation, environmental damage, famine, and drought.

They have also focused on the one thing that appears to have happened everywhere during the prolonged decline: As resources grew scarce, the kuhul ajaw lost their divine luster, and, with it, the confidence of their subjects, both noble and commoner. Instability and desperation in turn fueled more destructive wars. What had been ritualized contests fought for glory or captives turned into spasms of savagery like the one that obliterated Cancuén. Says Simon Martin of the University of Pennsylvania Museum: "The system broke down and ran out of control."

8. Which was the most important cause of the collapse of the Classical Mayan civilization?
   a. the conquest of Tikal in 378 by Fire Is Born
   b. the loss of confidence of the people in the system
   c. ritualized warfare for glory and captives
   d. the invasion of the Spanish Conquistadors

9. The Mayan rulers were called the _____.

Please use the following lyrics to answer questions 10 and 11.

"I Didn't Raise My Boy to Be a Soldier"
(1915)
Lyrics by Al Bryan, music by Al Piantadosi
I didn't raise my boy to be a soldier,
I brought him up to be my pride and joy.
Who dares to place a musket on his
    shoulder
To shoot some other mother's darling boy?
Let nations arbitrate their future troubles,
It's time to lay the sword and gun away;
There'd be no war today if mothers would
    all say,
"I didn't raise my boy to be a soldier."

"Over There"
(1917)
Music and Lyrics by George Cohan
Johnnie get your gun, get your gun, get
    your gun.
Take it on the run, on the run, on the run.
Hear them calling you and me, every son of
    liberty;
Hurry right away, no delay, go today.
Make your daddy glad to have had such a
    lad
Tell your sweetheart not to pine; to be
    proud her boy's in line.

10. These two popular American songs deal with the position of the United States at the time of World War I. What is the best conclusion based on these two sources?
    a. American parents were proud to have their children join the army.
    b. American soldiers in World War I fought for liberty.
    c. World War I was unnecessary.
    d. World War I was controversial and elicited different points of view.

11. Which propaganda technique is being used in "Over There"?
    a. testimonial
    b. name calling
    c. bandwagon
    d. fear

Please use the following excerpts to answer questions 12–14.

This excerpt is from the Declaration of Independence.

> We hold these truths to be self-evident, that all men are created equal, that they are endowed by their Creator with certain unalienable Rights, that among these are Life, Liberty and the pursuit of Happiness.—That to secure these rights, Governments are instituted among Men, deriving their just powers from the consent of the governed,—That whenever any Form of Government becomes destructive of these ends, it is the Right of the People to alter or to abolish it, and to institute new Government, laying its foundation on such principles and organizing its powers in such form, as to them shall seem most likely to effect their Safety and Happiness. Prudence, indeed, will dictate that Governments long established should not be changed for light and transient causes; and accordingly all experience hath shewn, that mankind are more disposed to suffer, while evils are sufferable, than to right themselves by abolishing the forms to which they are accustomed. But when a long train of abuses and usurpations, pursuing invariably the same Object evinces a design to reduce them under absolute Despotism, it is their right, it is their duty, to throw off such Government, and to provide new Guards for their future security.—Such has been the patient sufferance of these Colonies; and such is now the necessity which constrains them to alter their former Systems of Government. The history of the present King of Great Britain is a history of repeated injuries and usurpations, all having in direct object the establishment of an absolute Tyranny over these States. To prove this, let Facts be submitted to a candid world.

This excerpt is from the Second Treatise on Civil Government, by John Locke.

> To understand political power right, and derive it from its original, we must consider, what state all men are naturally in, and that is, a state of perfect freedom to order their actions, and dispose of their possessions and persons, as they think fit, within the bounds of the law of nature, without asking leave or depending upon the will of any other man.

12. Which sentence best represents the main idea expressed in the passage from the Declaration of Independence?

a. "We hold these truths to be self-evident, that all men are created equal, that they are endowed by their Creator with certain unalienable Rights . . ."

b. "That whenever any Form of Government becomes destructive of these ends, it is the Right of the People to alter or to abolish it, and to institute new Government . . ."

c. "The history of the present King of Great Britain is a history of repeated injuries and usurpations, all having in direct object the establishment of an absolute Tyranny over these States."

d. "To prove this, let Facts be submitted to a candid world."

13. The writers of the Declaration of Independence wanted the decent respect of the opinions of mankind. Their argument primarily
rested on what foundation?
   a. an appeal to reason
   b. a plea for emotional connection
   c. a demand for religious faith
   d. a request for partisan feeling

14. In considering the second excerpt and comparing it to the Declaration of Independence,
which ideas in the two excerpts are similar?
   a. Locke's ideas regarding a freedom created
   without asking leave or depending upon the
   will of any other man are similar to the
   Declaration's ideas regarding a government
   that secures men's rights.
   b. Locke's ideas regarding the state of perfect
   freedom are similar to the Declaration's
   ideas regarding unalienable rights.
   c. Locke's ideas regarding political power are
   similar to the Declaration's ideas regarding
   the pursuit of happiness.
   d. Locke's ideas regarding the consent of the
   governed are similar to the Declaration's
   ideas regarding the disposition of
   possessions and persons.

15. The following is an excerpt from an executive
order issued by a president of the United
States.

That on the first day of January, in the year
of our Lord one thousand eight hundred and
sixty-three, all persons held as slaves within
any State or designated part of a State, the
people whereof shall then be in rebellion
against the United States, shall be then,
thenceforward, and forever free; and the
Executive Government of the United States,
including the military and naval authority
thereof, will recognize and maintain the freedom of such persons, and will do no act or
acts to repress such persons, or any of them,
in any efforts they may make for their actual
freedom.

Who was the author of this executive order?
   a. George Washington
   b. Abraham Lincoln
   c. Thomas Jefferson
   d. James Madison

Please use the following excerpts to answer questions 16–18.

The following is an excerpt from the United States Supreme Court decision of *Plessy* v. *Ferguson* (1896).

> Legislation is powerless to eradicate racial instincts or to abolish distinctions based upon physical differences.

The following is an excerpt from the United States Supreme Court decision of *Brown* v. *Board of Education* (1954).

> To separate [children in grade and high schools] from others of similar age and qualifications solely because of their race generates a feeling of inferiority as to their status in the community that may affect their hearts and minds in a way unlikely to ever be undone . . . Whatever may have been the extent of psychological knowledge at the time of *Plessy v. Ferguson*, this finding is amply supported by modern authority . . . We conclude that in the field of public education the doctrine of "separate but equal" has no place.

The following is an excerpt from the First Amendment.

> Congress shall make no law respecting an establishment of religion, or prohibiting the free exercise thereof; or abridging the freedom of speech, or of the press; or the right of the people peaceably to assemble, and to petition the Government for a redress of grievances.

The following is an excerpt from the Sixth Amendment.

> In all criminal prosecutions, the accused shall enjoy the right to a speedy and public trial, by an impartial jury of the State and district wherein the crime shall have been committed, which district shall have been previously ascertained by law, and to be informed of the nature and cause of the accusation; to be confronted with the witnesses against him; to have compulsory process for obtaining witnesses in his favor, and to have the Assistance of Counsel for his defence.

The following is an excerpt from the Thirteenth Amendment.

> **Section 1.**
> Neither slavery nor involuntary servitude, except as a punishment for crime whereof the party shall have been duly convicted, shall exist within the United States, or any place subject to their jurisdiction.

The following is an excerpt from the Fourteenth Amendment.

> **Section 1.**
> All persons born or naturalized in the United States, and subject to the jurisdiction thereof, are citizens of the United States and of the State wherein they reside. No State shall make or enforce any law which shall abridge the privileges or immunities of citizens of the United States; nor shall any State deprive any person of life, liberty, or property, without due process of law; nor deny to any person within its jurisdiction the equal protection of the laws.

16. Which of the following statements is supported by evidence from the excerpts?
- **a.** The U.S. Supreme Court occasionally changes its mind.
- **b.** The *Brown* decision declared segregation was constitutional and overturned the *Plessy* decision.
- **c.** It is impossible to make laws to eliminate racial instincts.
- **d.** Interpretive problems can be solved by returning to the actual words of the Constitution.

17. Which of the following was central to the arguments presented to the Supreme Court in *Plessy* v. *Ferguson*?
- **a.** the First Amendment
- **b.** the Sixth Amendment
- **c.** the Thirteenth Amendment
- **d.** the Fourteenth Amendment

18. Which of the following was *least* likely to have influenced the Supreme Court's decision in *Brown* v. *Board of Education*?
- **a.** a statement signed by some of the leading experts in the fields of psychology, biology, cultural anthropology, and ethnology that rejected race theories and pseudo-science used to justify the Holocaust
- **b.** a study of race relations that detailed the obstacles facing African Americans in 1940s American society
- **c.** a study that found contrasts among children who attended segregated schools in Washington, D.C., versus those in integrated schools in New York
- **d.** the first African-American quarterback played in the National Football League during the modern era

19. Which of the following can you infer from this cartoon?

- **a.** Economic freedoms are the same as political freedoms.
- **b.** The economy has no effect on political freedoms in the United States.
- **c.** Political freedoms can be hindered by the economy.
- **d.** Race remains a key factor in the economic opportunities available to Americans.

Please use the following passage and painting to answer questions 20 and 21.

The following is an excerpt from "On Indian Removal," by President Andrew Jackson (1830).

What good man would prefer a country covered with forests, and ranged by a few thousand savages to our extensive Republic, studded with cities, towns, and prosperous farms embellished with all the improvements which art can devise or industry execute, occupied by more than 12,000,000 happy people, and filled with all the blessings of liberty, civilization and religion? . . .

  The tribes which occupied the countries not constituting the Eastern States were annihilated or have melted away to make room for the whites. The waves of population and civilization are rolling to the westward, and we now propose to acquire the countries occupied by the red men of the South and West by a fair exchange, and, at the expense of the United States, to send them to land where their existence may be prolonged and perhaps made perpetual.

The following is the painting *American Progress*, by John Gast (1872).

John Gast, *American Progress*, 1872.
Chromolithograph published by George A. Crofutt.
Source: Prints and Photographs Division, Library of Congress.

20. What element from the excerpt or the painting would be considered propaganda?

   a. The painting shows a progression of transportation ideas from horseback all the way to the steam-engine train, which matches the industrial movement of the time.

   b. The United States set aside land for displaced Indian tribes.

   c. The population of the United States was expanding westward.

   d. The woman in the painting representing American Progress wears white robes like a classical Greek or Roman sculpture.

21. In today's society, how would the concept of American Progress and President Andrew Jackson's removal plan be seen?

   a. as an infringement on the rights of individuals

   b. as valid and necessary for the reclamation of needed farmland

   c. as a removal of foreign peoples from American soil

   d. as an infringement on the rights of the states

Please use the following excerpts to answer question 22.

The following excerpt is from the Majority Decision of *Marbury* v. *Madison* (1803).

It is emphatically the province and duty of the Judicial Department [the judicial branch] to say what the law is. Those who apply the rule to particular cases must, of necessity, expound and interpret that rule. If two laws conflict with each other, the Courts must decide on the operation of each.

So, if a law [e.g., a statute or treaty] be in opposition to the Constitution, if both the law and the Constitution apply to a particular case, so that the Court must either decide that case conformably to the law, disregarding the Constitution, or conformably to the Constitution, disregarding the law, the Court must determine which of these conflicting rules governs the case. This is of the very essence of judicial duty. If, then, the Courts are to regard the Constitution, and the Constitution is superior to any ordinary act of the Legislature, the Constitution, and not such ordinary act, must govern the case to which they both apply.

Those, then, who controvert the principle that the Constitution is to be considered in court as a paramount law are reduced to the necessity of maintaining that courts must close their eyes on the Constitution, and see only the law [e.g., the statute or treaty].

This doctrine would subvert the very foundation of all written constitutions.

(Chief Justice John Marshall)

The following excerpt is from a letter to Abigail Adams from Thomas Jefferson (1804).

The Constitution . . . meant that its coordinate branches should be checks on each other. But the opinion which gives to the judges the right to decide what laws are constitutional and what not, not only for themselves in their own sphere of action but for the Legislature and Executive also in their spheres, would make the Judiciary a despotic branch.

22. What can be concluded from these two excerpts?
   a. Thomas Jefferson was supportive of the judiciary branch maintaining the Constitution.
   b. The judiciary branch prior to 1803 did not decide whether laws being formed by the other two branches were constitutional or not.
   c. The coordinate branches check and balance each other through the Constitution.
   d. The law should be blind to the Constitution and apply to each case as such.

Please use the following excerpts to answer question 23.

The following excerpt is from Adam Smith, *The Wealth of Nations*, Book V, Chapter 2 (1776).

> The subjects of every state ought to contribute towards the support of the government, as nearly as possible, in proportion to their respective abilities; that is, in proportion to the revenue which they respectively enjoy under the protection of the state. The expense of government to the individuals of a great nation is like the expense of management to the joint tenants of a great estate, who are all obliged to contribute in proportion to their respective interests in the estate.

The following excerpt is from *On the Duty of Civil Disobedience*, by Henry David Thoreau (1849).

> When a sixth of the population of a nation which has undertaken to be the refuge of liberty are slaves, and a whole country is unjustly overrun and conquered by a foreign army, and subjected to military law, I think that it is not too soon for honest men to rebel and revolutionize. What makes this duty the more urgent is the fact that the country so overrun is not our own, but ours is the invading army.
>
> . . . If a thousand men were not to pay their tax bills this year, that would not be a violent and bloody measure, as it would be to pay them, and enable the State to commit violence and shed innocent blood. This is, in fact, the definition of a peaceable revolution, if any such is possible.

23. Based on the two excerpts, what would you conclude to be true of the following statements?
   a. Adam Smith and Henry David Thoreau would agree on the distribution of taxation within the government.
   b. Adam Smith and Henry David Thoreau would agree on the definition of a peaceable revolution.
   c. Adam Smith and Henry David Thoreau would disagree on the use of military by the government.
   d. Adam Smith and Henry David Thoreau would disagree on the use of taxation as an avenue for government critique.

24. Using this chart, what can be concluded about the time when this population count was made?

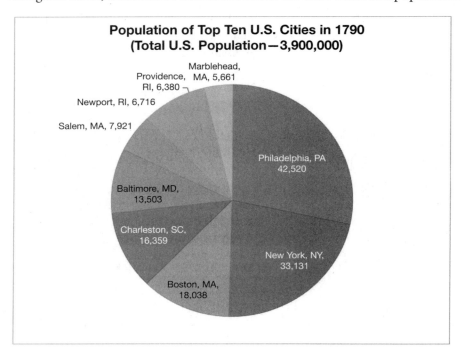

a. The American Revolution had drastically reduced the number of people living in cities.

b. The biggest cities had a more diverse population than the smaller cities.

c. Western expansion was in progress, but modern cities did not have big populations yet.

d. The majority of the total U.S. population was not located in cities.

25.

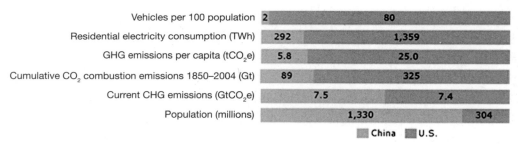

According to the graph, the energy statistic that shows the greatest difference between the United States and China is _____.

Select the correct answer from the following choices.

Vehicles per 100 population
Residential electricity consumption
GHG emissions per capita
Population (millions)

26. This map depicts the territories held by various empires in the years before and after European colonization of the Americas.

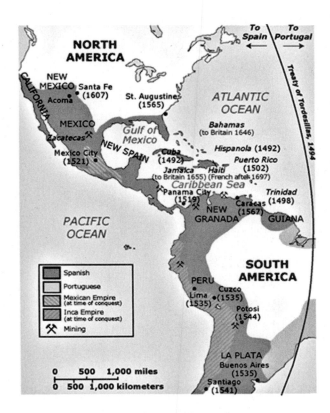

Which nation or people controlled the largest amount of territory in the Americas?
a. the Spanish
b. the Portuguese
c. the Mexican Empire
d. the Inca Empire

27. What is the exclusive control of the supply of a commodity called?
a. market power
b. price discrimination
c. monopoly
d. efficiency

Please use the following chart to answer questions 28 and 29.

The chart depicts the gross domestic product of the United States, China, and Japan between 1960 and 2011.

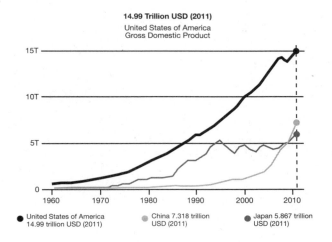

28. Which characteristic best describes the Japanese GDP trend between 1996 and 2010?
a. stable
b. turbulent
c. stagnant
d. all of the above

29. Which of the following accurately describes the United States GDP between 2008 and 2010?
a. It increased dramatically.
b. It decreased slightly before increasing.
c. It increased slightly before decreasing.
d. It decreased dramatically.

Please use the following cartoons to answer questions 30 and 31.

Abraham Lincoln and Andrew Johnson: "The Rail Splitter at Work Repairing the Union" (1865).

THE "RAIL SPLITTER" AT WORK REPAIRING THE UNION.

"Andrew Johnson Kicking out the Freedmen's Bureau," by Thomas Nast in *Harper's Weekly* (1866).

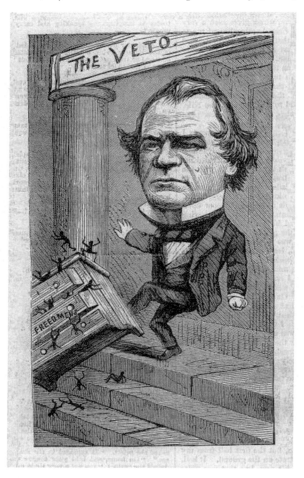

"This Little Boy . . . ," a political cartoon of President Andrew Johnson by Thomas Nast in *Harper's Weekly* (1868).

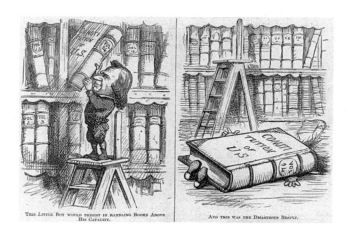

30. Viewing the three political cartoons, what can be surmised about Andrew Johnson's political career over the course of these years?
  a. Andrew Johnson continued the legacy of Abraham Lincoln's Restoration reforms.
  b. Andrew Johnson was well liked by political cartoonists and the populace.
  c. Andrew Johnson did what was necessary to work with the U.S. Constitution.
  d. Andrew Johnson succeeded Abraham Lincoln as president.

31. What aspects of the United States government are illustrated in these political cartoons?
  a. the amendment process and the power of veto
  b. the powers of the presidency
  c. the powers of Congress
  d. the Constitution and ratification

32. The following political cartoon appeared in *Harper's Weekly* (1868).

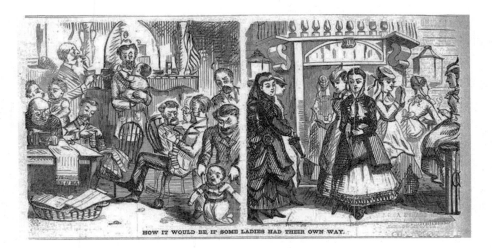

HOW IT WOULD BE, IF SOME LADIES HAD THEIR OWN WAY.

The following is an excerpt from *History of Woman Suffrage*, by Susan B Anthony, Elizabeth Cady Stanton, Matilda Joslyn Gage, and Ida Husted Harper (1886).

> We ask justice, we ask equality, we ask that all civil and political rights that belong to the citizens of the United States be guaranteed to us and our daughters forever."

In what way do these two references to the Women's Suffrage Movement diverge?
  a. The political cartoon is focused on women going out to work, while the quote is focused on daughters.
  b. The political cartoon is focused on babies, while the quote is focused on citizenship.
  c. The political cartoon is focused on women leaving men to take care of the children, while the quote is focused on equality.
  d. The political cartoon is focused on men spending time together, while the quote is focused on women spending time together.

Please use the following chart and excerpt to answer question 33.

UNITED STATES GOVERNMENT FINANCES, 1929–1941 (IN BILLIONS OF DOLLARS)			
FISCAL YEAR	EXPENDITURES	SURPLUS OR DEFICIT	TOTAL PUBLIC DEBT
1929	$3.127	$0.734	$16.9
1930	3.320	0.738	16.2
1931	3.577	−0.462	16.8
1932	4.659	−2.735	19.5
1933	4.598	−2.602	22.5
1934	6.645	−3.630	27.1
1935	6.497	−2.791	28.7
1936	8.422	−4.425	33.8
1937	7.733	−2.777	36.4
1938	6.765	−1.177	37.2
1939	8.841	−3.862	40.4
1940	9.589	−2.710	43.0
1941	13.980	−4.778	44.0

This excerpt is from President Herbert Hoover's annual message to the Congress on the State of the Union, presented in 1930.

> Economic depression cannot be cured by legislative action or executive pronouncement. Economic wounds must be healed by the action of the cells of the economic body—the producers and consumers themselves . . . The best contribution of government lies in encouragement of this voluntary cooperation in the community. The government—national, state, and local—can join with the community in such programs and do its part.

33. What do the chart and the excerpt indicate about the Great Depression?
- **a.** Hoover was correct: economic depression cannot be cured by legislative action or executive pronouncement.
- **b.** Hoover was incorrect: economic depression can be cured by legislative action or executive pronouncement.
- **c.** The Great Depression did not affect surplus or deficit.
- **d.** There is not enough data to truly evaluate the government's policies.

Please use the following map to answer questions 34 and 35.

This map illustrates the dates that each state joined the union.

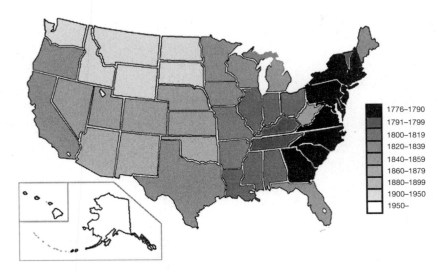

1776–1790
1791–1799
1800–1819
1820–1839
1840–1859
1860–1879
1880–1899
1900–1950
1950–

34. Which conclusion is supported by the map?
   a. The United States expanded from east to west.
   b. The United States expanded from west to east.
   c. The United States expanded from north to south.
   d. There is no general trend in United States expansion.

35. Which of the following statements is best supported by the data presented on the map?
   a. Wisconsin and Minnesota were once considered part of Canada.
   b. California was more difficult to reach than surrounding areas, resulting in a long delay before it became a state.
   c. Texas was considered part of the same territory as New Mexico until the late nineteenth century.
   d. West Virginia was originally part of Virginia but became a separate state at a later date.

Answers and Explanations

1. **Choice b is correct.** In presidential democracy, the president is separate from the legislature. Choice **a** is incorrect. Both in presidential and in parliamentary democracy, the people participate in voting. Choice **c** is incorrect. In parliamentary democracy, not presidential, the executive power, usually called the prime minister, is a member of parliament or the legislature. Choice **d** is incorrect. In parliamentary democracy, the parliament or legislature elects the president; this answer is incorrect because that is an attribute of parliamentary, not presidential, democracy.

2. **Choice d is correct.** In the United States, citizens elect representatives and vote to elect the president. In addition, the presidential powers are separate from legislative powers. These are all hallmarks of presidential democracy. Choice **a** is incorrect. This answer neglects the fact that U.S. citizens elect officials to represent them in the legislature. Choice **b** is incorrect. Although this is technically true, as one can see on the graph, it is not the most specific answer available. Choice **c** is incorrect. This answer is incorrect because it shows the reader does not understand the difference between parliamentary and presidential democracy, and how the United States fits the latter description.

3. **Choice a is correct.** In this type of democracy, people elect representatives who then make decisions on their behalf. People do not each get a vote on legislation. Choice **b** is incorrect. In this type of democracy, people elect representatives who then make the laws. In direct democracy, each individual's vote is represented. Choice **c** is incorrect. There is no evidence in this chart to support that conclusion; neither a president nor a prime minister's role is outlined here. Choice **d** is incorrect. Direct democracy and representative democracy are two separate branches.

4. **Choice d is correct.** This reflects the three branches of the U.S. government. Choice **a** is incorrect. This choice shows the reader does not comprehend the graphic and lacks basic understanding of the U.S. government. Choice **b** is incorrect. This choice shows a misinterpretation of the graphic. Choice **c** is incorrect. This choice shows a misreading of the graphic.

5. **The correct answer is judicial.** The judicial branch interprets and applies the law. This is the power of the judicial branch as listed in the Constitution. The Supreme Court reviews the laws through the lens of different cases and decides how the law should be understood and used. The legislative branch is responsible for writing the laws, and the executive branch is responsible for implementing and enforcing the laws written by the legislature.

6. **Choice a is correct.** By repeating the phrase "Ain't I a woman," Sojourner Truth makes it clear that all women have basic human rights. Choice **b** is incorrect. While she was a former slave and mentions slavery in her speech, it is not the main focus of her speech. Choice **c** is incorrect. Truth states that she worked hard, but that is not the main point of her speech. Choice **d** is incorrect. By describing her own tough life, she speaks out against special treatment and in favor of equal rights.

7. **Choice c is correct.** The directness and power of her language emphasize her moral strength. Her physical strength can be seen as a metaphor for her moral strength. Choice **a** is incorrect. Her physical toughness alone is only part of her credibility. Choice **b** is incorrect. Truth makes the point that she is not a dainty creature of privilege, and therefore beauty and charm would not form part of her powers of persuasion. Choice **d** is incorrect. Her eloquent and direct use of language may be persuasive and helps to clarify her moral character, but it is her character itself that is the ultimate source of her credibility.

8. **Choice b is correct.** Loss of confidence of the people in the system was the most important cause of the collapse of the Classical Mayan civilization. Choice **a** is incorrect. The conquest of Tikal in 378 by Fire Is Born was a key step in the collapse of the Mayan system, but it was only one part of a loss of confidence that spanned hundreds of years. Choice **c** is incorrect. Ritualized warfare was an important part of their stable religious system. Choice **d** is incorrect. The invasion of the Conquistadors happened hundreds of years later.

9. **The correct answer is kuhul ajaw.** The kuhul ajaw was a Mayan ruler. While the passage does not state this directly, it makes clear that the kuhul ajaw was the head of the society by what follows the phrase "kuhul ajaw"— "their divine luster . . . the confidence of their subjects."

10. **Choice d is correct.** The two songs take opposing views as to the value of enlisting and fighting in World War I. Choice **a** is incorrect. It is supported by "Over There" but not by "I Didn't Raise My Boy to Be a Soldier." Choice **b** is incorrect. It is supported by "Over There" but not by "I Didn't Raise My Boy to Be a Soldier." Choice **c** is incorrect. It is proposed by Al Bryan but rejected by George Cohan.

11. **Choice c is correct.** This technique entices the audience to follow the crowd by appealing to groups held together already by commonality of nationality, religion, race, and so forth. Bandwagon propaganda is a common technique used in wartime. Choice **a** is incorrect. A testimonial typically uses a celebrity in an attempt to have us agree with an idea, such as in a celebrity endorsement. This is not the case in "Over There." Choice **b** is incorrect. The name-calling propaganda technique connects a person, or idea, to a negative word or symbol in an effort to get the audience to reject the person or the idea. This is not the case in "Over There." Choice **d** is incorrect. Fear as a propaganda technique focuses on the negative outcomes if the desired course of action is not followed. This is not the case in "Over There."

12. Choice b is correct. This sentence correctly sums up the passage, whose main theme is the right of the United States to break away from an unfair government.

Choice **a** is incorrect. This is a reason that the United States' founding fathers are using to justify the document and its ideals, but it is not the main idea.

Choice **c** is incorrect. Although this is a sentence justifying the theme, it does not represent the main idea.

Choice **d** is incorrect. This sentence is only a transition sentence that introduces the facts.

13. Choice a is correct. The Declaration of Independence reads like a logical treatise. There is nothing in the excerpt that appeals to the reader's emotions, religious beliefs, or partisan feelings.

Choice **b** is incorrect. There is nothing in the excerpt that appeals to the reader's emotions.

Choice **c** is incorrect. There is nothing in the excerpt that appeals to the reader's religious beliefs.

Choice **d** is incorrect. There is nothing in the excerpt that appeals to the reader's partisan feelings.

14. Choice b is correct. John Locke's "state of perfect freedom" and the Declaration of Independence's "unalienable Rights" are similar concepts. John Locke's focus was that all men, through nature, are given this state of freedom, and the Declaration agreed that all men have rights that are not dictated by any other man.

Choice **a** is incorrect. John Locke, while influencing the Declaration of Independence, was more focused on man as an independent person without reliance on others, while the Declaration of Independence stated that government should protect any freedoms men could want. These ideas are not similar.

Choice **c** is incorrect. John Locke's ideas regarding political power are not fully addressed in this excerpt. These ideas may be similar, but are not the best choice.

Choice **d** is incorrect. John Locke did not write about "the consent of the governed," and the Declaration of Independence did not mention the disposing of possessions or persons. These ideas have been reversed, so this is not the best choice.

15. Choice b is correct. Lincoln is known for writing the Emancipation Proclamation, of which this is an excerpt, which freed all persons held as slaves.

Choice **a** is incorrect. This excerpt is dated "one thousand eight hundred and sixty-three," long after Washington's death.

Choice **c** is incorrect. This excerpt was written after Jefferson's death.

Choice **d** is incorrect. This choice neglects the evidence of time and content.

16. Choice a is correct. The *Brown* decision overturned the *Plessy* decision, thus demonstrating that the U.S. Supreme Court occasionally changes its mind.
Choice **b** is incorrect. The *Brown* decision did overturn the *Plessy* decision, but, in doing so, it declared segregation to be unconstitutional.
Choice **c** is incorrect. The *Plessy* decision held that laws could not eliminate racial instincts, but this does not make it a reasonable conclusion; indeed, Brown's authors completely disagreed.
Choice **d** is incorrect. Both decisions were based on the Fourteenth Amendment.

17. Choice d is correct. The Fourteenth Amendment protects the rights of Americans regardless of their race, which was the main issue in the case of *Plessy* v. *Ferguson*. However, the Supreme Court decided that "separate but equal" facilities offered to people of different races did not violate the Fourteenth Amendment. This viewpoint would stand as law until 1954, when the case *Brown* v. *Board of Education* essentially reversed this ruling.
Choice **a** is incorrect. The First Amendment deals with free speech and freedom of the press, which is not necessarily relevant in this case.
Choice **b** is incorrect. The Sixth Amendment guarantees the right to a speedy and public trial. This issue was not central to the arguments presented in *Plessy* v. *Ferguson*.
Choice **c** is incorrect. The Thirteenth Amendment outlawed slavery. Issues of slavery were not central to the arguments presented in *Plessy* v. *Ferguson*.

18. Choice d is correct. Although this was indeed a sign of the changing times in America, it did not influence the Supreme Court's decision in *Brown* v. *Board of Education*.
Choice **a** is incorrect. The Supreme Court's decision was, in fact, influenced by "The Race Question," a scholarly statement published by UNESCO in 1950.
Choice **b** is incorrect. The Supreme Court's decision was, in fact, influenced by "An American Dilemma: The Negro Problem and Modern Democracy," a 1,500-page study of race relations published in 1944.
Choice **c** is incorrect. The Supreme Court's decision was, in fact, influenced by a study that found contrasts between children who attended segregated schools in Washington, D.C., and those in integrated schools in New York.

19. Choice c is correct. This answer shows that the reader comprehends that the person in the cartoon cannot reach "political freedom" because he is being sat on by a piggy bank, a visual symbol of the economy.
Choice **a** is incorrect. There is no evidence or graphic representation in the cartoon that suggests the two are the same.
Choice **b** is incorrect. It neglects the visual representation of money, as symbolized by the piggy bank, as restricting the person from grabbing "political freedom."
Choice **d** is incorrect. The cartoon does not emphasize race as a component that can restrict economic opportunities or political freedoms.

20. Choice d is correct. By dressing this allegorical figure of American Progress in classical robes as though she were from Greek or Roman times, the painter is suggesting that the United States' displacement of native people is as important to civilization as the creation of democracy and republic in ancient times. This is propaganda. Choice **a** is incorrect. The painting does show this progression of transportation, but this would be seen more as illustrating the industry of the time rather than as propaganda. Choice **b** is incorrect. The United States did actually set aside land for displaced Indian tribes, but this is fact rather than propaganda. Choice **c** is incorrect. The population of the United States was actually expanding westward, but this is fact rather than propaganda.

21. Choice a is correct. American Indians are considered citizens, so in today's society, forcibly removing them would be seen as an infringement on the rights of individuals. Choice **b** is incorrect. Although much of where American Indians have lived has become farmland, this would not be seen as a valid reason to move citizens. Choice **c** is incorrect. Since American Indians are considered citizens, removing them would not be a removal of foreign people. Choice **d** is incorrect. Although this could be seen as infringing on the rights of the state, this is not the best choice.

22. Choice b is correct. By looking at both excerpts, we see that the judiciary branch, prior to *Marbury* v. *Madison*, was not ruling on whether a law set into place by the legislative and executive branches fell into agreement with the Constitution. Thomas Jefferson's letter shows that he is uncomfortable with the precedent of the judiciary branch having the final say over the creation of laws by the legislative and the executive, which means that this was not the case previously.
Choice **a** is incorrect. Thomas Jefferson does not support the judiciary branch maintaining the Constitution, as he uses the word "despotic" to describe what he fears it will become. Choice **c** is incorrect. This is only stated in the letter from Thomas Jefferson and is not referred to in the excerpt from *Marbury* v. *Madison*. Choice **d** is incorrect. This is only noted in the excerpt from *Marbury* v. *Madison* and is argued against within that ruling.

23. Choice d is correct. Since Adam Smith notes that all men ought to contribute via taxation to the government, it seems likely that he would disagree with Henry David Thoreau's notion that not paying taxes is a good way to disagree with government activities.
Choice **a** is incorrect. This is not something that it appears Adam Smith and Henry David Thoreau would agree on. Adam Smith notes that the government should be paid for the protections that each individual enjoys. This would suggest that Smith believes government should use those taxes for citizen protection, which might include military action. Thoreau, on the other hand, is against the use of tax money for military action, especially since he was protesting the Mexican-American war during this time.
Choices **b** and **c** are incorrect. Adam Smith does not refer to either concept.

24. Choice d is correct. The total population far exceeds the total population numbers listed for these cities. It can be inferred that most of the population was located not in cities, but in towns and rural areas.

Choice **a** is incorrect. This chart does not address the American Revolution casualties.

Choice **b** is incorrect. There is nothing in this chart to indicate the diversity of the cities at this time.

Choice **c** is incorrect. There is nothing in this chart to indicate the status of Western expansion.

25. The correct answer is Vehicles per 100 population. The United States has 80 cars per 100 people, while China only has 2; a 78-car difference. This is clearly shown on the graph, which has the United States taking up almost all of the bar for that characteristic.

26. Choice a is correct. A significant portion of the map is covered by the color that represents Spain.

Choice **b** is incorrect. In the map, the Portuguese conquests cover a relatively small portion compared to Spain.

Choice **c** is incorrect. The Mexican Empire was conquered; it covers only a small part of the map.

Choice **d** is incorrect. The Inca Empire was conquered; it takes up only a small part of the map.

27. Choice c is correct. This is the correct word for that definition.

Choice **a** is incorrect. This phrase indicates how a company can raise the market price of a good or service over its marginal costs in a profitable way.

Choice **b** is incorrect. This is a phrase used to describe the sales of identical goods and services at different prices from the same company.

Choice **d** is incorrect. This word means how well effort or cost is used.

28. Choice b is correct. The rate rises steadily before suffering turbulent ups and downs from around 1996 to 2010.

Choice **a** is incorrect. This would indicate that the rate rises increasingly without any drops; this is not true according to the graph.

Choice **c** is incorrect. This would indicate that the GDP does not increase at all, which is incorrect as shown on the graph.

Choice **d** is incorrect. The terms contradict each other, so they cannot all be true.

29. Choice b is correct. This answer correctly identifies that the graph drops before rising in the time period mentioned.

Choice **a** is incorrect. The graph obviously shows less dramatic changes during this time.

Choice **c** is incorrect. This choice does not accurately depict the graph.

Choice **d** is incorrect. The graph obviously shows less dramatic changes during this time.

30. Choice d is correct. The only choice that can be correctly surmised is that Andrew Johnson succeeded Abraham Lincoln as president. Between the first image, in which Abraham Lincoln is working on repairing the Union, and the second image, in which Andrew Johnson has the word "veto" above him, he has become president of the United States. A veto is an action exercised only by the president, and Abraham Lincoln would have been president during the reparation of the Union.

Choice **a** is incorrect. These political cartoons seem to show that Johnson did not continue the legacy of Lincoln's Restoration reforms.

Choice **b** is incorrect. These political cartoons do not seem to show Johnson in a favorable way.

Choice **c** is incorrect. One of the political cartoons shows Johnson flattened by the U.S. Constitution.

31. Choice a is correct. Both the amendment process and the power of the presidential veto are shown in these political cartoons. In the first image, Andrew Johnson and Abraham Lincoln are "repairing the Union" by introducing Amendments to the Constitution. In the second image, Andrew Johnson is shown exercising the right of veto. In the third image, Andrew Johnson is shown being flattened by the Constitution of the United States, which is the document to which Amendments are attached.

Choice **b** is incorrect. While the presidential power of veto is shown in these political cartoons, this is not the best choice.

Choice **c** is incorrect. These political cartoons do not show the powers of Congress.

Choice **d** is incorrect. The Constitution does appear in one of the political cartoons, but nothing about ratification appears.

32. Choice c is correct. The political cartoon shows women leaving the men to take care of the children, and the quote is focused on equality between the genders. The political cartoon reveals some of the fears of the time—that if women were given equal pay, the right to vote, and more, men would be forced into the position of caretakers and housewives. In contrast, the quote simply states a request for equal civil and political rights, without addressing the roles of men and women in the home.

Choice **a** is incorrect. The quote mentions daughters, but it is not focused just on daughters.

Choice **b** is incorrect. While there are babies in the political cartoon, the quote is not about citizenship.

Choice **d** is incorrect. The political cartoon is not about men spending time together, and the quote is not about women spending time together.

33. Choice d is correct. There is not enough data based on this chart to say whether the government policies affected the nation during the Great Depression. This would also require information based on cost of living per person, rates of employment and unemployment, and more to determine this.

Choice **a** is incorrect. There is nothing in the chart to indicate that President Hoover was correct regarding government spending during the Great Depression.

Choice **b** is incorrect. There is nothing in the chart to indicate that President Hoover was incorrect regarding government spending during the Great Depression.

Choice **c** is incorrect. According to information in the table, the Great Depression did affect the surplus and deficit.

34. Choice a is correct. Generally, as shown in the map, states joined chronologically from east to west.

Choice **b** is incorrect. States on the West Coast joined later than states on the East Coast.

Choice **c** is incorrect. Southern states joined the union earlier or at the same time as Northern states.

Choice **d** is incorrect. There is a clear trend indicating that the United States expanded from east to west.

35. Choice d is correct. West Virginia was admitted as a state in 1863, 75 years after most of its surrounding states. This suggests that it broke off from an existing state at a later date. Indeed, West Virginia was originally part of Virginia but separated during the Civil War—in which Virginia aligned with the Confederacy—and entered the Union as a free state.

Choice **a** is incorrect. None of the data shown on the map suggest that Wisconsin and Minnesota were once considered part of Canada.

Choice **b** is incorrect. California was admitted as a state on September 9, 1850, much sooner than most of the states surrounding it.

Choice **c** is incorrect. Texas was admitted as a state on December 29, 1845, while New Mexico was not admitted until 1912.

ADDITIONAL ONLINE PRACTICE

Using the codes below, you'll be able to log in and access additional online practice materials!

Your free online practice access codes are:
FVE54W3J6NJQK67W35SP
FVE78V14R5D3RXRM27OM

Follow these simple steps to redeem your codes:

- Go to **www.learningexpresshub.com/affiliate** and have your access codes handy.

  If you're a new user:
  - Click the **New user? Register here** button and complete the registration form to create your account and access your products.
  - Be sure to enter your unique access codes only once. If you have multiple access codes, you can enter them all—just use a comma to separate each code.
  - The next time you visit, simply click the **Returning user? Sign in** button and enter your username and password.
- Do not re-enter previously redeemed access codes. Any products you previously accessed are saved in the **My Account** section on the site. Entering a previously redeemed access code will result in an error message.

  If you're a returning user:
  - Click the **Returning user? Sign in** button, enter your username and password, and click **Sign In**.
  - You will automatically be brought to the **My Account** page to access your products.
- Do not re-enter previously redeemed access codes. Any products you previously accessed are saved in the **My Account** section on the site. Entering a previously redeemed access code will result in an error message.

  If you're a returning user with new access codes:
  - Click the **Returning user? Sign in** button, enter your username, password, and new access codes, and click **Sign In**.
  - If you have multiple access codes, you can enter them all—just use a comma to separate each code.
- Do not re-enter previously redeemed access codes. Any products you previously accessed are saved in the **My Account** section on the site. Entering a previously redeemed access code will result in an error message.

If you have any questions, please contact LearningExpress Customer Support at LXHub@Learning ExpressHub.com. All inquiries will be responded to within a 24-hour period during our normal business hours: 9:00 A.M.–5:00 P.M. Eastern Time. Thank you!

NOTES

NOTES

NOTES

NOTES

NOTES

NOTES